MW00800324

STRIVE FOR A 5
Preparing for the AP® United States History Exam

Warren Hierl
Career Center, Winston-Salem, North Carolina

Louisa Bond Moffitt
Marist School, Atlanta, Georgia

Nancy Schick
Los Alamos High School, Los Alamos, New Mexico

Kyle VanderWall
Grandville High School, Grandville, Michigan

This product was developed to accompany

Henretta's
AMERICA'S HISTORY
Tenth Edition

Rebecca Edwards • Eric Hinderaker • Robert O. Self • James A. Henretta

Bedford/St. Martin's Boston • New York

bedford, freeman & worth
high school publishers

Manufactured in the United States of America.

1 2 3 4 5 6 26 25 24 23 22 21

For information, write:
Bedford/St. Martin's
75 Arlington Street
Boston, MA 02116
(617-399-4000)

ISBN 978-1-319-33525-0

Acknowledgments

Text acknowledgments and copyrights appear at the back of the book on page 219, which constitute an extension of the copyright page. Art acknowledgments and copyrights appear on the same page as the art selections they cover. It is a violation of the law to reproduce these selections by any means whatsoever without the written permission of the copyright holder.

Contents

About the Authors

Warren Hierl taught Advanced Placement U.S. History at the Career Center in Winston-Salem, North Carolina, for twenty-eight years. He has conducted more than ninety one-day Advanced Placement workshops, more than eight five-week-long Advanced Placement Summer Institutes throughout the Southeast, and more than seventy pre-AP® workshops throughout the country. He was a member of the committee that wrote the original *Advanced Placement Social Studies Vertical Teams Guide* and, with Nancy Schick, the *Advanced Placement U.S. History Teachers Guide*. He has been a reader, a table leader, and an exam leader, and, for the past eight years, the question leader on the DBQ at the AP® U.S. History reading.

Louisa Bond Moffitt holds a Ph.D. in U.S. History and has been teaching AP® United States history at Marist School in Atlanta, Georgia, for more than twenty-eight years. She has been involved with the AP® U.S. History reading for many years, serving as an exam leader and assistant chief reader for that exam. She is currently working as the question leader for the alternate AP® U.S. History exam. In addition, she has been a member of the AP® U.S. History test development committee, as well as several other test development committees. She has also coauthored a number of textbooks dealing with international relations built around conversations among former U.S. secretaries of state and defense. She has been active in the field of Middle East studies and has been recognized by the Middle East Studies Association for her work with both students and teachers. She is the chair of the History Department at Marist School and leads numerous AP® U.S. workshops during the summers and throughout the school year.

Nancy Schick holds a B.A. in political science from Michigan State University and an M.A.T. from the University of Pittsburgh. She taught AP® U.S. History and AP® European History for nearly twenty years at Los Alamos High School in New Mexico. She has been a reader, table leader, and exam leader for AP® U.S. history for many years and served four years on the AP® U.S. History Development Committee. She has led over forty summer institutes and many workshops in several states and farther afield in Saipan and El Salvador. She has received grants from the National Endowment for the Humanities, the Gilder Lehrman Institute, the Goethe Institut, and the U.S. Institute of Peace. She was a Fulbright-Hays scholar in Southeast Asia, a Presidential Scholar Distinguished Teacher five times, and the 2005 New Mexico Teacher of the Year.

Kyle VanderWall has taught history for eighteen years at Grandville High School in Grandville, Michigan. For sixteen of those years, he has taught AP® U.S. History. Over that span, the program has grown significantly. The AP® U.S. History course at Grandville is designed for sophomores and has no prerequisites for admission. During the last ten years, Kyle has led numerous workshops around the country to help improve historical pedagogy. His instructional design and work focuses on increasing students' self-efficacy of historical inquiry. For the past ten years, he has participated in the AP® Reading as both a Reader and Table Leader scoring the Long-Essay and Document-Based Questions.

Preface

Welcome to the AP® U.S. History course, sometimes called APUSH. Your teacher is no doubt looking forward to teaching you not only the content of American history but also the concepts and historical skills. Although you may be concerned about the difficulty of the course and the AP® exam at the end of the school year, you will be well on your way to success as you learn to think like a historian and see the course as an exciting challenge.

Many resources are available to help you. One is your textbook, another is this test preparation manual, and a third is the College Board Web site (apcentral.collegeboard.com), where you can find much more information about the course and the exam.

Overview of the AP® U.S. History Course

The AP® U.S. History course is a comprehensive history of the parts of North America that became the United States from just before European contact in 1492 to the present. This course examines many aspects of U.S. history: political, cultural, social, economic, and diplomatic. Your teacher and your textbook will help you to understand how these threads are woven together into a diverse and complex American tapestry.

You will also learn how to analyze and interpret primary source materials, connect issues of one time period with those of another, and write clearly and succinctly in order to support a thesis. As you "strive for a 5," the highest score on the AP® exam, you will master the historical content, understand the AP® Themes, and develop the critical thinking skills essential to both the AP® U.S. History course and the exam.

Your teacher will explain how the APUSH course is structured. For more detail, go to apcentral.collegeboard.org/courses/ap-united-states-history for the curriculum framework, course description, and exam description. This course has been revised multiple times in the past few years, so using older test preparation guides and exams will not be as helpful and could mislead you about what to expect on the exam.

Briefly, the course is divided into nine historical periods, and there are eight themes that cut across all nine periods. The periods are:

- Period 1: 1491–1607
- Period 2: 1607–1754
- Period 3: 1754–1800
- Period 4: 1800–1848
- Period 5: 1844–1877
- Period 6: 1865–1898
- Period 7: 1890–1945
- Period 8: 1945–1980
- Period 9: 1980–Present

The AP® themes are:

- American and National Identity
- Work, Exchange, and Technology
- Geography and the Environment
- Migration and Settlement

- Politics and Power
- America in the World
- American and Regional Culture
- Social Structures

Each theme weaves through the more than five hundred years of U.S. history and is accompanied by a set of AP® Themes. In addition, each of the nine periods requires that you examine key concepts that are broken down into subconcepts and specific examples. This may sound complicated, but the curriculum framework that establishes this structure is designed to show you clearly just what it is that you are expected to know and to do.

In addition to the historical content, you will develop historical thinking skills and reasoning processes.

Historical Thinking Skills

- Developments and Processes: Be able to explain historical process and change using specific factual information.
- Sourcing and Situation: Analyze primary documents looking for the significance of the author, audience, historical situation, and point of view of the document.
- Claims, Evidence, and Sources: Compare two secondary source documents for main idea, similarities, differences, and specific examples which support contrasting points of view.
- Contextualization: Set the stage for a discussion by looking at what is going on before, during or after the questions making certain to relate the collateral events to the question.
- Making Connections: Identify trends, patterns, and similarities/difference between different time periods.
- Argumentation: Develop a defensible thesis or claim and support that claim with relevant historical factual information.

Historical Reasoning Processes

AP® US History Exam DBQs and Long Essays will focus on one of the following:

- Comparison: Be able to explain the historic similarities and/or differences between historical developments and/or processes.
- Causation: Be able to describe, explain, and clearly express the significance of cause and effect on historical developments and processes.
- Continuity and Change: Be able to identify and explain the significance of change and continuity in historical development and processes.

How the *Strive* for a 5 will help you with the exam

Preparation is the key to success in the AP® U.S. History course. This *Strive for a 5,*and along with your textbook, *Henretta's America's History,* Tenth Edition, by Rebecca Edwards, Eric Hinderaker, Robert O. Self, and James A. Henretta, are important resources. With these, you have the tools you need to earn a top score.

Section 1 follows the organization of the AP® U.S. History course and correlates course themes and key concepts with *America's History,* Tenth Edition. Both the course and *America's History* are divided into nine chronological periods, or parts. Within each period, you will find a period overview, a list of key terms, and focus questions to consider as you read and study. Also included is a thematic timeline, followed by chapter summaries from *America's History.* Following the chapter summaries, you will find practice questions—multiple-choice, short-answer, and either a long essay or a document-based question.

Section 2 explains how to register for the exam and make a review plan for yourself. Here you will also find explanations of and guidelines for how to respond to the four types of questions on the AP® U.S. History Exam: multiple-choice questions, short-answer questions, document-based question, and long essay questions. Following this information, you'll find two full-length AP® U.S. History style practice exams that require you to put all of your preparation into action. These are designed to follow the AP® exam format and prepare you for the real thing. Our goal is for you to build confidence by knowing what to expect from the exam and reviewing the most important elements of the APUSH course.

Notice this guide does not include answers to the exam questions. This is because some teachers like to use these practice exams for credit. Your teacher has access to the practice exam answers (for essays: what good answers will include), and can provide them to you, depending on his or her plans for utilizing this book.

SECTION 1

PERIOD 1, 1491-1607

Period 1 focuses on the North American continent from 1491 until 1607, the years from just before the arrival of European explorers to the founding of the Jamestown colony by the British. These years include the initial contacts between American Indians and the earliest explorers, as well as the introduction of West African slaves to the Western Hemisphere.

The overview begins with an examination of the various native populations that migrated to and spread across North America—their origins and the different ways each group adapted to the conditions they faced in the regions they settled. The American Indian societies that developed shared some common characteristics, but all had to make unique adjustments to the environments they encountered. The result was the creation of societies of varying complexity.

American Indians living in present-day Mexico and the American Southwest relied on the cultivation of maize, with the addition of a mix of foraging and hunting to sustain their communities. Settlement of the western Great Plains was limited until the arrival of horses with the Spanish made possible a nomadic lifestyle based on hunting. Those who settled in the Northeast and Southeast relied on both agriculture and hunting, practices that led to more permanent towns and villages.

The arrival of European explorers in the fifteenth and sixteenth centuries brought significant changes to both the Eastern and Western Hemispheres. The introduction of trade goods and agricultural products, as well as diseases on both sides of the Atlantic, set off a series of changes that had a lasting impact on the entire world. Called the Columbian Exchange, this series of contacts and interactions initiated demographic, social, and economic changes that reshaped the history of all the regions involved. Areas where the Spanish and Portuguese explored saw the emergence of a racially mixed population, one made even more diverse by the introduction of West African slaves. The Spanish justified slavery by labeling it the *encomienda* system, arguing that offering conversion to Christianity offset the disadvantages of being enslaved. The introduction of horses, pigs, and cattle further altered the economy and lifestyles of those who lived in the Western Hemisphere.

European rivalries led to intense competition for control of the Western Hemisphere. The desire for wealth, the wish to extend political power, and the determination to spread Christianity fueled these rivalries. European nations experienced growth in both population and wealth, furthering the shift from a feudal economy to more modern capitalism.

Changes in technology and better business organization also boosted international trade, leading to more rapid changes for the economies of all involved.

Colonization led to significant changes in how Europeans, American Indians, and West Africans viewed each other. Europeans tended to judge all peoples by European standards and saw anyone different from themselves as backward and in need of "civilization." This belief in white superiority led to the justification and extensive use of slavery and other methods of control, such as forced conversion to Christianity. In spite of these hardships, both American Indians and West Africans managed to adapt to the harsh conditions they faced while still finding ways to maintain cultural and linguistic aspects of their distinct heritages, as well as some measures of autonomy in their daily lives.

Key Terms, Period 1:

The following are key terms either included in the Curricular Framework of the Course and Exam Description or serve as concrete examples of key concepts that may be specifically tested on the Advanced Placement® U.S. History Exam.

Columbian Exchange (3, 37, 42–44)
Maize culture (10, 13, 15–16, 44, 116)
Hunter-gatherer (8, 10, 15–16)

Capitalism (250)
Joint Stock Company (48–63)
Encomienda system (43)

Focus Questions

As you study Period 1, keep the following thematic questions in mind.

American and National Identity

- In what ways did American Indians and Africans struggle to maintain their identity and autonomy in the face of Europeans' attempts to subjugate them?

Work, Exchange, and Technology

- Why did the economies of native societies differ so much?
- What advantages and disadvantages accrued to both European and native societies as a result of the Columbian Exchange?
- What impact did technological advancements have on Portuguese and Spanish exploration to the New World?

Geography and the Environment

- How did different American Indian societies confront the environmental challenges?
- How did the varied environments in North and South America shape the emergence of vastly different economic, social, and political development among American Indian societies?

Migration and Settlement

- What forces resulted in the emergence of diverse native societies in both North and South America?
- Why were Europeans able to develop and maintain an extensive slave trade?
- Why did African slaves replace American Indian labor in Spanish New World colonies?
- In what ways did the Spanish presence in the Western Hemisphere shape native social, economic, and political development?

Politics and Power

- In what ways was European colonization of the New World promoted by national conflicts in Europe?
- What factors led American Indian societies to resist the European domination and influence?
- What shape did American Indian resistance take, and how successful was it?

America in the World

- How did economic and political rivalries in Europe affect the forms of colonization in North America?
- What effects did Spanish and Portuguese colonists have on the American Indian population?
- What effects did the Columbian Exchange have in Europe, Africa, and the Americas?

American and Regional Culture

- In what ways did overseas expansion change how Europeans viewed Africans and American Indians?
- How and why did Africans and American Indians both adapt some aspects of European culture and resist European attempts to change their values and beliefs?

Social Structures

- What religious and social beliefs promoted Spanish and Portuguese colonization in the New World?

Thematic Timeline

TIME	Key Events
1450	
	American and National Identity • Castile and Aragon join to create Spain; the Inquisition helps create a sense of a Spanish identity • John Calvin establishes a Protestant commonwealth in Geneva, Switzerland
	Work, Exchange, and Technology • Diversified economies of Native America • Rise of the Ottoman Empire blocks Asian trading routes of the Italian city-states • Europeans fish off North American coast • Portuguese traders explore African coast
	Geography and the Environment • Native American burning practices alter North American landscapes • Martellus map underestimates distance from Europe to Asia (1489) • Yellow fever, malaria, and dysentery help keep European traders from African interior • Columbian Exchange begins to transform global ecology
	Migration and Settlement • Christopher Columbus explores the Bahamas and West Indies (1492–1504) • Pedro Alvares Cabral makes landfall in Brazil (1500) • Spanish conquest of Mexico and Peru (1519–1535)
	Politics and Power • Rise of monarchical nation-states in Europe • Aztecs and Incas consolidate their empires • Probable founding of the Iroquois Confederacy • Rise of the Songhai Empire in Africa
	America in the World • Amerigo Vespucci gives America its name • Spain and Portugal begin to tap American resources
	Social Structures • Protestant Reformation (1517) sparks century of religious warfare • Henry VIII creates Church of England (1534) • Founding of Jesuit order (1540)

TIME	Key Events
1550	
	American and National Identity • English conquest and persecution of native Irish • Growing Protestant movement in England **Work, Exchange, and Technology** • Growth of the outwork system in English textile industry • Spanish *encomienda* system organizes native labor in Mexico • Inca mita system is co-opted by the Spanish in the Andes **Geography and the Environment** • Plantation complex brings sugarcane agriculture to the Americas • Steep Native American population decline in Hispaniola, Mesoamerica, and the Andes **Migration and Settlement** • Castilians and Africans arrive in Spanish America in large numbers • English colonies in Newfoundland, Maine, and Roanoke fail **Politics and Power** • Elizabeth's "sea dogs" plague Spanish shipping • English monarchs adopt mercantilist policies • Defeat of the Spanish Armada (1588) **America in the World** • Protestant nations challenge Catholic control of the Americas • American gold and silver flow to Europe and Asia **Social Structures** • Philip II defends the Roman Catholic Church against Protestantism • Elizabeth I adopts Protestant Book of Common Prayer (1559)
1600	
	American and National Identity • Pilgrims and Puritans seek to create godly commonwealths • Powhatan and Virginia Company representatives attempt to extract tribute from each other **Work, Exchange, and Technology** • First staple exports from the English mainland colonies: furs and tobacco • Subsistence farms in New England • Transition to sugar plantation system in the Caribbean islands **Geography and the Environment** • Chesapeake colonists suffer from unbalanced sex ratios and subtropical illnesses • New England colonists benefit from balanced sex ratios and healthy climate • Native American burning practices decline in the eastern woodland

Migration and Settlement

- First set of Anglo-Indian wars
- African servitude begins in Virginia (1619)
- Caribbean islands move from servitude to slavery
- Growing gentry immigration to Virginia
- White indentured servitude shapes Chesapeake society
- Africans defined as property rather than people in the Chesapeake

Politics and Power

- James I claims divine right to rule England
- Virginia's House of Burgesses (1619)
- English Puritan Revolution
- Native Americans rise up against English colonists in Virginia (1620s and 1640s) and New England (1630s)
- Restoration of the English crown (1660)
- English conquer New Netherland (1664)
- Native American revolt against colonial authority in New England (1670s) and New Mexico (1680s)
- Bacon's Rebellion

America in the World

- Opportunities for trade and settlement in America attract European investment
- American colonies become a prime destination for bound labor
- England's American colonies become a destination for free migrants

American and Regional Culture

- Persecuted English Puritans and Catholics migrate to America
- Established churches set up in Puritan New England and Anglican Virginia
- Metacom's War in New England (1675–1676)
- Bacon's Rebellion calls for removal of American Indians and end of elite rule

Social Structures

- Salem witchcraft crisis (1692)
- Dissenters settle in Rhode Island

1700

American and National Identity

- Social mobility for Africans ends with collapse of tobacco trade and increased power of gentry

Work, Exchange, and Technology

- Tobacco trade stagnates
- Maturing yeoman economy and emerging Atlantic trade in New England

Migration and Settlement

- Three types of colonies formed in America: tribute, plantation, and neo-European

Geography and the Environment

- French merchants found New Orleans

America's History Chapter Summaries

(required AP® content in bold)

Chapter 1

Colliding Worlds, 1491-1600

Chapter 1 discusses the earliest inhabitants of the Western Hemisphere, their migration from Asia, and the different societies that developed as they adapted to new surroundings. The chapter also looks at Western Europe and West and Central Africa on the eve of first contact. It then examines the earliest explorations of the Spanish and the Portuguese into Africa and the Americas.

The first Americans migrated across a land bridge from Siberia in far eastern Asia across the Bering Strait into what today is Alaska. Over time, Native Americans spread across the Americas and adapted to a **variety of environments and developed unique politics, economies, language, and social structures.** Mesoamerica was home to the Aztec Empire, and the Andes region was dominated by the Incas. Both societies were led by priests and warrior-kings who managed large, agriculturally-based populations with complex political and religious systems. While nothing on the scale of the Aztecs and Incas developed north of Mexico, **maize cultivation spread from Mexico into the Rio Grande Valley and beyond** (ex: Cahokia, Pueblos). **Along the Atlantic coast, native peoples practiced both agriculture and hunting-gathering**. American Indians living on the **edges of the Western Plains established a more mobile lifestyle.**

By the late 1400s, European explorers began to arrive in the Americas by sea, **seeking to expand their empires**. The Spanish and the Portuguese were the first to "discover" the Americas as they looked for sea routes to Asia. The Spanish conquistadors began to systematically conquer native empires in Mesoamerica and Peru, **destroying civilizations and introducing diseases that killed millions.** The Indians of Mesoamerica and South America were better organized and able to offer some resistance to European conquerors, while those of North America were weaker lineage-based societies that were more easily subjugated.

Europe in the mid-1400s was largely a land of peasants farming manorial land. Hierarchical authority rested in the hands of the monarchs, the nobility, and the Church, although all of these institutions were on the verge of change with the arrival of the Renaissance. **New technologies made exploration and trade easier.** The power of the merchant class grew as **Europeans became aware of the immense riches to be found in Asia and other parts of the world.** The Portuguese were the first to branch out toward Africa in search of a lucrative gold trade. It was through this trade that the Portuguese adopted the system of acquiring African slaves. As their African trade networks expanded, other European countries also looked for ways to both exploit Africa and find a quicker route to the Far East. **Trade in African slaves soon became a lucrative international business** that would have a lasting impact on four continents.

The Spanish soon replaced the Portuguese as the leading empire builders, sending expeditions around Africa as well as across the Atlantic. Native tribes in the West Indies as well as in Mesoamerica fell at the hands of Spanish conquistadors. Many of those who survived the initial onslaught later **died of epidemic European diseases** (ex: smallpox, measles). Paying little attention to American Indian culture and traditions, the **Spanish justified their conquests, seeing themselves as bearers of "civilization."** The Spanish created their own bureaucratic empire in the New World, establishing institutions such as the **Catholic Church to convert native peoples** and the Spanish legal code, as well as organizing **American Indians into their labor force in a system known as the *encomienda*. The Spanish justified the subjugation of Africans and American Indians by claiming superiority and offering them the opportunity to become Christians.**

Chapter 2

American Experiments, 1521-1700

Chapter 2 explores the three types of distinctive colonies that emerged in the Americas: the Spanish colonies in Mexico and Peru that relied on the wealth and labor of American Indian peoples, the plantation colonies of the tropics and subtropics where slave labor worked to product sugar and other crops, and the colonies where

Europeans sought to establish societies similar to the ones they knew in Europe. All of these colonial endeavors brought disease, displacement, or subjugation to native people, but there were **significant differences in the Europeans' approaches to colonization.**

The Spanish came to the New World in search of gold and silver, relying on conquistadors to establish military control and then sending priests to work for the **conversion of native people to Catholicism.** Many Spanish soldiers eventually took American Indian wives, leading to the **creation of a society that included large numbers of mixed-race people.** The Spanish used the ***encomienda* system** to commandeer American Indian lands and labor. **Some American Indian groups resisted Spanish control and attempted to retain some of their cultural traditions (ex: The Pueblo Revolt). When African slaves replaced native labor, they too managed to retain much of their own cultures.**

The **Columbian Exchange** is the term given to the movement of peoples, diseases, plants, and animals among societies on both sides of the Atlantic Ocean. Beginning with the Spanish and the Portuguese, **epidemic diseases from the Old World,** such as smallpox, influenza, measles, and yellow fever, decimated Native American populations. The exchange of **new crops and livestock** transformed the American landscape.

The plantation colonies that emerged first in Brazil saw **the introduction of plantation-based African slave labor to the Americas who replaced Native Americans,** who had succumbed in large numbers to disease. Later **plantation societies emerged in the Caribbean,** based on a single crop: sugar. In the colony of Virginia, established at Jamestown in 1607, tobacco cultivation based on the plantation model emerged as the dominant economic system. At first, planters used indentured servants from England, but as the **supply of indentured servants dwindled, the colony came to rely on slaves imported from Africa.** Slavery as an institution became more rigid and harsher, and a **slave's status became permanent and hereditary.** Although they had few rights, **slaves managed to find ways to resist their bondage.** Continuing **competition for land led to conflicts between American Indians and settlers as well as conflicts among the settlers themselves** (ex: Bacon's Rebellion).

The Dutch colony of New Netherland and the French colony of New France both began as fur trading enterprises. French and Dutch trappers and traders often **intermarried with American Indians, building trade alliances in order to obtain valuable furs**. In New France, Jesuit missionaries made concerted efforts to convert Native Americans to Catholicism, allowing some incorporation of native traditions into Catholic rituals.

The British colonies in New England, settled by Separatists and Puritans, established **closely knit communities that stressed family and religious principles. They founded small villages and towns and organized their economy around farming and commerce.** They also brought with them British forms of government, establishing the first representative assemblies in the New World. As the Puritan population grew and settlements expanded, they came into **direct conflict with American Indians** (ex: Puritan-Pequot War, Metacom's War).

Period 1 Practice Questions
Multiple-Choice Questions

Questions 1–3 refer to the map below.

Native American Peoples, 1492

1. Which of the following represents the most important historical factor for why American Indians and Europeans held varying views of land use?
   (a) Different technologies
   (b) Opposing views over mineral wealth
   (c) Divergent worldviews
   (d) Different social diversification

2. Which of the following characterize an element of American Indian culture in the New World prior to European exploration?
   (a) Most American Indian nations held common languages
   (b) Most American Indian nations established trade networks over large swaths of territory
   (c) Very few wars over territory among American Indian nations
   (d) A lack of adaptation to the physical environment

3. Which of the following is true about American Indian cultures prior to contact with Europeans?
   (a) They experienced frequent epidemic diseases
   (b) They had developed wheeled vehicles pulled by livestock
   (c) They exchanged goods with African societies
   (d) They developed economics based on the environment

Questions 4–7 refer to the map below.

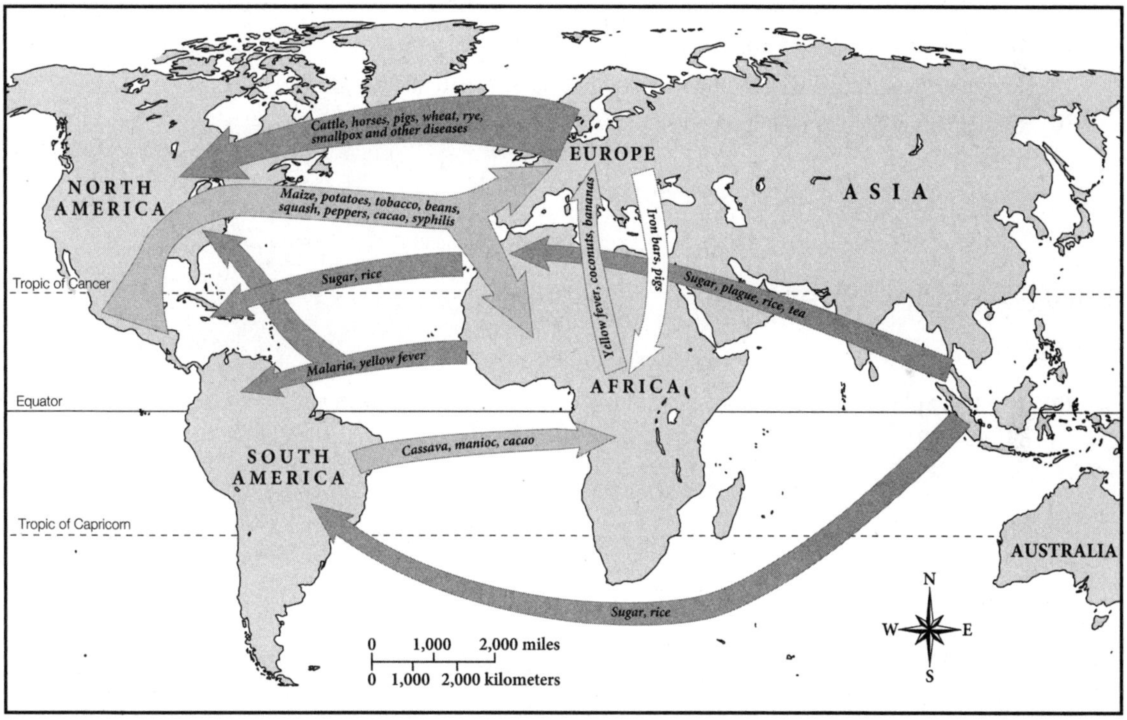

The Columbian Exchange

4. Which of the following represents the most important long-term benefit of the Columbian Exchange?
   (a) the exchange of diverse crops between Europe and the Americas
   (b) the introduction of horses into Europe
   (c) the introduction of cattle into Europe
   (d) the exchange of architectural design techniques between the two continents

5. The primary negative consequence of the Columbian exchange was
   (a) food products that led to debilitating illnesses for both American Indians and Europeans.
   (b) concepts of autocratic governments that delayed the development of democracy.
   (c) epidemiological disasters spread by Europeans in the Americas.
   (d) the transition from feudalism to capitalism.

6. Which of the following represents the most significant outcome of the Columbian Exchange in Europe?
   (a) European religious rivalries
   (b) Varied intellectual and religious rationale for colonization
   (c) The introduction of sugar to the European diet
   (d) Large population growth

7. Which of the following developments represents Spanish exploration patterns prior to 1600?
   (a) The movement through a Northwest Passage route to Asia
   (b) Migration to and within South America only
   (c) Migration and settlement throughout large areas of North and South America
   (d) Settlement along the northeast coast of North America

END OF MULTIPLE-CHOICE SECTION

Short-Answer Question

1. Answer a, b, and c.
   (a) Briefly explain ONE difference in worldviews between the Spanish and American Indians prior to 1650.

   (b) Briefly explain ONE difference between the economic systems of the Spanish and American Indians prior to 1650.

   (c) Briefly explain ONE historical factor that accounts for the interactions between the Spanish and American Indians.

END OF SHORT-ANSWER SECTION

PERIOD 2, 1607-1754

Overview

Period 2 begins in 1607 when the English established the first permanent North American colony at Jamestown, Virginia. The period focuses on colonial development and European rivalries in North America up to the eve of the French and Indian War. Included are comparisons of European interactions with American Indians, as well as the imperialist powers' approaches to colonization.

European colonizers had differen t goals and methods as each sought to expand their hold on North American territory. The Spanish maintained tight control of the areas they conquered, relying on military garrisons and working to convert the native population to Catholicism. The French and the Dutch were much less disruptive, working to forge trade alliances that involved fewer Europeans and often intermarrying with American Indians as they sought to build networks to acquire furs and other goods for European markets. The English sought to establish permanent colonies, clearing large tracts of land for agriculture, which disrupted American Indian hunting and resources, leading to hostile encounters.

Because English colonists often came as family groups, they rarely intermarried with the native population or with Africans who were brought over as slaves, thereby creating a society marked by strict social and racial lines. As English indentured servants became fewer and the demand for labor to produce goods for European markets grew, southern colonists in particular increasingly turned to slave labor. Slavery in the English colonies gradually became more widespread and rigid, with slaves and their offspring held in perpetuity. In spite of these difficult circumstances, Africans managed to maintain many of their cultural and traditional values, and they found numerous ways to resist their captors.

Differences in climate, geography, and available resources resulted in striking regional differences among the British colonies in North America. New England, settled mainly by Puritans, developed into a closely knit region with an economy built around shipping, commerce, and farming. The middle colonies were the most diverse, relying on trade as well as agriculture. The Chesapeake region depended on tobacco, relying first on the labor of indentured servants and then increasingly on slaves. Farther south and in the West Indies, colonists grew other staple crops, sugar in particular, and depended heavily on slave labor.

As the European empires expanded in North America, they competed for land and resources and came into conflict with each other and with American Indians. They often tried to make alliances with various American Indian groups to further their own interests. When the emerging British Empire attempted to assert imperial control over its North American colonies, the colonists began to find themselves at odds with the mother country.

American Indians grew alarmed as the colonial holdings expanded. Threats to their traditional ways of life and the dangers of European diseases began to outweigh their desire for European trade goods. Although the Spanish made some accommodations to American Indian culture after the Pueblo Revolt in 1680, English colonists refused to make concessions. Conflicts between American Indians and Europeans were made more destructive by the introduction of European weapons and alcohol.

Colonies in eighteenth-century North America were part of the commercial, political, and cultural network known as the Atlantic world. Goods traveled to and from the Americas and Europe, and Africa became the source of slave labor for the New World.

The British colonies exhibited many characteristics of life in England, including political institutions, religious denominations, commercial interests, and an admiration for the ideals of the Enlightenment. The growing reliance on slave labor and the reluctance to accept either slaves or American Indians as equals led to a colonial society with clearly drawn racial divisions, unlike those of the French or the Spanish.

The British government attempted to assert stricter control over their North American colonies as they grew more important to the economy and prestige of the empire. Periods of benign neglect had led the colonists to recognize their ability to be self-reliant and to lessen their sense of being distinct regions.

They began to realize their similar interests and advantages, which often did not fit neatly with the demands of the British government. British mercantilist policies often went against colonial interests, and resistance to imperial control became more frequent.

This period of history ends with colonial resistance on the rise as the colonists became more experienced in self-government, more accepting of religious diversity, more dissatisfied with British imperialist economic control, and more interested in the ideals of the Enlightenment.

Key Terms

Be sure that you understand the meaning of these terms and their relevance in U.S. history. Page numbers from the textbook are provided.

Atlantic slave trade (27, 37, 90–103)
Chesapeake Colonies (47–52, 81–82)
Fur trade (58, 60)
Cash crop (48, 52)
Indentured servants (54, 56, 119)
Puritans (62–69, 112–113)
Middle Atlantic colonies (117–122)
New England colonies (62–69, 80–81)
Plantation economies (91–92)
Town meetings (67)
Elected assemblies (106)
Mercantilism (83–85, 107–108)
Metacom's (King Phillip's) War (69–70)
Pueblo Revolt (70–71)
First Great Awakening (128–131)
Enlightenment ideas (124–127)
Protestant evangelism (317–318)

Focus Questions

As you study Period 2, keep the following thematic questions in mind.

American and National Identity

- To what extent did British American colonists develop a sense of identity separate from that of English men and women?
- What factors encouraged and what factors impeded the development of an "American" identity?
- What group and regional identities emerged in the thirteen British American colonies?
- Why and how did the English, the Spanish, and the French develop different views on race?

Work, Exchange, and Technology

- How did patterns of exchange shape the societies that emerged in North America between 1607 and 1754?
- How did British American colonists react to the implementation of the British economic policies of the late seventeenth and early eighteenth centuries?
- How did new technologies lead to increasingly destructive conflicts between European and American Indians?

Geography and the Environment

- How did the colonial environment shape the lives of the colonists in ways that contributed to their eventual separation from England?
- What was the role of the natural environment in shaping regional and group identities in colonial North America?

Migration and Settlement

- What were the various models of colonization that the Spanish, French, Dutch, and English in North America adopted?
- What settlement patterns emerged in this period in North America, and how did these shape colonial society?
- What factors shaped the institution of slavery in the British North American colonies?

Politics and Power

- In what ways did British American colonists model their political institutions on England? How did these colonists adapt these institutions in a way that seemed uniquely "American"?
- What were the sources of conflict between native peoples and Europeans in the seventeenth century and the first half of the eighteenth century? How did the resolution of these conflicts change the lives of American Indians and those of European descent?
- In what ways did African Americans resist slavery?

America in the World

- What factors led to increasing opposition to both British and Spanish authority in North America?
- How did rivalries and competition between European nations affect the lives of colonists, American Indians, and African Americans in North America?

American and Regional Culture

- How did cultural differences shape the relationships among Europeans, Native Americans, and African Americans in colonial America?
- What regional differences in religion, family life, and community values emerged in the British American colonies? What accounted for these differences?

Social Structures

- How did religion shape the development of colonial societies?
- What role did religious discord play in colonial communities?

Thematic Timeline

TIME	Key Events
1607	
	American and National Identity • English colonies founded without an overarching imperial system • English civil war allows colonial "big men" to govern themselves **Work, Exchange, and Technology** • Indentured servitude provides labor for the Chesapeake tobacco economy • Yeoman society takes root in New England **Geography and the Environment** • Tobacco takes root in the Chesapeake

TIME	Key Events
	Migration and Settlement • Young male laborers dominate migration to the Chesapeake • Migration to New England brings intact households **Politics and Power** • New England, Chesapeake, and West Indies elites establish their authority • King Charles I beheaded by Parliament (1649) **America in the World** • England intermittently ignores its American colonies **Social Structures** • Puritan magistrates and tobacco planters govern the colonies
1660	
	American and National Identity • Restoration makes England a monarchy again; royalist revival • The Glorious Revolution makes England a constitutional monarchy • Massachusetts loses its charter (1684) and gains a new one (1691) **Work, Exchange, and Technology** • South Atlantic System links plantation and neo-European colonies • Mercantilist legislation in England: Navigation Acts (1651, 1660, 1663) • New York inherits Hudson River Valley manors from the Dutch; Carolina proprietors fail to institute a manorial system • Migrants to Pennsylvania seek freehold lands • Rapid expansion of African slave imports undergirds sugar, tobacco, and rice plantation systems **Geography and the Environment** • Native American populations of the eastern woodlands decline catastrophically • African Americans are imported to tropical and semitropical colonies in large numbers **Migration and Settlement** • The Middle Passage shapes Africans' experiences of arrival • American Indian slave trade emerges in South Carolina • First Mennonites arrive in Pennsylvania (1683) **Politics and Power** • Dominion of New England (1686–1689) • Glorious Revolution (1688–1689) • War of the League of Augsburg (1689–1697) • Founding of the Restoration Colonies: the Carolinas (1663), New York (1664), New Jersey (1664), Pennsylvania (1681) **America in the World** • England's proprietary colonies claim much of the Atlantic coast of North America **American and Regional Culture** • Collapse of the Puritan Commonwealth leads to toleration in England • Isaac Newton publishes *Principia Mathematica* (1687)

1690

American and National Identity

- Colonists gain autonomy in the post–Glorious Revolution era
- Tribalization develops among Native American peoples

Work, Exchange, and Technology

- New England shipbuilding industry and merchant community dominate the coastal trade
- Agricultural labor and artisanal skills in high demand in the Middle colonies

Geography and the Environment

- Rice cultivation begins in the Carolina and Georgia low country
- New England fish feed southern Europe and Caribbean Slaves

Migration and Settlement

- Quakers emigrate to Pennsylvania and New Jersey Second wave of Germans arrives in Pennsylvania, Shenandoah Valley

Politics and Power

- Parliament creates Board of Trade (1696)
- War of the Spanish Succession (1702–1713)

America in the World

- European wars begin to spill onto American shores
- Pennsylvania begins to draw large numbers of Scots-Irish and German migrants

American and Regional Culture

- John Locke publishes *Two Treatises on Government* (1690)
- Print revolution begins the press (1798)

Social Structures

- Rise of toleration among colonial Protestants

1720

American and National Identity

- African American community forms in the Chesapeake
- Planter aristocracy emerges in the Chesapeake and South Carolina
- Culture of gentility spreads among well-to-do

Work, Exchange, and Technology

- The price of wheat rises (doubles in Philadelphia, 1720–1770)
- British trade dominates the Atlantic
- Opportunity and inequality in the Middle colonies
- Ohio Company of Virginia receives 200,000 acres (1749)

Geography and the Environment

- The pace of transatlantic shipping accelerates
- A road network begins to knit together colonial towns

Migration and Settlement

- Scots-Irish begin migrating to Pennsylvania (c. 1720)
- Parliament charters Georgia (1732)
- Penns make Walking Purchase from the Delawares (1737)

TIME	Key Events
	America in the World • The South Atlantic System connects America, Africa, and Europe • Mercantilism shapes England's policies toward its American colonies **Politics and Power** • Robert Walpole is prime minister (1720–1742) • Stono Rebellion (1739) • War of Jenkins's Ear (1739–1741) • War of the Austrian Succession (1740–1748) • The South Atlantic System connects America, Africa, and Europe • Mercantilism shapes England's policies toward its American colonies **American and Regional Culture** • Benjamin Franklin founds American Philosophical Society (1743) **Social Structures** • George Whitefield's visit to America sparks the Great Awakening (1739)
1754	
	American and National Identity • Victory in the Great War for Empire sparks pro-British pride in the colonies • Desire for political autonomy and economic independence grows **Work, Exchange, and Technology** • Freehold society in crisis in New England • Half of Middle colonies' white men landless • Conflicts over western lands and political power (1750–1775) • British industry being mechanized; colonial debt crisis **Geography and the Environment** • The vast geographical scale of North America challenges European armies in the French and Indian War **Migration and Settlement** • 40,000 Germans and Swiss emigrate to Pennsylvania (1749–1756) • Anglo-Americans push onto backcountry lands **Politics and Power** • French and Indian War/Seven Years' War (1754–1763) • The Albany Congress (1754) • The Treaty of Paris (1763) • Pontiac's Rebellion (1763) **America in the World** • Britain wins the Great War for Empire and claims eastern North America **American and Regional Culture** • New colleges, newspapers, magazines • Neolin promotes nativist revival among Ohio Indians (1763) **Social Structures** • At least twelve religious denominations in Philadelphia

America's History Chapter Summaries

(required AP® content in bold)

Chapter 3
The British Atlantic World, 1607–1750

Chapter 3 examines the changes in politics and society in the British North American colonies in the century leading up to the American Revolution. The British government sought to tighten control over colonial commerce with the imposition of numerous Navigation Acts, which only increased the colonists' desire to regulate their own trade. King James II further angered the northern colonies when he abolished their own assemblies and created his own Dominion of New England, an organization that fell apart during England's Glorious Revolution in 1688. The years that followed saw sporadic periods of salutary neglect when colonists were able to regulate their own affairs, though the British periodically reasserted control, which led to even more colonial resentment. These years also saw the enormous expansion of the slave trade and slave system, particularly in the southern colonies and the West Indies, a system of labor that had an impact of workers throughout the colonies.

In the 1660s, King Charles II of England reinvigorated colonial expansion with the creation of the Carolina colony, the establishment of the colony of Pennsylvania, and the acquisition of New York and New Jersey. He sought to give Britain a **mercantilist advantage and to maximize British profits** by restricting colonial trade with a series of Navigation Acts. After his death, his brother, James II, continued these policies, adding another layer to colonial control with the imposition of his Dominion of New England, which gave the king and his representative authority in decisions about local government, trade, and charters. These restrictions were weakened by the Glorious Revolution, though the British reasserted their authority in various ways. The colonists began to see both the **advantages of self-government and their own abilities to be successful at managing their own affairs**.

The colonists were further disillusioned by their involvement in England's colonial wars with European rivals, as they found themselves fighting proxy battles. The **colonists were often dissatisfied with the territorial settlements that ended these wars**. The wars also led to increasing conflicts with American Indians, as the various tribes sought to make alliances with both Europeans and each other that they thought might benefit them. Few of these alliances had any long-term rewards for the American Indians.

The growth of the Atlantic world economy and the North American slave trade brought tremendous wealth to England and its colonies, but at tremendous cost to the peoples of West and Central Africa. Millions of Africans were captured, transported across the Atlantic in unspeakable conditions, and sold into slavery in the New World. The **enormous number of Africans transported had a significant impact on life in Africa and in the colonies**. Those who survived the dreaded Middle Passage were destined for a life of hardship. West Indian-style slavery came to the Carolinas and Chesapeake to cultivate rice and tobacco. In spite of the harsh conditions under which they lived, the slave communities that emerged were marked with distinct signs of African cultural traditions and values. Major rebellions were few in the early days of slavery, but **many more subtle forms of resistance were common**. Southern colonies in particular developed a **rigid social hierarchy**, setting the landowners apart from the landless and all whites apart from the slaves.

As the southern colonies became increasingly dependent on slave labor, the northern colonies developed a thriving maritime economy and a more urban society. Wealthy merchants headed society, but a middle class of artisans and shopkeepers slowly developed. Propertyless workers made up the next tier of society, with a relatively small percentage of slaves at the bottom.

During the occasional periods of salutary neglect that the colonists enjoyed, interest grew in self-government. Colonial assemblies became increasingly powerful and outspoken, challenging the restrictions of the **British mercantilist system**. Periods of salutary neglect led colonists to long for more permanent control over their own affairs. The British responded with determination to reassert control over what they saw as **rebellious subjects who posed a threat to the imperialist system**. The stage was being set for a political showdown between the colonies and Great Britain.

Chapter 4
Growth, Diversity, and Conflict, 1720–1763

Chapter 4 examines the social changes that occurred in British North America in the mid-eighteenth century. It begins by tracing the changes in the New England colonies and then examines the diversity of the middle colonies. It also explores the tremendous cultural changes that were the result of advances in transportation and print technology, the ideas that emanated from the Enlightenment, and the major religious upheavals in both the northern and southern colonies. The final section focuses on the French and Indian War (also known as the Seven Years' War) and the continuing struggle over land and expansion.

The New England colonies experienced dramatic population growth in the eighteenth century, largely the result of natural increase. Closely knit Puritan **families and communities continued to rely on a mixed economy**. While colonists saw their communities as models of democracy, women remained second-class citizens, and a social hierarchy grew as some families were able to increase their wealth while many others remained relatively poor. The fast-growing population also strained the New England colonies as good farmland became scarce.

The **middle colonies were quite diverse**, with Dutch colonists in New York and the Hudson Valley, Quaker Englishmen and women in Pennsylvania, and Presbyterian Scots-Irish and German Protestants of various denominations throughout the region. The cities of Philadelphia and New York were centers of trade and destinations for new immigrants, giving the region a flourishing economy. Most groups retained characteristics of their different cultures.

A road network developed that supplemented the "Great Wagon Road" that ran through the Shenandoah Valley. These roads carried people, produce, and merchandise east and west, along with newspapers and pamphlets. The **print revolution that was occurring in Europe quickly spread to the British colonies, bringing with it new ideas that would reshape the colonial mind set.**

Colonial culture was also influenced by the ideas of the European Enlightenment, the religious revival known as the Great Awakening, and the impact of British trade. The old idea that political authority was given by God to monarchs was replaced with the concept of natural rights; that is, the idea that people had the right to change governments if they felt their needs were not being met. Traditional religion was also challenged with some speculating that they might be better served by rational thought and scientific solutions to their problems rather than worrying about appeasing a vengeful Calvinist God. Some colonial intellectuals like Benjamin Franklin and Thomas Paine leaned toward deism, relying on **"natural reason" to help them define right and wrong**. Others sought to renew interest in religion through Pietism, the belief that worship should be more emotional and personal, a shift away from the academic approach of the earlier Puritan clergy. New England saw the rise of charismatic preachers like Jonathan Edwards and George Whitefield, leaders in what became known as the Great Awakening.

As these changes were sweeping the colonies, more challenges to traditional ways of life were brewing in Europe. Britain and France, along with their various American Indian allies, fought each other in **several imperial wars**. The largest of these conflicts, the Seven Years' War (also known as the French and Indian War), resulted in the final **defeat of the French in North America**. At the same time, **British colonists were demanding the right to move farther west, regardless of the potential for conflicts with both European powers and American Indians.**

Period 2 Practice Questions

Multiple-Choice Questions

Questions 1–3 refer to the excerpt below.

> "And it is further enacted by the authority aforesaid, that from and after the first day of April, which shall be in the year of our Lord one thousand six hundred sixty-one, no sugars, tobacco, cotton-wool, indigoes, ginger, fustic, or other dyeing wood, of the growth, production, or manufacture of any English plantations in America, Asia, or Africa, shall be shipped, carried, conveyed, or transported from any of the said English plantations to any land, island, territory, dominion, port, or place whatsoever, other than to such other English plantations as do belong to his Majesty, his heirs and successors, or to the kingdom of England or Ireland, or principality of Wales, or town of Berwick upon Tweed, there to be laid on shore . . ."

Excerpt from the Navigation Acts, 1660–1696

1. The policy described in the excerpt represent the British attempt to
   (a) encourage the British North American colonies to develop self-sufficient commodities.
   (b) assert imperial enforcement of a mercantile economic system.
   (c) increase colonial production of manufactured goods.
   (d) establish a high protective tariff on colonial goods entering Great Britain.

2. The excerpt above best illustrates which of the following historical developments?
   (a) the attempt by the British to establish a coherent economic system
   (b) the rigid and successful enforcement of the British economic system
   (c) the attempt to establish Atlantic trade networks
   (d) conflicts with colonists over the fur trade with the Iroquois

3. Which of the following is NOT true of the series of English acts that regulated trade during the seventeenth century?
   (a) They benefitted both the colonies and England in certain ways
   (b) They were largely ignored by the American colonies if they were not beneficial
   (c) They required that colonial goods be carried in English ships with English crews
   (d) They sparked frequent violent rebellions over British authority beginning with King Philip's (Metacom's) War

Questions 4-6 refer to the excerpt below.

> "[New Englanders] are at present a numerous and thriving people and in 20 years more are likely . . . to be mighty rich and powerful and not at all careful of their dependence upon old England. . . . I take the way of roughness and peremptory orders, with force to back them, to be utterly unadvisable. For they are already too strong to be compelled . . . and though I apprehend them yet not at that point to cast us off voluntarily and of choice; yet I believe if we use severity towards them in their government civil or religious, that they will (being made desperate) set up for themselves and reject us."

Earl of Sandwich, "Comments upon New England," 1671

4. Which of the following is best reflected by the above passage?
   (a) New England was threatening the world trade dominance of Great Britain in the late seventeenth century
   (b) The success of the Atlantic Trade throughout the British West Indies
   (c) Economic prosperity that led to calls for rebellion from England
   (d) Colonists' experiencing both Anglicization and a spirit of economic independence

5. The above passage indicates that the New England colonies
   (a) were successfully developing a diverse economy.
   (b) rejected the Anglican Church, leading to English repression.
   (c) dominated trade with American Indians, reducing British profits.
   (d) were dependent on Great Britain for raw materials.

6. Which of the following best represents a reason for the development of the New England colonies as expressed by the Earl of Sandwich?
   (a) The commitment of British troops to protect the New England colonists from American Indian allies of the French
   (b) The continued naval dominance of the Spanish fleet
   (c) British preoccupation with internal and European affairs
   (d) The failure of New England to provide England with useful raw materials

Questions 7–9 refer to the excerpt below.

"Now, know ye, that we, being willing to encourage the hopeful undertaking of our said loyal and loving subjects . . . that our royal will and pleasure is, that no person within the said colony, at any time hereafter shall be any wise molested, punished, disquieted, or called in question, for any differences in opinion in matters of religion, and do not actually disturb the civil peace of our said colony; but that all and every person and persons may, from time to time, and at all times hereafter, freely and fully have and enjoy his and their own judgments and consciences, in matters of religious concernments, throughout the tract of land hereafter mentioned."

Charter of Rhode Island and Providence Plantations, July 8, 1663

7. The excerpt above best serves as evidence of which of the following?
   (a) Varied relations with American Indian
   (b) European colonization and settlement in the New World
   (c) Colonial opposition to enslavement
   (d) Cultural and religious norms varied across the British North American colonies

8. Provisions such as those in the Rhode Island charter would ultimately encourage movement toward which of the following principles in colonial America?
   (a) Increased tolerance over belief systems
   (b) Devotion to egalitarianism
   (c) The establishment of peaceful relations with American Indians
   (d) The use of enslaved labor

9. Which of the following regions represented similar belief structures to that described in the excerpt?
   (a) Carolinas
   (b) Middle Colonies
   (c) New England
   (d) Chesapeake

Questions 10–12 are based on the excerpt below.

"That for all persons . . . which during the next seven years after Midsummer Day 1618 shall go into Virginia with intent there to inhabit, if they continue there three years or die after they are shipped there shall be a grant made of fifty acres for every person . . . which grants to be made respectively to such persons and their heirs at whose charges the said persons going to inhabit in Virginia shall be transported."

Virginia Company Instructions to Sir George Yeardley, November 18, 1618

10. The system described above was primarily initiated to
    (a) protect colonists settling in Virginia from attacks by American Indians.
    (b) encourage the growth of an elite class of plantation holders.
    (c) provide an adequate labor force to make the land profitable.
    (d) encourage the deportation of the displaced class from England.

11. Which of the following best describes an historical consequence of the system described above?
    (a) Enslavement replaced indentured servitude as the chief labor source prior to 1650
    (b) A majority of English people emigrating to Virginia came as indentured servants prior to 1650
    (c) There was little dissension between the backcountry and the Tidewater prior to 1700
    (d) The Anglican Church was firmly established as the state church of Virginia by 1660

12. Because no such system was established in New England,
    (a) the average size of landholdings was smaller in New England than in the Chesapeake.
    (b) New England was the last colonial region to become "overpopulated."
    (c) African slaves became the chief labor source in New England.
    (d) the Chesapeake colonies became more homogeneous than New England in both religion and ethnic background.

END OF MULTIPLE-CHOICE SECTION

Short-Answer Question

"SIR, Having notice that under color of a trade to Newfoundland for fish, great quantities of wine, brandy and other European goods, are imported from thence into his Majesty's plantations, particularly New England, on an allegation, that the said New Foundland is accounted as one of the said plantations. To which purpose, it is now become a Magazine of all sorts of goods brought thither directly from France, Holland, Scotland, Ireland and other places, which is not only contrary to law, but greatly to the prejudice of his Majesty's Customs, and to the trade and navigation of this Kingdom. To the end, therefore, that so destructive and growing an evil may be timely prevented, we desire you . . . to give public notice to all persons concerned . . . that they be very careful not to suffer any European goods, other than what are by the aforesaid law and Proclamation accepted, to be imported into New England."

Commercial Orders to Governor Andros (1686–1687)

1. Using the excerpt above, answer a, b, and c.
    (a) Briefly describe ONE change in the economic relationship between the British North American colonies and England from the period 1607-1754.

    (b) Briefly describe ONE change in the political relationship between the British North American colonies and England from the period 1607-1754.

    (c) Briefly describe ONE continuity in the political or economic relationship between the North American colonies and England form the period 1607-1754.

END OF SHORT-ANSWER SECTION

Document-Based Question

Directions: The following question in based on the accompanying documents. The documents have been edited for this exercise. Spend approximately 15 minutes planning and 45 minutes writing your answer.

Write an essay that does the following:

- States an appropriate thesis that directly addresses all parts of the question.
- Supports the thesis or argument with evidence from all or all but one of the documents AND your knowledge of U.S. history beyond the documents.
- Analyzes all or all but one of the documents.
- Explains the significance of the author's point of view, author's purpose, historical context, and/or audience for at least three documents.
- Uses historical evidence beyond the documents to support your argument.
- Places the argument in the context of broader regional, national, or global processes.
- Incorporates all of the elements above into a convincing essay.

Question: Evaluate the extent to which different settlement patterns shaped the New England and Chesapeake colonies from the period 1607-1754.

Document 1

Source: Letter from indentured servant in Virginia to His Parents in England, 1623

I am not half a quarter so strong as I was in England, and all is for want of victuals, for I do protest unto you, that I have eaten more in [a] day at home th[a]n I have allowed me here for a week.

Document 2

Source: John Winthrop, *A Modell of Christian Charity,* 1630

We shall be as a City upon a hill. The eyes of all people are upon us. So that if we shall deal falsely with our God in this work we have undertaken, and so cause him to withdraw his present help from us, we shall be made a story and a by-word throughout the world.

Document 3

Source: John Underhill, *Newes from America; Or, A New and Experimentall Discoverie of New England* (London, 1638).

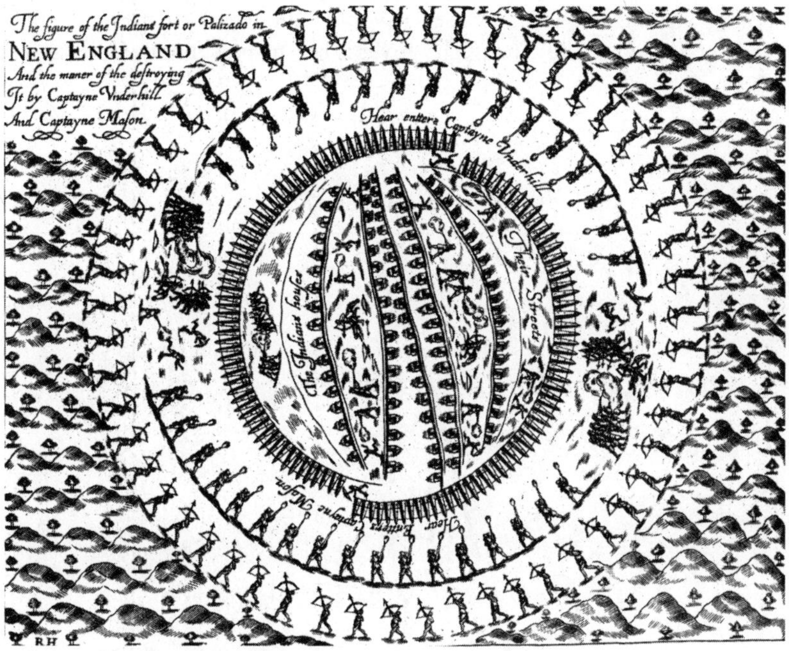

Pequot Village Massacre Woodcut

Document 4

Source: Nathaniel Bacon, *Declaration,* 1676

Another main article of our guilt is our open and manifest aversion of all, not only the foreign but the protected and darling Indians.

Document 5

Source: An act for preventing Negroes Insurrections, Statutes of Virginia, June 1680–ACT X

Be it enacted by the kings most excellent majesty by and with the consent of the general assembly, and it is hereby enacted by the authority aforesaid, that from and after the publication of this law, it shall not be lawful for any negro or other slave to carry or arm himself with any club, staff, gun, sword or any other weapon of defense or offense, nor to go or depart from of his masters ground without a certificate from his master, mistress or overseer and such permission not to be granted but upon particular and necessary occasions.

Document 6

Source: Benjamin Wadsworth, selection from a Puritan marriage manual, 1712

Though the husband is to rule his family and his wife, yet his government of his wife should not be with rigor, haughtiness, harshness, severity; but with the greatest love, gentleness, kindness, tenderness that may be. Though he governs her, he must not treat her as a servant, but as his own flesh.

Document 7

Source: U.S. Bureau of the Census

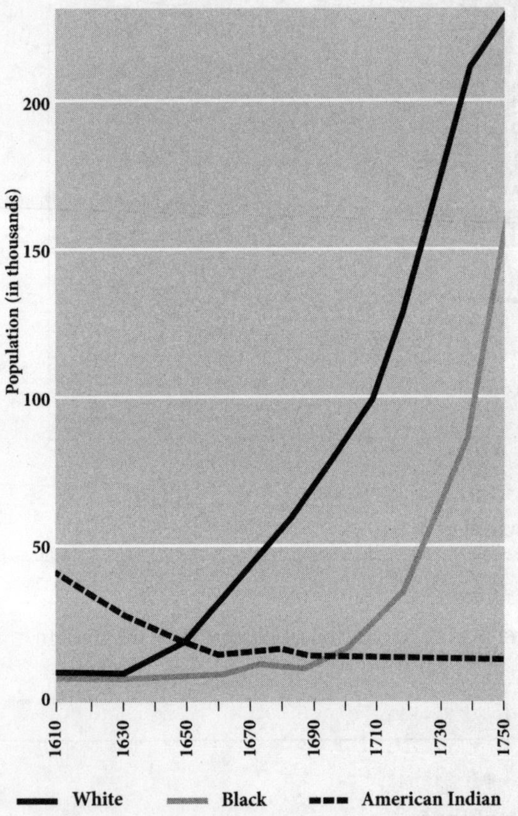

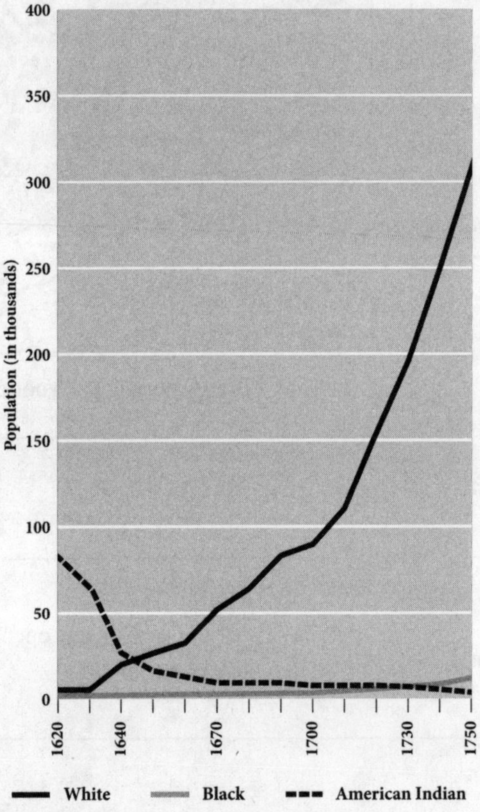

END OF DOCUMENT-BASED SECTION

PERIOD 3, 1754-1800

Overview

Period 3 traces the developments that led to the expulsion of the French as a factor in the imperial struggle for North America and the subsequent American Revolution. It then focuses on the efforts by the new United States to define its government, policies, identity, and place in the world.

Although the British were victorious over France in the Seven Years' War ending in 1763, they faced new problems with their North American colonies and the American Indian tribes. British acquisition of lands west of the Appalachians and in the Ohio Valley meant dismantling of the French-Indian trade networks and new waves of colonial settlers. The opening of lands west of the Appalachians led to rapid settlement and renewed conflicts with both American Indians and the British who remained in the Ohio Valley. Colonists in the backcountry developed an independent yeoman culture, increasing tensions as they sought to defend their new homes. American Indians tried to form new alliances to ward off these threats, and the British sought to limit migration of settlers into western territories.

Colonists, frustrated at attempts to stop western settlement, were also angered when the British began to tighten control over trade and taxes in an effort to clear debts left from the Seven Years' War. Colonial resistance was fueled by the ideas of the Enlightenment as well as the determination to be treated fairly under British law. In spite of British military and financial advantages, the resulting revolution succeeded due to colonial resilience, ideological commitment, and timely foreign intervention.

The late eighteenth century was a time of international debate about religion, politics, and new forms of government, leading to new theories that challenged old imperial systems and beliefs. Americans embraced the ideals of the Enlightenment, hoping to create a model republican government that would guarantee natural rights and protect the people from both autocratic leaders and the rule of the mob. Thomas Paine's *Common Sense* made the case for a republic. The first attempt at government of the new country was the Articles of Confederation, which concentrated power in the hands of the legislature and had no chief executive. This document proved too limited and the central government it created was too weak to be effective. The Articles were replaced by the Constitution after long deliberations about the proper role of the federal government and a series of compromises about representation. Ratification almost failed when some states felt there were not strong enough guarantees of individual rights, but the addition of the Bill of Rights calmed those fears. Continuing debates in the new government over federal power, foreign policy, and economics eventually led to the formation of political parties.

The new United States also had to deal with foreign policy issues. Early leaders felt the best course to take with Europe was that of neutrality in order to protect the new nation's borders and secure favorable trade alliances. The French Revolution presented a special challenge because the French had aided the colonists in their own revolution. President Washington restated his belief in the importance of neutrality, though others in government continued to debate the wisdom of this approach.

Slavery remained a point of disagreement among the states in the new nation. Many felt the existence of slavery ran counter to the ideals of the American Revolution and the Declaration of Independence. To ensure passage of the Constitution, debates over slavery were postponed, though the issue continued to be at the forefront of political debate for decades.

In California, the Spanish continued to expand their mission settlements, which offered some social mobility to soldiers and settlers. The Northwest Ordinance created an orderly way for land to be sold and new states to be admitted, while also providing for public education and prohibiting slavery. American Indian claims and rights remained unaddressed, however, and they continued to lose land to settlers. Increasing need for access to the Mississippi River led to new problems for the new country with both the Spanish and the British.

People in the United States still wrestled with the tension between regional identity and loyalty and their loyalties to the federal government. The South's determination to expand slavery into new territories conflicted with states in other parts of the country that were moving to end the institution. Women also confronted the disconnect between the ideals of equality promoted by the Enlightenment and the Revolution with their second-class status in the new country. White women had to be content with the ideal of "republican motherhood," seeing their role as that of forming good citizens as they raised their children at home rather than playing a role in public life.

Key Terms

Be sure that you understand the meaning of these terms and their relevance in U.S. history. Page numbers from the textbook are provided.

Seven Year's (French and Indian) War (131–134)
Proclamation of 1763 (135, 138)
Salutary neglect (107–108, 150)
Enlightenment Ideals (124–127)
Benjamin Franklin (184, 189, 203)
Thomas Paine (Common Sense) (173)
Declaration of Independence (106-108)
Patriots (178–179)
Tories (Loyalists) (169, 172, 176, 178, 193)
George Washington (178-179, 187–188)
Republican motherhood (287, 339)
Articles of Confederation (193-197, 199–200)
Northwest Ordinance (194–197)
Constitutional Convention (200–205)
International slave trade (226)
Federalists (204-206, 212-223)
Anti-federalists (205–206)
Alexander Hamilton (199, 206, 213–215, 223)
James Madison (172, 199, 201–202, 214–215)
John Adams (189, 198, 220–223)
Democratic-Republicans (215)
Thomas Jefferson (173–174, 220–223)
Washington's farewell address (234)

Focus Questions

As you study Period 3, carefully consider each theme and the questions that relate to that theme.

American and National Identity

- What accounted for the emergence of an American identity in the years between the French and Indian War and the beginning of the American Revolution?
- What factors accounted for the formation of regional and group identities in the years between 1754 and 1800?

Work, Exchange, and Technology

- What economic factors influenced the decision of the American colonists to wage a war for independence from Britain?
- What beliefs guided the founders as they set about establishing the American economic system in the years following the American Revolution?

Geography and the Environment

- What environmental factors influenced settlement patterns and the formation of regional identities in this period?

Migration and Settlement

- How did the movement of English colonists to the west affect relations with the French and American Indian nations in the mid-eighteenth century?

Politics and Power

- What factors led to the outbreak of war between the French and British in both Europe and North America?
- Why and how did both the French and the British forge alliances with American Indians in the French and Indian War?
- What goals did native groups hope to achieve by making alliances with the French and British before and during the French and Indian War?
- What accounted for the colonial victory over the British?
- What values were reflected in the political institutions that Americans established during and after the American Revolution?
- What factors accounted for the continued tensions between white Americans and American Indians after the end of the Revolution?
- What tensions emerged in the debate over the writing of the Constitution? Why did this occur, and how were these tensions resolved?
- Why did political factions, and eventually political parties, emerge in the years after the American Revolution?

America in the World

- How did events in Europe exacerbate the tensions between the British and the American colonists in the years between 1754 and 1776?
- What factors determined the foreign policy of the new nation during the Washington and Adams presidencies?
- How successful was the American government in asserting itself on the world stage during this period?

American and Regional Culture

- What influence did Enlightenment thinkers have on the colonists' decision to go to war against Britain?
- Why did the Articles of Confederation prove ineffectual, and how did the framers of the Constitution attempt to remedy their shortcomings?
- What are republican values, and how were they manifested in American political, religious, and cultural institutions in the last half of the eighteenth century?

Social Structures

- In what ways did Americans' beliefs about race and gender change in the years following independence from Britain?

Thematic Timeline

TIME	Key Events
1754	
	American and National Identity • Concept of popular sovereignty gains force • Colonists claim rights of Englishmen
	Work, Exchange, and Technology • Merchants defy Sugar and Stamp Acts • Patriots mount three boycotts of British goods, in 1765, 1767, and 1774 • Boycotts spur Patriot women to make textiles
	Geography and the Environment • The trans-Appalachian west attracts the interest of settlers and investors • Ohio Indians resist Anglo-American expansion
	Migration and Settlement • Migration into the Ohio Valley after Pontiac's Rebellion • Quebec Act (1774) allows Catholicism
	Politics and Power • Stamp Act Congress (1765) • First Continental Congress (1774) • Second Continental Congress (1775)
	America in the World • France and Spain cede all their territories east of the Mississippi River to Britain in the Treaty of Paris (1763) • Patriots invade Canada (1775)
	American and Regional Culture • Patriots call for American unity
	Social Structures • The idea of natural rights challenges the institution of chattel slavery
1776	
	American and National Identity • Thomas Paine's *Common Sense* (1776) causes colonists to rethink political loyalties • New state constitutions rely on property qualifications to define citizenship rights
	Work, Exchange, and Technology • Manufacturing expands during the war • Cutoff of trade and severe inflation threaten economy • War debt grows
	Geography and the Environment • The vast geographical scale of the American Revolution poses challenges for its combatants
	Migration and Settlement • Declining immigration from Europe (1775–1820) enhances American identity • African American slaves seek freedom through military service

Politics and Power

- The Declaration of Independence (1776)
- States adopt republican constitutions (1776 on)
- Articles of Confederation ratified (1781)
- Treaty of Paris (1783)

America in the World

- Thomas Paine's *Common Sense* (1776) assaults monarchy
- U.S. alliances with France (1778) and Spain (1779) virtually ensure a Patriot victory

American and Regional Culture

- Emancipation of slaves begins in the North
- Virginia enacts religious freedom (1786)

Social Structures

- Judith Sargent Murray publishes "On the Equality of the Sexes" (1779)

1787

American and National Identity

- American Indians form Western Confederacy (1790)
- Second Great Awakening (1790–1860)
- Emerging political divide between South and North

Work, Exchange, and Technology

- Bank of the United States founded (1791)
- Land speculation increases in the West
- Whiskey producers rebel against taxes (1794)
- War in Europe raises wheat prices in Chesapeake and Middle colonies
- Invention of cotton gin creates boom in cotton production

Geography and the Environment

- The Northwest Ordinance and sham American Indian treaties open western land to settlement

Migration and Settlement

- State cessions, land ordinances, and American Indian wars create national domain in the West
- The Alien Act makes it harder for immigrants to become citizens and allows for deporting aliens (1798)

Politics and Power

- U.S. Constitution drafted (1787)
- Conflict over Alexander Hamilton's economic policies
- First national parties: Federalists and Republicans

America in the World

- War between Britain and France puts American neutrality at risk
- The French Revolution divides Americans

American and Regional Culture

- Bill of Rights ratified (1791)
- Sedition Act limits freedom of the press (1798)

Social Structures

- Politicians and ministers deny vote to women; praise republican motherhood

TIME	Key Events
1800	

American and National Identity
- Marshall's Supreme Court affirms national over state powers

Work, Exchange, and Technology
- Congress cuts off Atlantic slave trade (1808)
- Eastern farmers change crop mix and upgrade equipment

Geography and the Environment
- The Louisiana Purchase (1803) nearly doubles the size of the United States
- The West is explored by Lewis and Clark (1804–1806)

Migration and Settlement
- Conflicts with Native Americans increase as settlers move west

Politics and Power
- Jefferson reduces activism of national government; end of First Party System
- Chief Justice Marshall asserts federal judicial powers
- "Era of Good Feeling" in politics

America in the World
- Napoleonic Wars lead to British impressment of American sailors
- Jefferson enacts Embargo Act of 1807
- Battle of Tippecanoe eliminates threat from Western Confederacy
- War of 1812 fought; Jackson's victory raises nation's pride
- Monroe Doctrine (1823) asserts American leadership in Western Hemisphere

American and Regional Culture
- Handsome Lake preaches a middle path between American Indian and Christian traditions

Social Structures
- Northern states move to abolish slavery

America's History Chapter Summaries

(required AP® content in bold)

Chapter 5
The Problem of Empire, 1754–1776

Chapter 5 covers the period of time between the beginning of the French and Indian War (also known as the Seven Years' War) and the formal Declaration of Independence of the American colonists from Great Britain. It details Britain's attempts to affirm control over the North American colonies and colonial resistance to these efforts, culminating in the American Revolution. Poor British leadership, enormous imperial debt, and an aggressive Parliament ran headlong into colonial demands for more political and financial autonomy, along with their determination to expand settlement into territories they felt they had earned due to their participation in the war. The clash led to the emergence of a new nation.

The end of the Seven Years' War left the British with a huge debt, which they expected their American colonists to help pay. The colonists, however, had long been used to being able to manage their own affairs to a large degree. The British hoped to make up wartime expenses by stricter enforcement of taxation and tariff collection in the colonies. Additional **fears of French rebellions in Canada and American Indian uprisings in the Ohio Valley led to decisions to increase military strength in North America as well**. The British were angered when the colonial merchants and assemblies resented what they saw as military occupation and extortion.

Prime Minister George Grenville was the first to propose a series of laws designed to boost the British treasury at the colonists' expense. The Stamp Act of 1765 led to the first open confrontation with colonists, who convened the Stamp Act Congress and demanded an end to taxes within the colonies they were not allowed to vote on themselves—what they called "internal taxes." They rejected the British claim that they had "virtual representation" and **claimed what they felt were their rights as British citizens**. Britain responded with sending even more troops under a new Quartering Act, requiring the colonists to provide food and shelter for troops. The Stamp Act Congress was followed by violence in the streets, with citizens' groups such as the Sons of Liberty destroying stamp warehouses and attacking the British stamp agents. The colonists based their actions on **both the traditions of British common law and the ideas of the Enlightenment. What they saw as imperial oppression did not fit with new ideas of natural rights and the obligations of the government to the governed**.

These popular resistance movements caught the attention of Parliament. Charles Townshend replaced Grenville as prime minister, and the Declaratory Act repealed the Stamp Act, while still maintaining that the British government had the right to tax the colonies. Townshend imposed a new round of taxes and duties that led to **renewal of colonial resistance**. Colonial women led the call for nonimportation of British products they could make themselves. Men followed their lead, and British commercial profits dropped. The British responded by increasing the number of troops stationed in the colonies.

New troubles were brewing in the Ohio Valley as **colonial settlers ignored the Proclamation Line of 1763, which prohibited any new settlements west of the mountains in what was then American Indian country**. Thousands had already moved west, and they were not likely to be driven back. Lord North replaced Townshend in 1770, and he agreed to repeal most of the Townshend duties. As Parliament debated Lord North's proposals, trouble broke out in Boston in March 1770 when British soldiers fired on a group of colonists. Though the soldiers were later acquitted, the event became known as the Boston Massacre and further inflamed sentiment against imperial power.

While the repeal of the Townshend duties restored order for a while, colonial resentments were never far beneath the surface. Several colonial assemblies set up committees of correspondence to keep in touch without having to use British mails in the event of a crisis. Such a moment was not long in coming when **Parliament passed a new Tea Act in 1773 to bolster the fortunes of the imperial East India Company**. Colonists reacted to the proposed monopoly with new calls for boycott, and in Boston they dumped an entire shipment of tea into the harbor. The British responded with the Coercive Acts, hoping to make an example of Boston and the Massachusetts colony. The Quebec Act opening the Ohio Valley to Canadian settlers inflamed the colonists even more.

The First Continental Congress was called to meet in Philadelphia in September 1774. Some who attended wanted more boycotts, others favored a move to independence, and still others hoped for compromise. They agreed to demand repeal of the Coercive Acts and threatened complete boycott if the British refused. The colonies remained deeply divided as to how to respond to British policies. Some remained loyal to the crown while others simply wanted to be left alone. Growing tensions in the Ohio Valley and in New England pushed people on all sides into open conflict by spring 1775. The British occupying Boston heard claims of armed militia in the countryside and sent troops out to capture colonial leaders and supplies. The battles that ensued at Lexington and Concord became the opening round of the American Revolution.

The Second Continental Congress set up a temporary government and authorized raising a militia as the British prepared to launch another attack on Boston. King George III and the British Parliament ignored last-ditch efforts at compromise by the Congress, and skirmishes broke out in the South and West as well as New England. **Pamphleteer Thomas Paine sought to rally the undecided to the Patriots' cause with the publication of *Common Sense* in which he made the case to end the tyranny of monarchy and establish a republic**. In the summer of 1776, the Declaration of Independence was signed, **using the ideas of the European Enlightenment to make the case for independence and the rule of popular sovereignty**.

Chapter 6
Making War and Republican Governments, 1776-1789

Chapter 6 examines two related sets of events. The first is the American Revolution against the British Empire, which began in 1776 and ended in 1783. The **colonists won through a combination of outstanding leadership, the resilient Continental army and militia, and support from allies abroad**. The second focuses on the Patriots' attempts to build an effective form of republican government, culminating in the ratification of the Constitution of 1787, the national charter that endures today.

Colonial leaders **wrote and signed the Declaration of Independence in 1776**, just as the British began large-scale military assaults in New England. The British seemed to have more advantages in the conflict, as the colonists were economically and militarily weak. After a number of setbacks in the early years of the war, the Patriots' prospects improved dramatically in 1778 when they formed a formal alliance with France. The British tried to focus on the South, where they thought they would find greater Loyalist support. They also hoped to win slaves to the British cause by offering freedom to any who would rebel against their colonial masters. However, by October 1781, the British were forced to concede defeat at the seaport of Yorktown, Virginia, thus ending the American Revolution.

Shortly after the signing the Declaration of Independence, the Continental Congress adopted the **Articles of Confederation, a document that created a loose union of the states as an association of equals**. Although the Confederation held powers to make war and treaties, requisition funds from the states, and manage American Indian affairs, there were major weaknesses as well. The Articles provided for no chief executive or federal judiciary, could not tax, and lacked the power to enforce its provisions. Even so, ratification came after a dispute involving land claims in the Ohio Valley was settled by the creation of a federally administered Northwest Territory. The Northwest Ordinance of 1784 and the Land Ordinance of 1785 later provided for the orderly settlement of the territory and included a ban on slavery. While a boon for settlers, **these policies effectively ended American Indian claims to any of the lands in the Ohio Valley**.

Financial problems quickly emerged as the war ended and states began to deal with their war debts. Some states tried to clear these debts by raising taxes, which placed a heavy burden on already financially strapped small farmers. Revolt broke out in Massachusetts with Shays's Rebellion, led by former Patriot soldiers who now faced the possibility of losing the land they had fought for because they could not pay the new taxes. The **national government under the Articles of Confederation had no way to help solve such problems, and many began to support demands for the creation of a stronger central government**.

In May 1787, a national convention met in Philadelphia to consider changes in the Articles. The delegates quickly realized that revisions would be inadequate; the country needed a completely new framework. The **result of their deliberations and compromises was the creation of the U.S. Constitution**, a document that created a stronger federal government with a chief executive and a judiciary, yet one that would still share many powers with the individual states. The final Constitution created a two-house legislative branch. Smaller states got equal representation in the Senate, while larger states won representation based on population in the House of Representatives. The issue of slavery was too controversial to deal with definitively, so the new Constitution simply set a time for the end of the international slave trade but **left the question of slavery for another generation to solve**. Those who hoped the new government would move to end slavery altogether were disappointed. Southern delegates did get the right to count slaves proportionally in determining representation in the House of Representatives. Women who hoped the new Constitution would offer citizenship to them were disappointed as well. They were relegated to continuing **their roles as wives and mothers and contenting themselves with raising good future citizens**.

The ratification process proved to be more difficult than the framers had expected. Two camps quickly emerged: the Federalists, who felt a strong national government was a necessity, and the Antifederalists, who worried that the states were giving up too much power. Legislators in Massachusetts declared **they would vote against ratification if a more explicit Bill of Rights were not added to the document, spelling out certain individual rights they felt were left too vague in the Constitution itself**. With the promise of the addition of a Bill of Rights, states voted to ratify the Constitution and the new government was officially established. Nevertheless, **debates over the limits of federal and state power would continue for some time**.

Chapter 7
Hammering Out a Federal Republic, 1787–1820

Chapter 7 explores three interrelated themes: public policy (both domestic and foreign), party politics, and westward expansion. The chapter discusses the rise of mass democracy, the struggle to define the limits of state versus federal power, the first major extension of national boundaries beyond the Mississippi River, the growth of the first political parties, and the social pressures that accompanied this rapid expansion of political, economic, and technological change. It examines the breakup of the old Federalist order with the election of Thomas Jefferson and then moves to the development of the First Party System with the rise of the Virginia Dynasty presidents and the Democratic-Republicans. The addition of the Louisiana Territory meant changes for the nation in terms of rapid westward expansion, more complicated international diplomacy, new economic opportunities, and new social and cultural issues. The United States moved from its status as a small emerging nation to one with the beginnings of a world presence, even though many internal social and political issues still needed resolution

During the 1790s, the new nation debated its role in foreign conflicts, especially the war between Great Britain and France triggered **by the French Revolution, which was itself partially inspired by the American Revolution. The American Revolution also helped spark the Haitian Revolution** beginning in 1791, which established the first black republic in the Atlantic world.

Prior to 1800, during the first administration of President George Washington, the government ratified **the Bill of Rights**. Throughout the 1790s, the nation moved to **more participatory democracy** with the development of new political parties, with the **Democratic-Republicans** successfully challenging the Federalists in the election of 1800. The Supreme Court played a role in defining the **supremacy of federal power over state power and solidified the role of the judiciary in making determinations about the meaning of the Constitution** (ex: *Marbury v. Madison*; *McCulloch v. Maryland*).

The country also experienced **growing regional economic diversification**, which also led to political and social differences. **The expansion of slavery** became a central issue for the nation, especially **as slavery expanded west across the Lower South** with the **increasing demand for cotton for the newly emerging textile industry.** The acquisition of lands from the **Louisiana Purchase** led to further debate about the expansion of slavery, an issue settled only temporarily by the **Missouri Compromise** in 1820.

Expansion also led to increased **conflicts with American Indians** who resisted expansion (ex: Tecumseh) yet often found themselves on the unfavorable side of increasingly restrictive treaties (ex: Treaty of Greenville). **Homesteaders and entrepreneurs sought to push farther west**, leading to a constant demand for more land.

While the United States was intent on expanding its national borders, the new nation also wished to stay out of European conflicts. Even so, foreign involvement was inevitable, as the government negotiated the **purchase of the Louisiana Territory** from France and later **sought to control the North American continent**, leading in part to further conflict with Great Britain. While the nation's leaders talked of isolation, **the country was slowly finding itself involved in world affairs.**

Period 3 Practice Questions

Multiple-Choice Questions

Questions 1–3 refer to the image below.

Source: Library of Congress, 1770

Anne S.K. Brown Military Collection, Brown University Library

The Bloody Massacre on 5th March 1770 (coloured engraving)

1. The image above most directly reflects which of the following developments?
   (a) The use of political propaganda for colonial unity
   (b) Reactions of the British toward American Independence
   (c) Economic shortages during the Revolutionary War
   (d) The effort to prevent colonists from moving westward

2. All of the following are in the context of the event portrayed in the engraving EXCEPT
   (a) imperial control over North American markets.
   (b) British implementation of what colonials believed to be unfair taxation.
   (c) the British navy's refusal to protect colonial interests from the Barbary pirates.
   (d) Great Britain's massive debt from the Seven Years' War.

3. The engraving above represents which of the following trends of colonial discontent?
   (a) Anger over perceived threats
   (b) British victory in the Seven Years' War
   (c) British military occupation in port cities
   (d) The trade networks between the British and Iroquois

Questions 4–6 refer to the excerpt below.

"The next wish of this traveler will be to know whence came all these people? They are a mixture of English, Scotch, Irish, French, Dutch, Germans, and Swedes.

"What then is the American, this new man? He is either an European, or the descendant of an European, hence that strange mixture of blood, which you will find in no other country. I could point out to you a family whose grandfather was an Englishman, whose wife was Dutch, whose son married a French woman, and whose present four sons have now four wives of different nations. He is an American, who leaving behind him all his ancient prejudices and manners, receives new ones from the new mode of life he has embraced, the new government he obeys, and the new rank he holds. He becomes an American by being received in the broad lap of our great Alma Mater."

St. Jean de Crèvecoeur, "What Is an American?" *Letters from an American Farmer*, 1782

4. The excerpt above best serves as evidence of which of the following developments?
   (a) The effort of Americans to mirror British views on religion
   (b) The social mobility of Americans in the northeast after the American Revolution
   (c) New American cultures as the result of migration and settlement patterns
   (d) Egalitarian views on race and ethnicity in America after the revolution

5. Which of the following represents a short-term consequence of the ideas expressed in the excerpt?
   (a) Agreements with American Indians over contested territory
   (b) Cultural tension between frontier and coastal communities
   (c) The expansion of enslavement in the South
   (d) New alliances with European nations

6. The above passage supports which of the following statements about the American Revolution?
   (a) Great Britain hired mercenaries to assist them in fighting the Patriots
   (b) Increasing calls for greater political democracy in several state goverments
   (c) American Indians tended to side with the British rather than the colonists
   (d) The Revolution began because Great Britain prohibited people from other nations to emigrate to the colonies

Questions 7–9 refer to the excerpt below.

"Art. II. Each State retains its Sovereignty, Freedom, and Independence, and every Power, Jurisdiction, and Right, which is not by this Confederation expressly delegated to the United States in Congress assembled.

"Art. V. In determining Questions in the United States, in Congress assembled, each State shall have one vote.

"Art. VIII. The Taxes for paying that Proportion shall be laid and levied by the Authority and Direction of the Legislatures of the several States, within the Time agreed upon by the United States in Congress assembled.

"Art. IX. All Controversies concerning the private Right of Soil claimed under different Grants of two or more States, whose Jurisdictions, as they may respect such Lands . . . shall, on the Petition of either Party to the Congress of the United States, be finally determined . . .

"Art. XIII. . . . And we do further solemnly plight and engage the Faith of our respective Constituents, that they shall abide by the Determinations of the United States in Congress assembled, on all Questions which by the said Confederation are submitted to them, and that the Articles thereof shall be inviolably observed by the States we respectively represent, and that the Union shall be perpetual."

Articles of Confederation, November 1777 (ratified 1781)

7. The primary reason the Articles of Confederation restricted the power of the federal government was fear
   (a) that the national government would create a monarchy.
   (b) that anarchy would sweep the nation following victory over Great Britain.
   (c) of strong central governments because of their experiences under British rule.
   (d) that the French would attempt to recapture land they had lost in the French and Indian War.

8. Despite its weaknesses, the Articles of Confederation experienced their greatest success in
   (a) securing from Spain the right to peacefully navigate the entire length of the Mississippi River.
   (b) designing a system for admitting new states in western territories.
   (c) removal of the British from the Northwest forts.
   (d) agreement from the French to halt the impressments of American sailors.

9. Disagreement over determining state representation in the Articles of Confederation Congress led to the Constitutional Convention to incorporate which of the following into the Constitution?
   (a) The first ten amendments limiting the power of the federal government
   (b) A federal system that divided power between the national and state governments
   (c) A clause that allowed Congress to stretch its power as necessary
   (d) The division of Congress into two branches, the House of Representatives and the Senate

Questions 10–12 refer to the excerpt below.

" 'Why did I go?'

'Yes,' I replied; 'My histories tell me that you men of the Revolution took up arms against intolerable oppression.'

'What were they? Oppressions? I didn't feel them.'

'What, were you not oppressed by the Stamp Act?'

'I never saw one of those stamps. . . . I am certain I never paid a penny for one of them.'

'Well, what then about the tea-tax?'

'Tea-tax! I never drank a drop of that stuff; the boys threw it all overboard.'

'Then I suppose you had been reading Harrington or Sidney and Locke about the eternal principles of liberty.'

'Never heard of 'em. We read only the Bible, the Catechism, Watt's Psalms and Hymns, and the Almanac.'

'Well, then, what was the matter? and what did you mean in going to the fight?'

'Young man, what we meant in going for those red-coats was this: we always had governed ourselves, and we always meant to. They didn't mean we should.' "

Interview of Ninety-Year-Old American Revolutionary War veteran Captain Preston, 1842

10. The above account best reflects which of the following about the American Revolution?
    (a) It was fueled by specific acts of British oppression
    (b) It was in part the result of serious propaganda campaigns by the colonial elite
    (c) It was in part the result of a changing American identity
    (d) It resulted in a serious divide between Loyalists and Patriots

11. Which of the following developments could be used as proof of the ideas expressed in the excerpt?
    (a) Colonial commitment to republican ideals
    (b) The influence of the Great Awakening
    (c) The effects of Thomas Paine's *Common Sense* pamphlet
    (d) Inter-colonial rivalry after the American Revolution

12. The above excerpt best illustrates the fact that colonists
    (a) had developed a sense of self-government before the Declaration of Independence.
    (b) would call for a strong central government following the Revolution.
    (c) developed a lasting sense of egalitarianism following the Revolution.
    (d) supported the expansion of natural rights to disadvantaged classes before the Revolution.

END OF MULTIPLE-CHOICE SECTION

Short-Answer Questions

"And be it further enacted, That if any person shall write, print, utter or publish, or shall cause or procure to be written, printed, uttered or publishing, or shall knowingly and willingly assist or aid in writing, printing, uttering or publishing any false, scandalous and malicious writing or writings against the government o tates, or either house of the Congress of the United States, or the President of the United States, . . . then such person, being thereof convicted before any court of the United States having jurisdiction thereof, shall be punished by a fine not exceeding two thousand dollars, and by imprisonment not exceeding two years."

The Alien and Sedition Acts, July 14, 1798

1. Using the quotation above, answer a, b, and c.
    (a) Briefly explain ONE specific historical development in the period from 1787 to 1800 that influenced the ideas expressed in the excerpt above.

(b) Briefly explain ONE specific historical event or development in the period from 1787 to 1800 that occurred as a result of the ideas expressed in the excerpt above.

(c) Briefly explain ANOTHER specific historical event or development in the period from 1787 to 1800 that occurred as a result of the ideas expressed in the excerpt above.

2. Using the map on the following page, answer a, b, and c.

(a) Briefly explain ONE specificw historical factor that caused the events depicted on the map.

(b) Briefly explain ONE significant historical event or development resulting from the events depicted on the map.

(c) Briefly explain ANOTHER significant historical event or development resulting from the events depicted on the map.

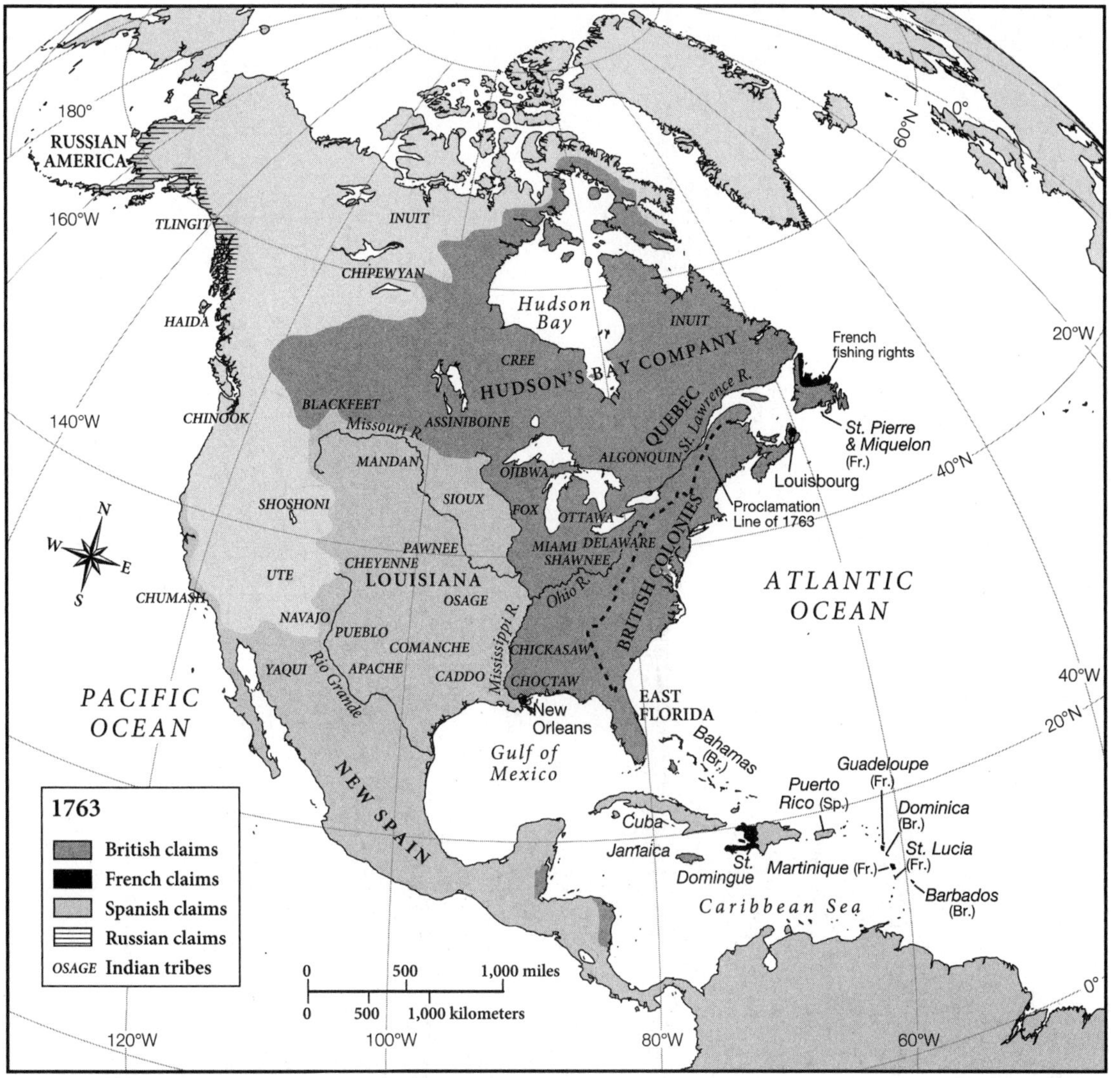

Europe Redraws the Map of North America, 1763

END OF SHORT-ANSWER SECTION

Long Essay Question

Question: Evaluate extent of change in American political ideas in the United States during the period 1776–1800.

END OF LONG ESSAY SECTION

NOTES:

PERIOD 4, 1800-1848

Overview

Period 4 focuses on the history of the United States between 1800 and 1848. This division highlights the new nation's move from an emerging postcolonial country to one that controlled most of a continent and had to redefine the meaning of both democracy and citizenship. This was an era of competing political, social, and economic "revolutions," as dramatic changes in voting rights, the economy, and society led to a mass democracy and a growing, if contested, sense of a national identity.

The end of the Federalist era and the emergence of the Democratic-Republicans marked the beginning of the process of broadening participatory democracy. The four decades that followed the turn of the nineteenth century saw the broadening of the franchise (the right to vote) from the privileged few to most white males. To be sure, many were still left without voting rights—women, American Indians, most African Americans (whether enslaved or not), and many newly arrived immigrants—but the move toward a more open definition of citizenship gained momentum.

The creation of modern political parties also began during this period as the United States moved from the Federalist decade of the 1790s to the formation of the Democratic-Republicans and later the Democratic and Whig parties. As the voter base broadened and the nation expanded, questions arose about the proper role of the federal and state governments in the growing republic and the expanding economy. Some of these issues were decided by the U.S. Supreme Court; for example, in *McCulloch v. Maryland*, the Supreme Court decided that state laws could be ruled unconstitutional. Other issues surfaced in the context of new economic conditions that saw the emergence of factories in the North and the development of slavery as a uniquely southern institution. The diverging economic structures of the North and South led to a sharpening of distinct regional identities. All of these changes left many Americans struggling to match democratic ideals with the harsher realities surrounding them, touching off a series of reform efforts—the Second Great Awakening, the movement for women's rights, and abolition (the move to abolish slavery)—that ultimately served both to unite and divide the country.

During this period, the United States also embarked on unprecedented territorial and economic expansion. The boundaries of the United States doubled with the Louisiana Purchase in 1803, opening the prospect of landownership to millions and beginning the rapid westward movement that transformed the continent. Along with access to new lands came revolutionary changes in technology and economic specialization that brought both prosperity and increased focus on regional interests that had an impact on markets as well as politics. This rapid development resulted in significant changes in the lives of everyone regardless of gender, race, ethnicity, or socioeconomic group. Many people were able to take advantage of new opportunities, while others, such as American Indians like the Cherokee and the Iroquois nation, found themselves further marginalized in the name of "progress."

Rapidly changing technology fueled the expansion of American commerce into the global market as factories expanded in the North and cotton cultivation came to dominate the southern economy. Efforts to organize the national economy, including proposals such as the American System, which sought to use tariff revenues to fund internal improvements, strengthened economic ties between the North and the newly opening West but further isolated the slaveholding South. Efforts to modernize transportation fostered regional division, as canals and roads tended to connect the Northeast to the West, while the South continued to rely on rivers for transportation and trade. The lives of people in all parts of the country were affected by this economic growth as the nature of the workplace changed.

Entry into the global economy also complicated U.S. foreign policy. Territorial expansion and growing markets required involvement with the rest of the world. At the same time, the United States sought to remain isolated from European political conflicts. Territorial expansion also raised questions about the role of slavery in the newly acquired areas. The existence and expansion of slavery emerged during this period as issues of overarching national concern. The slavery question was settled temporarily by political expediency, such as the Missouri Compromise, which divided the Louisiana Territory into free and slave areas, but there was no final resolution to the debate over slavery in this era.

Key Terms

Be sure that you understand the meaning of these terms and their relevance in U.S. history. Page numbers from the textbook are provided.

Market Revolution (253–258, 272–273)
Second Great Awakening (316–319)
Participatory democracy (850)
Universal white male suffrage (285–286)
Transportation Revolution (245, 254–258)
Agricultural Revolution (254–255)
Adams-Onis (Florida Purchase) Treaty (240)
McCulloch v Maryland (239)
Marbury v Madison (228, 238–239)
Louisiana Purchase (229–230)
American System (291–292)
Missouri Compromise (290–291, 399–400)
Monroe Doctrine (240)
Interchangeable parts (248, 270)
Whigs (245)
Henry Clay (291-292)
Abolitionism (289-290, 334–339)
Seneca Falls Convention (343–344)
Nat Turner's Rebellion (309, 336)
Utopian communitarianism (322–335)
War of 1812 (233–238, 254, 299)
Indian Removal Act (245, 301–302)

Focus Questions

As you study Period 4, keep the following thematic questions in mind.

American and National Identity

- What characteristics of national identity emerged in the first half of the nineteenth century?
- What factors encouraged and which impeded the formation of a national identity?
- Why during this period did Americans form both a national and a regional identity, and how did the two conflict with each other?
- How did government policies shape the formation of regional identities in the North, South, and West?
- How did both free and enslaved African Americans preserve their identity and their culture in the face of increased barriers that confronted them?

Work, Exchange, and Technology

- How were Americans affected by innovations in markets, technology, and transportation in the first half of the nineteenth century?
- How did changes in both agriculture and manufacturing change labor systems and affect the lives of American workers?
- How did government policies affect the manufacture and distribution of goods in the United States?

Geography and the Environment

- How did environmental factors contribute to the western movement that occurred in the first half of the nineteenth century?
- What was the impact of western migration on American Indians?

Migration and Settlement

- What caused the emergence of nativism in the mid-nineteenth century?
- In what ways did immigration change the social, economic, and political fabric of America?
- How did technological changes affect immigration patterns?

Politics and Power

- Why did political parties emerge in the early years of the Republic?
- In what ways, and why, did the positions taken by the Federalists and the Democratic-Republicans change over time?
- How did the Supreme Court help shape the political and economic landscape of the United States in the first half of the nineteenth century?
- Why and how did many Americans attempt to expand democratic ideals in the early and mid-nineteenth century?
- What were the similarities and differences between the Jeffersonian Republicans and the Jacksonian Democrats? Account for these similarities and differences.

America in the World

- What were some turning points in the development of American foreign policy?
- Why were these turning points so important?
- How did the U.S. government use foreign policy to advance its interests?

American and Regional Culture

- How did the Second Great Awakening shape reform in education, women's rights, abolitionism, temperance, and the prison system?
- What were the characteristics of the new national culture?

Social Structures

- In what ways did literary and philosophical movements in the first half of the nineteenth century reflect changes in the economic and social order?

Thematic Timeline

TIME	Key Events
1800	
	American and National Identity • Neomercantilist policies support banking, transportation, and communication systems **Work, Exchange, and Technology** • Cotton output and demand for African labor expands • Congress approves funds for a National Road (1806) **Geography and the Environment** • Louisiana Purchase nearly doubles the land mass of the United States (1803) • Lewis and Clark explore the West (1804–1806) **Migration and Settlement** • Congress outlaws Atlantic slave trade (1808)

TIME	Key Events
	Politics and Power • Jefferson reduces activism of national government • Chief Justice Marshall begins to assert federal judicial powers **America in the World** • Embargo Act prohibits trade with Great Britain (1807) **American and Regional Culture** • Rural white Americans share a common culture
1810	
	American and National Identity • Emma Willard founds Middlebury Female Seminary for young women (1814) • American Colonization Society founded (1817) • Notion of the self-made man spreads **Work, Exchange, and Technology** • Construction on National Road begins (1811) • First American textile factory opens in Waltham, Massachusetts (1814) **Geography and the Environment** • Road and turnpike construction facilitate travel • The cotton frontier moves inland **Migration and Settlement** • Andrew Jackson forces Creeks to relinquish millions of acres during War of 1812 **Politics and Power** • Expansion of white male political rights begins • Martin Van Buren creates first statewide political machine (1817–1821) • Missouri crisis (1819–1821) over slavery **America in the World** • Africans from Congo region influence black culture for decades • U.S. and Great Britain agree to joint control of Oregon Country (1818) **American and Regional Culture** • African Methodist Episcopal Church founded (1816)
1820	
	American and National Identity • David Walker's *Appeal . . . to the Colored Citizens* (1829) attacks slavery • Public schools, female academies strengthen literacy and civic engagement • Domesticity and ideal of "separate spheres" emerge in middle class **Work, Exchange, and Technology** • Erie Canal completed (1825) • Henry Clay proposes "American System" of government-assisted development **Geography and the Environment** • Canals and steamboats shrink space • Major Stephen H. Long labels the Great Plains the "Great American Desert" **Migration and Settlement** • Internal slave trade forces thousands of African Americans west in cotton boom • Rise of cities and manufacturing towns prompts migration from rural areas • Violence drives over a thousand African Americans out of Cincinnati (1829)

Politics and Power

- Rise of Andrew Jackson and Democratic Party
- Anti-Masonic and Working Men's parties rise and decline

America in the World

- Mexico gains independence from Spain (1821)

American and Regional Culture

- Second Great Awakening; Charles Finney begins Protestant revival campaigns (1823)

1830

American and National Identity

- More distinct middle-class and working-class identities emerge with industrialization
- Nat Turner's uprising in Virginia (1831)
- American Anti-Slavery Society founded (1833)
- First wave of married women's property laws (1839–1845)
- Abolitionist Grimké sisters defend public roles for women

Work, Exchange, and Technology

- U.S. textiles compete with British goods
- Canal systems expand trade in eastern United States
- Cotton complex expands
- Financial panic of 1837 begins six-year depression

Geography and the Environment

- U.S. immigration into Texas accelerates
- Emergence of commercial cities in the Old Northwest
- Indian Removal Act (1830) leads to mass relocation

Migration and Settlement

- Indian Removal Act (1830) forces Native peoples west
- Cherokee Trail of Tears (1838)

Politics and Power

- Tariff battles and nullification crisis (1828, 1832)
- Whig Party forms (1834)
- Jackson destroys Second National Bank, expands executive power
- Congress adopts "gag rule" to block antislavery petitions (1836)

America in the World

- Emerson and others draw on European romanticism in developing transcendentalist ideas
- Texas declares its independence from Mexico (1836)

American and Regional Culture

- Emerson champions transcendentalism
- Benevolent Empire of reform movements
- Immense popularity of blackface minstrel shows

Social Structures

- Joseph Smith founds Mormon church (Latter-day Saints) (1830)
- Horace Mann begins public school expansion in Massachusetts (1837)

TIME	Key Events
1848	
	American and National Identity • Margaret Fuller publishes *Woman in the Nineteenth Century* (1844) • Seneca Falls Convention seeks women's equal rights (1848) **Work, Exchange, and Technology** • American machine tool industry expands **Geography and the Environment** • Immigration to the Oregon Country increases dramatically **Migration and Settlement** • Brigham Young leads Mormons to Salt Lake (1846) • Increased immigration from Ireland and Germany **Politics and Power** • Heyday of Second Party System (Democrats vs. Whigs) • Liberty Party runs James G. Birney for president (1844) • U.S.-Mexico War (1846–1848) **America in the World** • United States declares war on Mexico (1846) • Treaty with Britain divides Oregon Country (1846) • American troops capture Mexico City (1847) **American and Regional Culture** • Dorothea Dix promotes hospitals for the mentally ill (1841) • Henry Thoreau spends a year at Walden Pond (1845) • John Humphrey Noyes establishes cooperative experiment at Oneida (1848)

America's History Chapter Summaries
(required AP® content in bold)

Chapter 8
Economic Transformations, 1800–1848

Chapter 8 examines the causes of the economic transformation of the first half of the nineteenth century, as well as the consequences that resulted from these changes. The two driving forces of economic growth during this period were the Industrial Revolution and the development and expansion of the market economy. These developments brought with them social transformations as well: the rise of an urban society, growing ties between the Northeast and the Midwest along with the further isolation of the South, and increased tensions among different social groups throughout the country, including newly arriving immigrants from Ireland and Germany.

In the years following the American Revolution, the growth of the market economy led a number of states, as well as the federal government, to support private businesses that **expanded technology and transportation** and thus contributed to regional and national growth (ex: Lancaster Turnpike, canals). **These economic developments precipitated profound changes in business, manufacturing, and agriculture** and in the lives of many Americans. Rural families that previously relied on farming became the nation's first factory workers, while others **in rural areas began to produce goods for distant markets**, making them more prosperous but also more dependent on the market.

Industrialization unfolded in the United States between 1790 and 1860 and included the development and growth of the modern factory system, with a distinct division of labor and enormous increases in production. Textile factories in particular illustrated the favorable combination of new technologies, newly discovered power sources, identification of new labor pools, and the support of **government economic policies such as protective tariffs**. The creation of interchangeable parts further aided the growth of manufacturing.

Many of the early workers in textile factories were women, though their labor was soon supplemented **by low-skilled men**, who produced the goods that supplied both local and international markets. Many soon found themselves at odds with management over low pay and harsh working conditions, leading to early labor organization and disagreements about what the rights of working classes should be. Advances in manufacturing technology led to greatly increased production in many new industries, particularly **textiles** (ex: Lancaster model, Lowell model, Samuel Slater, the Boston Associates, Eli Whitney).

The national economy benefitted from advances in the construction of roads and canals, transportation networks that facilitated both commerce and **movement of settlers to the West**. Cities and towns grew along these trade routes, while Atlantic seaports remained centers of both foreign and domestic trade.

The rapidly expanding domestic and international market economy led to debates about both the government's role in that expansion and the **regional differences** that were developing. **State-sponsored roads and canals** facilitated that expansion and led to calls for more government involvement in such infrastructure improvements (ex: **American System**, the Erie Canal, the National Road).

The Market Revolution **widened the gap between the rich and poor**, creating a business elite in many towns and cities, as well as a growing middle class **that set themselves apart** from the working classes. Women who could stay at home saw themselves as the guardians of the futures of their children, continuing the **transformation of gender and family roles**. This transformation separated middle-class women from women who did not have the luxury of staying out of the workplace. For middle-class men, many came to see their success as a result of their willingness to work, giving rise to the image of the self-made man. This perception obscured the hard work done by those at the poorer end of the economic scale and led to further class divisions.

Chapter 9
A Democratic Revolution, 1800–1848

Chapter 9 examines the causes and consequences of the political changes that accompanied the economic transformation of the early nineteenth century. It follows the rise of popular politics and the decline of the dominance of the wealthy "notables"—northern landlords, southern planters, and seacoast merchants. The chapter also explores the rise and presidency of Andrew Jackson and the emergence of the Second Party System.

The **growth of mass democracy began** as the right to vote was extended to more white men, though many still remained unable to claim full citizenship. Concurrent with the expansion of democracy was the rise of political parties, often run by professional politicians such as lawyers or journalists. The election of 1824 pitted the older "notables"—John Quincy Adams and Henry Clay—against William Crawford, a protégé of Thomas Jefferson, and Andrew Jackson, the rising hero of the War of 1812. Jackson, backed by a group of supporters who called themselves "democrats" to emphasize their egalitarian policies, won the most electoral votes but did not win a majority, and the House of Representatives voted to elect John Quincy Adams as president. As president, John Quincy Adams faced fierce **opposition to his support of protective tariffs** and his support of Clay's proposed **American System**.

Andrew Jackson's run for the presidency in 1818 produced a huge voter turnout that signaled the real beginning of mass democracy in the United States. As president, Jackson enjoyed support for his policies of decentralization, but he also confronted some of his own supporters in South Carolina who tried to assert **state's right to reject federal law** in the nullification crisis. Jackson also struck at both the American System and **supporters of centrally controlled economy**, which symbolized the Bank of the

United States. Jackson also threw his full support behind the Indian Removal Act, which called for the **relocation of American Indians**. The Cherokees attempted to use the **Supreme Court's power** to fight the state of Georgia and removal. Although the Supreme Court sided with the Cherokees in *Worcester v. Georgia* (1832), Jackson's negotiators pushed through the fraudulent Treaty of New Echota to effect removal. By the time Jackson left office in 1837, the **Second Party System, consisting of the Democrats and the newly formed Whig Party**, had emerged. The economic chaos that resulted from the Panic of 1837 led to disillusionment with Jackson's successor, President Martin Van Buren, resulting in a Whig victory in the election of 1840.

Chapter 10
Religion, Reform and Culture, 1820–1848

Chapter 10 examines a number of reform movements in the first half of the nineteenth century. The transcendentalist movement led to unique American art and culture and emphasized individualism, especially among the middle class. The chapter also explores the rise of utopian movements and religion and looks at the rise of urban popular culture and a wave of European immigration. Finally, it focuses on the rise of abolitionism and the women's rights movement.

American religious and secular beliefs both changed in the early nineteenth century. Beginning in the 1790s, a series of religious revivals led to **the Second Great Awakening, based on the belief in human perfectibility**. These new beliefs, grounded in romanticism, also sparked a wave of **voluntary organization dedicated to social reform**. Women in particular began to take up reform work in areas that fit with white women's traditional concerns: raising children, the home, and campaigns for moral reform. Women increasingly played a role in other reform movements as well, finding opportunities to work for better education for children, temperance, and abolition. The **Second Great Awakening** also led to changes in Protestantism, how many people viewed the role of religion in national life, and the increasing insistence that Christians had an obligation to bring about meaningful reform in society.

A number of communitarian movements emerged in the middle years of the nineteenth century, growing out of the **Second Great Awakening's support for the doctrine of perfectibility** and the search for utopia on earth (ex: Brook Farm, the Shakers, the Oneida Colony, the Fourier communities). The Mormons also emerged during this period. Out of Brook Farm, in particular, a number of American artists and writers helped create a distinctly **American national culture through literature and art** (ex: Ralph Waldo Emerson, Henry David Thoreau, Walt Whitman, Nathaniel Hawthorne, Herman Melville, Charles Willson Peale).

During these same years, a new urban popular culture arose as East Coast cities grew in size and population. Part of this expansion was **due to a wave of immigration from Europe**. While cities seemed to promise success and adventure, many found a much harsher reality there, living on subsistence wages in poor housing. Immigrants often confronted particularly virulent **xenophobia**.

This reform era also saw the expansion of abolitionist and women's rights movements. The **abolitionist movement in particular found support among free African Americans** (ex. David Walker) **and from enslaved African Americans** (ex. Nat Turner). Growing out of the abolitionist movement, the early women's rights movement drew on **middle-class women's experiences** as they stepped out of their culturally prescribed roles to advocate for property and voting rights (ex: Seneca Falls).

Chapter 11
Imperial Ambitions, 1820–1848

Chapter 11 traces the expansion of the South and the plantation culture from the Upper South to the Mississippi Valley and beyond during the first half of the nineteenth century. It focuses first on the culture of white southerners, then looks at the culture of southern African Americans, both enslaved and free. It also examines the idea of Manifest Destiny and the westward expansion beginning in the 1840s, as well as the impact of the Mexican War (1846–1848).

The invention of the cotton gin led to the rapid spread of short-staple cotton cultivation in areas that had not been suitable for the long-staple cotton that had to be cleaned by hand. **Southern cotton furnished raw materials for manufacturing and fueled the internal slave trade**. Cotton was critical to the national economy, and slavery was a critical piece of cotton agriculture.

As plantation agriculture spread west in the first half of the nineteenth century, slavery spread with it. Slaves came into the newly opened regions through the international slave trade only until 1808, when the Constitution abolished the international slave trade. After the end of the international slave trade, slaves moved from the Upper South to the Mississippi Valley through the internal or domestic slave trade. This trade involved the breaking up of families and forced migration to new parts of the country. Slaves who were "sold South" rarely saw their loved ones again.

Most of the political leaders in the South had some stake in the slave system, and few emancipation initiatives ever got very far in southern legislatures. In fact, **many Americans in the South felt pride in the institution of slavery and insisted that the federal government should defend the institution**. John C. Calhoun, a U.S. senator from South Carolina who had served as Andrew Jackson's first vice president, called slavery a "positive good." While most southern whites did not personally own slaves, most were caught up in the society the slave system created.

The slave economy resulted in southern dependence on foreign and domestic trade for other necessities, particularly manufactured goods. Even the development of schools and municipal institutions languished because the slaveholding elite voted down taxes that would have paid for such advances.

The settlement and eventual annexation of Texas in the 1820s and 1830s became entangled with the slavery issue. Indeed, throughout the nineteenth century, the **American acquisition of new lands in the West led to heated debate over the extension of slavery**.

Within the context of slavery, **enslaved and free African Americans created communities** that were a synthesis of African- and European-derived cultures. Many African Americans relied heavily on the **evangelical Christianity of the Second Great Awakening**. The church became a core institution in the black community. Free blacks in both the North and the South worked in various ways to negotiate rights and further the cause of abolition. In the North, African Americans were **prominent in the abolitionist movement**.

Many state governments continued to restrict African Americans' citizenship. Freed blacks in the South and most in the North were treated as second-class citizens without the right to vote, attend public schools, or attend white churches. Only in Massachusetts could African Americans testify in court. The federal government did not allow blacks to work for the postal service, claim public lands, or hold a U.S. passport.

The decade of the 1840s saw Americans embrace the concept of Manifest Destiny—the belief that they had a God-given right to extend the blessings of **republican government across the continent to the Pacific**. This "right" carried with it the assumption of Anglo-American superiority. Oregon was the first target, followed soon by California, with little attention paid to the Spanish, Mexicans, and American Indians who were in those territories already. The Plains Indian culture had been made possible by the introduction of European horses and weapons. **The descendants of those same people now threatened the Indians' way of life**.

The presidential election of 1844 brought in an administration that revered expansionism, particularly into Texas and Oregon. The desire to annex Texas soon helped spark war with Mexico, a war that was fought on many different fronts in the Southwest. American victories in both California and Mexico itself led to the surrender by the Mexican government and a treaty that added vast new territories to the United States. Even before the treaty was ratified, **the issue of whether to allow the extension of slavery into these new territories began to split Congress along regional lines**.

Period 4 Practice Questions
Multiple-Choice Questions

Questions 1–3 refer to the excerpt below.

"We admit, as all must admit, that the powers of the Government are limited, and that its limits are not to be transcended. But we think the sound construction of the Constitution must allow to the national legislature that discretion with respect to the means by which the powers it confers are to be carried into execution which will enable that body to perform the high duties assigned to it in the manner most beneficial to the people. Let the end be legitimate, let it be within the scope of the Constitution, and all means which are appropriate, which are plainly adapted to that end, which are not prohibited, but consist with the letter and spirit of the Constitution, are Constitutional."

U.S. Supreme Court, *McCulloch v. Maryland*, 1819

1. The above quotation most focuses on which of the following debates that characterized the new republic?
   (a) The extension of slavery into the territories
   (b) The formation of a national currency
   (c) Federal vs. state power
   (d) The application of the Bill of Rights to states

2. The above decision reflected which of the following tendencies of the early Supreme Court?
   (a) To side with big business over labor
   (b) To assert its role as an equal branch of government
   (c) To uphold the sanctity of contract
   (d) To look unfavorably on the institution of slavery

3. Which of the following groups would be most likely to support the above decision?
   (a) Western farmers
   (b) Jacksonian Democrats
   (c) Know-Nothings
   (d) Former Federalists

Questions 4–6 refer to the excerpt below.

"We might feel a pride in the reflection, that our young country . . . was the first to adopt with any efficacy, the penitentiary system of prison discipline, and the first to attempt to prevent the commission of crimes, by seeking out the youthful and unprotected, who were in the way of temptation, and by religious and moral instruction, by imparting to them useful knowledge, and by giving them industrious and orderly habits, rescuing them from vice, and rendering them valuable members of society. . . . To confine these youthful criminals . . . where no, or scarcely any, distinction can be made between the young and the old, or between the more or less vicious, where little can be learned but the ways of the wicked, and from whence they must be sent to encounter new wants, new temptation, and to commit new crimes, is to pursue a course, as little reconcilable with justice as humanity: yet, till the House of Refuge was established there was no alternative."

Society for the Reformation of Juvenile Delinquents in the City of New York,
Fourth Annual Report, 1829

4. The above account best reflects what growing reform sentiment during the period 1820 to 1848?
   (a) Belief in democratic reforms
   (b) Commitment to egalitarianism
   (c) Acceptance of transcendental philosophy
   (d) Commitment to the philosophy of predestination

5. Reform movements concerned with all of the following emerged in the same time period EXCEPT
   (a) women's rights.
   (b) environmental preservation.
   (c) temperance.
   (d) public education.

6. During the period 1800 to 1848, reform movements were most successful in achieving their goals in which of the following?
   (a) The creation of utopian communities
   (b) The emancipation of enslaved people in the South
   (c) State laws focused on improving public education
   (d) Women's Suffrage

Questions 7–9 refer to the excerpt below.

"This transformation of the condition of the country from gloom and distress to brightness and prosperity, has been mainly the work of American legislation, fostering American industry, instead of allowing it to be controlled by foreign legislation, cherishing foreign industry. The foes of the American System, in 1824, with great boldness and confidence, predicted, first, the ruin of the public revenue, and the creation of a necessity to resort to direct taxation; The gentleman from South Carolina (General Hayne), I believe, thought that the tariff of 1824 would operate a reduction of revenue to the large amount of eight millions of dollars; secondly, the destruction of our navigation; thirdly, the desolation of commercial cities; and fourthly, the augmentation of the price of objects of consumption, and further decline in that of the articles of our exports. Every prediction which they made has failed, utterly failed."

Henry Clay, *In Defense of the American System*, 1832

7. The system that Henry Clay describes above was designed to amplify
   (a) government ownership of the means of production.
   (b) a foreign trade system that favored Great Britain over France.
   (c) a national market economy.
   (d) dominance of state government over the national government.

8. Which of the following was a component of the American System that Henry Clay envisioned?
   (a) Locally funded internal improvements
   (b) A second Bank of the United States
   (c) Government ownership of railroads
   (d) Tariffs to protect the textile industry

9. By 1848, which component of the American System was still used to benefit business?
   (a) A third Bank of the United States
   (b) Providing business with free raw materials from government-owned land
   (c) A protective tariff
   (d) The completion of transcontinental railroads

Questions 10–12 refer to the excerpt below.

"In 1831 Lowell was little more than a factory village. Several corporations were started, and the cotton-mills belonging to them were building. Help was in great demand; and stories were told all over the country of the new factory town, and the high wages that were offered to all classes of work-people,—stories that reached the ears of mechanics' and farmers' songs, and gave new life to lonely and dependent women in distant towns and farmhouses. . . . Troops of young girls came by stages and baggage-wagons, men often being employed to go to other States and to Canada, to collect them at so much a head, and deliver them at the factories."

Harriet Hanson Robinson, *Loom and Spindle,* 1898

10. The above account best represents a departure from which of the following beliefs about the role of women in the early nineteenth century?
    (a) Prevalence of the concept of "republican motherhood"
    (b) Aspirations of women to become "career" women
    (c) Aspiration of women to become "visible saints"
    (d) Prevalence of the concept of "the cult of domesticity"

11. Early industry began in the Northeast for all of the following reasons EXCEPT
    (a) swift-flowing streams that provided a good source of power.
    (b) a relatively high population density to supply both labor and markets.
    (c) the mechanization of the workplace through the assembly line.
    (d) an efficient mean of transportation provided by good natural harbors.

12. The original mill girls mentioned above were subsequently replaced by which of the following groups?
    (a) Immigrant women
    (b) Native-born children
    (c) Retired farmers
    (d) Immigrant children

END OF MULTIPLE-CHOICE SECTION

Short-Answer Questions

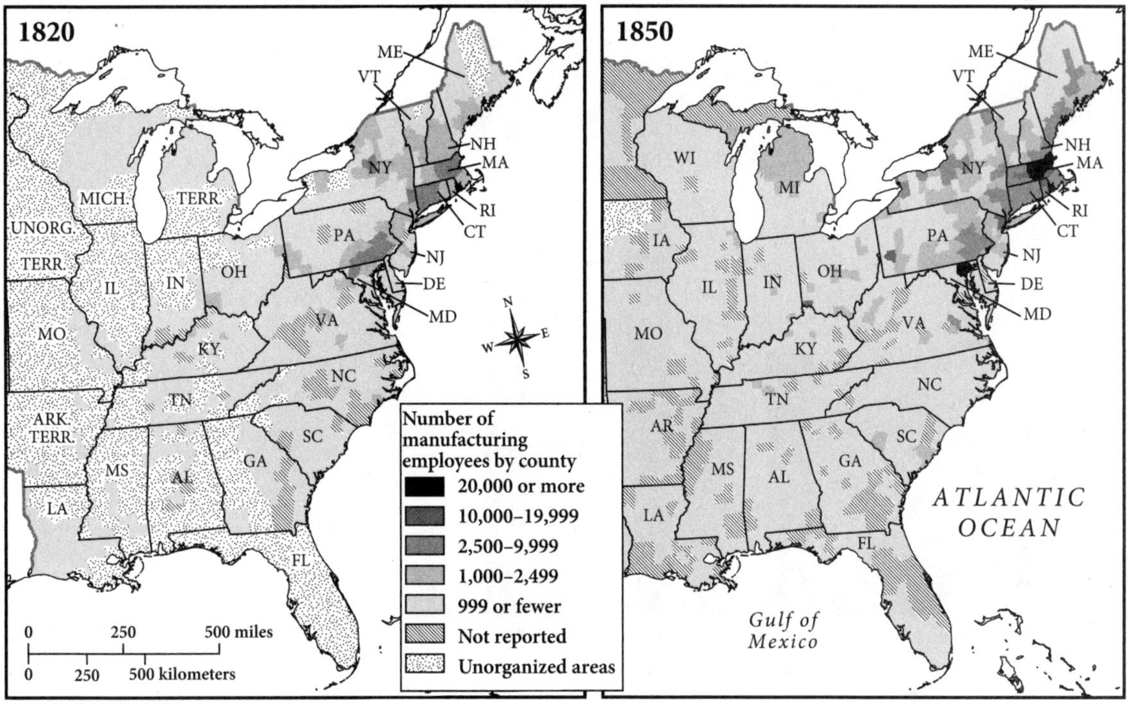

U.S. Manufacturing, 1820 and 1850

1. Using the two maps above, answer a, b, and c.
   (a) Briefly explain ONE historical continuity referenced in the maps above during the period from 1820 to 1850.

   (b) Briefly explain ONE historical change referenced in in the maps above during the period from 1820 to 1850.

   (c) Briefly explain ONE historical factor that accounts for the change you explained in part (b).

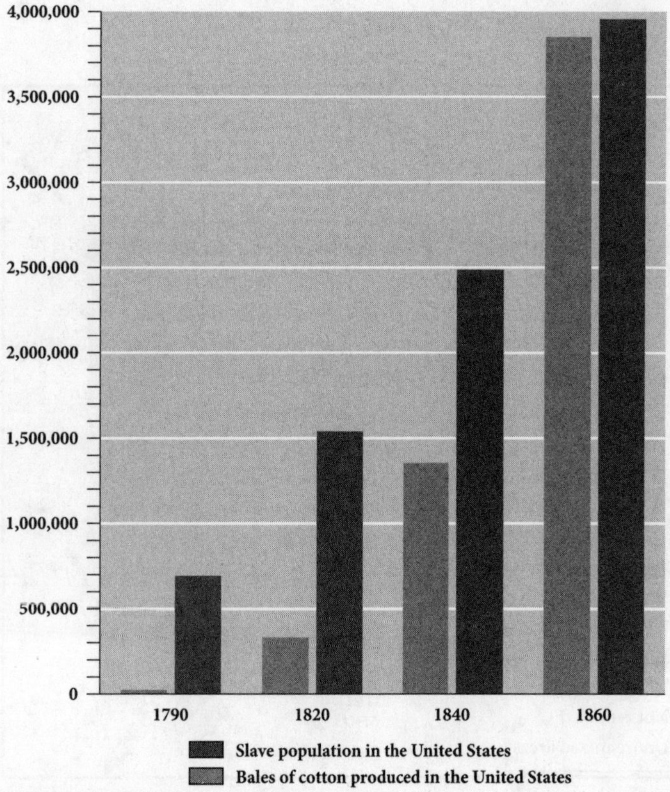

Growth of Cotton Production and the Slave Population, 1790–1860

2. Using the figure above, answer a, b, and c.

(a) Briefly describe a cultural impact from 1790-1840 on the growth shown in the figure above.

(b) Briefly describe an economic impact from 1790-1840 on the growth shown in the figure above.

(c) Briefly describe a political impact from 1790-1840 on the growth shown in the figure above.

END OF SHORT-ANSWER SECTION

Document-Based Question

Directions: The following question is based on the accompanying documents. The documents have been edited for this exercise. Spend approximately 15 minutes planning and 45 minutes writing your answer. Write an essay that does the following:

- States an appropriate thesis that directly addresses all parts of the question.
- Supports the thesis or argument with evidence from all or all but one of the documents AND your knowledge of U.S. history beyond the documents.
- Analyzes all or all but one of the documents.
- Explains the significance of the author's point of view, author's purpose, historical context, and/or audience for at least three documents.
- Uses historical evidence beyond the documents to support your argument.
- Places the argument in the context of broader regional, national, or global processes.
- Incorporates all of the elements above into a convincing essay.

Question: Evaluate the relative importance of different causes for the westward movement of Americans during the period from 1800 to 1848.

Document 1

Source: The USCen Web Census Project, www.US-Census.org

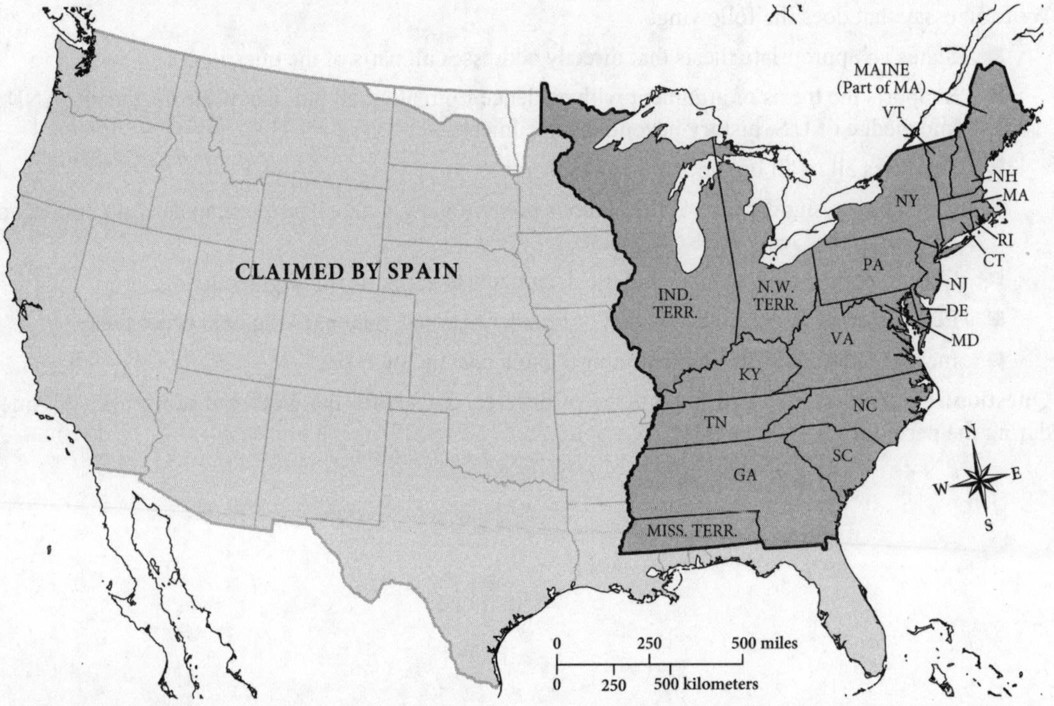

1800 U.S. Census

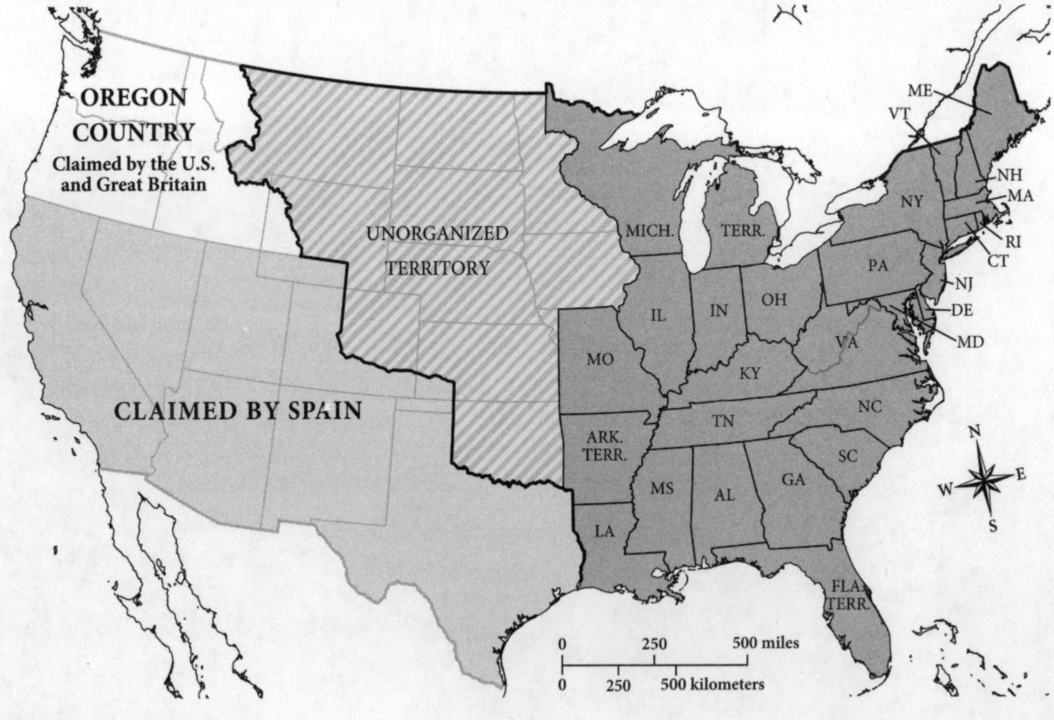

1830 U.S. Census

Document 2

Source: American Explorer Zebulon Pike, 1806

From these immense prairies may arise one great advantage to the United States, viz: The restriction of our population to some certain limits, and thereby a continuation of the Union. Our citizens being so prone to rambling and extending themselves on the frontier will through necessity be constrained to limit their extent to the west to the borders of the Missouri and Mississippi, while they leave the prairies incapable of cultivation to the wandering and uncivilized aborigines of the country.

Document 3

Source: Land Act of 1820

That from and after the first day of July next [1820], all the public lands of the United States, the sale of which is, or may be authorized by law, shall when offered at public sale, to the highest bidder, be offered in half quarter sections [80 acres]; and when offered at private sale, may be purchased, at the option of the purchaser, either in entire sections [640 acres], half sections [320 acres], quarter sections [160 acres], or half quarter sections [80 acres].

Document 4

Source: John William Hill, *View of the Erie Canal*, 1829

Bettmann/Getty Images

Document 5

Source: Xu Naiji, a senior official and advisor to Qing Emperor Daoguang, "An Argument for Legalization," 1836. "Memorial from Heu-Naetse," in *Blue Book—Correspondence Relating to China* (London, 1840).
Source: President Andrew Jackson's Case for the Removal Act, First Annual Message to Congress, December 8, 1829

It gives me pleasure to announce to Congress that the benevolent policy of the Government, steadily pursued for nearly thirty years, in relation to the removal of the Indians beyond the white settlements is approaching to a happy consummation. Two important tribes have accepted the provision made for their removal at the last session of Congress, and it is believed that their example will induce the remaining tribes also to seek the same obvious advantages. . . .

Toward the aborigines of the country no one can indulge a more friendly feeling than myself, or would go further in attempting to reclaim them from their wandering habits and make them a happy, prosperous people. I have endeavored to impress upon them my own solemn convictions of the duties and powers of the General Government in relation to the State authorities. For the justice of the laws passed by the States within the scope of their reserved powers they are not responsible to this Government. As individuals we may entertain and express our opinions of their acts, but as a Government we have as little right to control them as we have to prescribe laws for other nations.

Document 6

Source: John O'Sullivan on America's "Manifest Destiny," 1839

America is destined for better deeds. It is our unparalleled glory that we have no reminiscences of battle fields, but in defense of humanity, of the oppressed of all nations, of the rights of conscience, the rights of personal enfranchisement. Our annals describe no scenes of horrid carnage, where men were led on by hundreds of thousands to slay one another, dupes and victims to emperors, kings, nobles, demons in the human form called heroes. We have had patriots to defend our homes, our liberties, but no aspirants to crowns or thrones; nor have the American people ever suffered themselves to be led on by wicked ambition to depopulate the land, to spread desolation far and wide, that a human being might be placed on a seat of supremacy. . . .

The far-reaching, the boundless future will be the era of American greatness. In its magnificent domain of space and time, the nation of many nations is destined to manifest to mankind the excellence of divine principles; to establish on earth the noblest temple ever dedicated to the worship of the Most High—the Sacred and the True. Its floor shall be a hemisphere—its roof the firmament of the star-studded heavens, and its congregation an Union of many Republics, comprising hundreds of happy millions, calling, owning no man master, but governed by God's natural and moral law of equality, the law of brotherhood—of "peace and good will amongst men."

Document 7

Source: Adapted from Table 40 in Lewis Cecil Gray, *History of Agriculture in the Southern United States to 1860*, vol. 2 (Gloucester, MA: Peter Smith, 1958), 1026.

American Production of Raw Cotton, 1790–1860 (bales)					
Year	Production	Year	Production	Year	Production
1790	3,135	1815	208,896	1840	1,346,232
1795	16,719	1820	334,378	1845	1,804,223
1800	73,145	1825	532,915	1850	2,133,851
1805	146,290	1830	731,452	1855	3,217,417
1810	177,638	1835	1,060,711	1860	3,837,402

END OF DOCUMENT-BASED SECTION

NOTES:

NOTES:

PERIOD 5, 1844-1877

Overview

The years of Period 5 see the nation expand across the continent, though that growth comes with confrontations over slavery and different views of the place of the United States in the world. Many believed in the concept of Manifest Destiny—that the United States was ordained by God to rule the continent through a combination of racial and cultural superiority. As the country grew, however, the controversy over the extension of slavery followed. Another minority, American Indians, faced increasing pressure as more of their lands were forcibly taken from them. U.S. economic, diplomatic, and cultural interests even began to look beyond the West Coast to the possible extension of American influence into Asia.

As immigrants continued to pour into the United States, tensions grew between the new arrivals and established communities. Immigrants were often met with violent nativist movements, particularly aimed at Catholics. Many sought refuge in the West in the years after the Civil War. The need for labor to promote economic development often trumped nativist sentiment. As the settlement of the West progressed, Hispanics and American Indians came under particular hardship as many refused to accept their assimilation into American society.

Tensions between the North and the South over issues involving slavery came to a head in the 1840s and 1850s. The North relied increasingly on free labor, while the South grew more dependent on slave-based agriculture. Abolitionist groups became more outspoken and activist, leading to a growing paranoia among slaveholders. Southerners responded with states' rights claims, nullification bills, and increased reliance of racial stereotyping to bolster their case for maintaining slavery.

The 1850s saw repeated attempts to defuse the conflict, resulting in the Compromise of 1850, the Kansas-Nebraska Act, and the *Dred Scott* decision by the Supreme Court. Nothing seemed to slow down the growing sectionalism. Issues of slavery and nativism led to the realignment of political parties, with the Republican Party emerging in the Midwest and North, while Democrats still tried to hold the northern and southern factions of their party together. The election of Lincoln in 1860 on a platform calling for the end of the extension of slavery into new territories proved to be the tipping point that led to the breakup of the Union and the Civil War.

The Union victory in the war ended the constitutional issues of slavery and secession but left unresolved many disputes over what should be the limits of federal power. The North triumphed over the South in the war through a combination of industrial power, leadership, and the moral high ground of calling for an end to slavery. Lincoln's decision to issue the Emancipation Proclamation gained the Union cause support in Europe and mobilized many African Americans to fight for the northern cause. Northern strength eventually overcame southern resistance, as the war destroyed both the South's environment and its infrastructure.

While the Union victory settled the question of slavery once and for all, Reconstruction left unresolved many questions about federal versus state power, as well as many prewar social and economic patterns. The Thirteenth Amendment ended slavery, but many former slaves fell into the almost equally oppressive sharecropping system during Reconstruction and beyond. Some temporary progress was made in terms of African American voting rights and political participation, but these gains were short-lived when the rest of the country began to lose interest in Reconstruction programs as the country put the Civil War behind it. The Fourteenth and Fifteenth amendments promised full citizenship and voting rights to African American men, but as interest in Reconstruction faded, so did a commitment to the enforcement of these promises. Women felt particularly betrayed when the Fifteenth Amendment specified male voting rights but left women out altogether. In spite of these shortcomings, these two amendments became the basis for effective civil rights legislation in the twentieth century.

Key Terms

Be sure that you understand the meaning of these terms and their relevance in U.S. history. Page numbers from the textbook are provided.

Manifest Destiny (359–368, 370)
Mexican American War (369–372, 383–386)
American exceptionism (643)
Compromise of 1850 (377, 389–390)
Nativist movement (398–399)
Irish immigration (395–400)
Free-soil movement (383–386)
Kansas-Nebraska Act (377, 400–401)
Dred Scott v Sanford (384, 402–403)
Republican Party (377, 400–401)
Abraham Lincoln (376, 417–418, 423–425)
Emancipation Proclamation (424-425, 429, 444)
Gettysburg Address (437, 439)
Confederacy (377, 408, 427)
Thirteenth Amendment (452, 477)
Fourteenth Amendment (455, 457, 474–475, 486)
Fifteenth Amendment (450, 457–458, 477)
Reconstruction (453–455, 468–475)
Sharecropping (461–463, 476)

Focus Questions

As you study Period 5, keep the following thematic questions in mind.

American and National Identity

- How did westward expansion and the quest for "manifest destiny" both reflect and shape Americans' views on progress and identity?
- What effect did the debate over slavery have on shaping regional identities in the period 1844–1877?
- How did the Civil War and its aftermath change people's views about what it means to be American?

Work, Exchange, and Technology

- How did the differing economies of the North and South contribute to both the outbreak of the Civil War and its outcome?
- In what ways did events during the Civil War years, 1861–1865, shape the postwar economy?

Geography and the Environment

- What effect did geography have on Americans' quest for economic progress in the antebellum era?
- To what extent did geography have an impact on the events leading up to and during the Civil War?
- How was the western environment transformed as more and more settlers moved west in the mid-nineteenth century?

Migration and Settlement

- How did the influx of immigrants in the mid-nineteenth century change America?
- Why did Americans and immigrants move west, and how did the federal government promote westward expansion?

Politics and Power

- How and why did political alignments change as a result of events in the period from 1844 to 1877?
- How did reformers and writers shape the arguments about slavery in the years before the Civil War?
- How successful was political compromise at resolving the issues facing the nation in the antebellum period? Account for the successes and failures of compromise.
- How did various groups use the Constitution to buttress their beliefs about slavery and post–Civil War reconstruction?

- What issues were left unresolved as the Civil War ended, and how were these addressed between 1865 and 1877?
- How did the Civil War and Reconstruction affect the balance of power between branches of the federal government and between the federal government and the states?
- How successful was Reconstruction in achieving its goals? Account for the successes and shortcomings of the effort to rebuild the nation and to guarantee the slaves rights and opportunities that others had.

America in the World

- In what ways did American efforts to increase the power and prestige of the United States bring the country into conflict with other nations?
- Why was the Mexican War, which ended in 1848, such an important factor in leading the U.S. into a civil war thirteen years later?
- How did foreign involvement help determine the outcome of the Civil War?

American and Regional Culture

- How did Americans' views about race and ethnicity shape their views on expansion and the treatment of immigrants?
- How did the power of the pen shape Americans' views on slavery and the conflict between North and South?
- In what ways was expansion of republican ideals at the heart of debates over Manifest Destiny, slavery, and Reconstruction?

Social Structures

- What were the unifying factors that linked the abolitionist movement to the efforts to achieve an expanded role for women in the mid-nineteenth century?

Thematic Timeline

TIME	Key Events
1844	
	American and National Identity • Free Soil Party forms (1848) • Foreign Miner's Tax enacted in California (1850) **Work, Exchange, and Technology** • Gold discovered in California (1848) **Migration and Settlement** • Great Irish famine prompts mass immigration to United States (1845–1851) • "Forty-niners" seek gold in California (1849) **Politics and Power** • James K. Polk elected president (1844) • Wilmot Proviso approved by House but not by Senate (1846) **America in the World** • Congress supports Polk's recommendation and declares war on Mexico (1846) • Treaty of Guadalupe Hidalgo transfers Mexican lands to United States (1848)

TIME	Key Events
1850	
	American and National Identity • American (Know-Nothing) Party forms (1851) • *Dred Scott v. Sandford* allows slavery in all U.S. territories (1857) • John Brown raids federal arsenal at Harpers Ferry (1859) **Work, Exchange, and Technology** • Comstock silver lode discovered in Nevada (1859) **Politics and Power** • Compromise of 1850 • Kansas-Nebraska Act tests popular sovereignty (1854) • Republican Party forms (1854) • Rep. Preston Brooks canes Sen. Charles Sumner on Senate floor (1856) **America in the World** • Treaty of Kanagawa opens U.S. coaling stations in Japan (1854) • Ostend Manifesto urges U.S. seizure of Cuba (1854) • William Walker deposes Nicaraguan government, sets up "filibuster" regime (1856) • President Buchanan seeks to buy and annex Cuba as a slave state (1858) **American and Regional Culture** • Harriet Beecher Stowe publishes *Uncle Tom's Cabin* (1852)
1860	
	American and National Identity • General Butler declares refugee slaves "contraband of war" (1861) • Dakota Sioux uprising in Minnesota (1862) • Lincoln issues preliminary emancipation proclamation (Sept. 1862) • Union initiates draft, sparking riots in New York City (1863) • Lincoln delivers Gettysburg Address (1863) • Ex-Confederate states pass Black Codes to limit freedpeople's rights (1865) • Civil Rights Act passed over President Johnson's veto (1866) • Wyoming Territory grants women suffrage (1869) **Work, Exchange, and Technology** • Legal Tender Act authorizes greenback currency (1862) • Explosion kills munitions workers in Pittsburgh (1862) • Long Drive of Texas longhorns begins (1865) • Transcontinental railroad completed (1869) **Geography and the Environment** • Homestead Act passed (1862) • Yosemite Valley reserved as public park (1864) • Sherman's army devastates Georgia and South Carolina (1864–1865) **Migration and Settlement** • African Americans escape slavery and become "contrabands" behind Union lines (1861–1865) **Politics and Power** • Lincoln elected president (1860) • Deep South states secede (1860–1861) • Confederate forces fire on Fort Sumter (April 1861)

- Upper South secedes (1861)
- Confederates win First Battle of Bull Run (July 1861)
- Union wins battles of Gettysburg and Vicksburg (July 1863)
- Lincoln reelected (1864)
- Robert E. Lee surrenders to Grant (April 1865)
- Lincoln assassinated (1865)
- Reconstruction Act (1867)
- Impeachment of Andrew Johnson (1868)
- Fourteenth Amendment (1868)
- Ulysses S. Grant elected president (1868)

America in the World

- Britain and France refuse recognition to the Confederacy; Britain impounds Confederate ships being built in British shipyards (1863)
- Burlingame Treaty with China (1868)

American and Regional Culture

- U.S. Sanitary Commission formed (1861)
- Morrill Act funds public state universities (1862)

Social Structures

- Women's rights advocates form Woman's Loyal National League (1863)
- Louisa May Alcott publishes *Hospital Sketches* (1863)

1877

American and National Identity

- Utah Territory grants women suffrage (1870)
- *Minor v. Happersett:* Supreme Court rules that Fourteenth Amendment does not extend national voting rights to women (1875)
- Sioux, Cheyennes, and Arapahos win Battle of Little Big Horn (1876)

Work, Exchange, and Technology

- Panic of 1873 ushers in severe economic depression (1873)
- United States begins to move to gold standard (1873)

Geography and the Environment

- General Mining Act (1872)
- Yellowstone National Park created (1872)

Migration and Settlement

- Nez Perce forcibly removed from homelands in Northwest (1877)

Politics and Power

- Congress passes Enforcement Laws to suppress Klan (1870)
- Fifteenth Amendment (1870)
- Grant reelected; Crédit Mobilier scandal (1872)
- *Slaughterhouse Cases* (1873)
- Sweeping Democratic gains in congressional elections (1874)
- *Munn v. Illinois* (1877)

American and Regional Culture

- Ku Klux Klan at peak of power (1870)
- Beecher-Tilton scandal dominates headlines (1875)

Social Structures

- Victoria Woodhull declares support for "free love" (1871)

America's History Chapter Summaries

(required AP® content in bold)

Chapter 12
Sectional Conflict and Crisis, 1844–1861

Chapter 12 examines four related themes: the impact of traders and settlers on the Great Plains and in California, the disintegration of the two-party system as debates over the extension of slavery grew more acrimonious, the rise of Abraham Lincoln and the Republican party, and the effect of the secession of the South. Every addition of new territory to the Union brought with it the debate over whether that territory would be slave or free. The question was settled temporarily with the Compromise of 1850, but arguments over the Fugitive Slave Act and southerners' determination to open new lands to slavery made any future compromises difficult. The Whig Party disintegrated and was replaced by the Republican Party, dedicated to limiting slavery to the states and territories where it already existed. The Democratic Party splintered as well into a northern faction that looked for a way to limit slavery and a southern one devoted to protecting the institution. The 1850s was a decade that saw less and less room for compromise.

This issue of whether any new states would be slave or free reached a crisis point quickly when gold was discovered in California and the population of the West Coast grew rapidly. **Rights of Mexicans and American Indians were pushed aside as gold miners crowded in and began to stake claims. California had the added attraction of being a port of call toward Asia, a possibility many American merchants already appreciated.** Constitutional crisis followed California's application for statehood. Southern threats to leave the Union were temporarily put off with the passage of the Compromise of 1850, though many of the provisions of this bill led to more controversy. A free California was balanced by opening the rest of the territory gained from Mexico through popular sovereignty, and the South got a new, **more stringent Fugitive Slave Law**. The old **Two Party System crumbled as more aggressive antislavery advocates took the political stage. The Democrats splintered along regional lines while the new Republican Party replaced the divided Whigs.**

Northern abolitionists were quick to try and undermine the new Fugitive Slave Law, and antislave literature gained widespread popularity. Southerners responded with defense of the system, citing what they felt was the "positive good" of the institution. The economies of both North and South continued to move apart, with the North relying more and more on free labor while the South became ever more dependent on slaves.

Expansion continued as Congress sought to put the **Kansas and Nebraska territories** on the statehood track. The decision to handle the issue of slavery through popular sovereignty stirred up even more controversy, as the bill cancelled out the earlier Missouri Compromise and threw **these two territories open for renewed fighting over whether they would be slave or free**. The new Republican Party began to take the lead in the fight to contain slavery where it already was but to allow no new slave territories for states to be created. Fighting broke out in Kansas almost immediately, but Congress was able to do nothing to resolve the conflict. The next challenge to the Compromise of 1850 came in the form of a court case brought by a slave, Dred Scott, who asked that he be declared free because he was taken into free territory. The Supreme Court, dominated by southerners, not only denied his petition but went on to add that no one could be prevented from taking their "property" wherever they chose, **a position that undercut all political attempts to limit the spread of slavery**.

This was the political atmosphere in which **Abraham Lincoln won the office of the presidency in 1860, a Republican elected on a platform of protecting slavery where it already existed but preventing its spread into any new territories**. Many in the South viewed Lincoln's victory as the end of their chances to live a prosperous life in the United States. Secessionist fervor swept through the Deep South, beginning with South Carolina. All attempts at compromise failed, and Lincoln took office with a divided Union. **Both sides faced disagreements among their people, but the final division fell along the lines of slave or free states.**

Chapter 13
Bloody Ground: The Civil War, 1861–1865

Chapter 13 surveys the dramatic events of the Civil War. Although the South enjoyed early successes, the lack of industry, disrupted agriculture, and the weight of the slave system eventually combined to make the southern cause a lost one. The North began the war with weak military leadership but with industrial advantages, financial resources, and enormous manpower, it eventually gained the upper hand. Congress worked to create a more efficient banking system to finance the war effort. Lincoln changed the nature of the war with his Emancipation Proclamation, pushing the end of slavery to the forefront of Union war aims. His choice of better military leadership led the Union to victory. The war was hard on civilians on both sides. They faced high taxes, food shortages, inflation, and the constant fear of conscription and the deaths of loved ones. Although the North won, personal losses were heavy on both sides of the war.

South Carolina was the site of the first fighting in the Civil War with the attack on Fort Sumter in 1861, following the election of Abraham Lincoln. The South had a slight advantage in the first year of the war, as Lincoln sought a reliable general to lead the northern troops. A surprise victory at Antietam led **Lincoln to change the focus of the war by announcing the Emancipation Proclamation, making the end of slavery a northern war aim**. The Union strategies of blockade and the fight to control the Mississippi River soon left the South without supply lines, and the course of the war began to change. **Lincoln's choice of Ulysses S. Grant gave him the military leadership he needed to bring total war to the South**.

The war touched all parts of society in both the North and the South. **Conscription, wartime deprivations, and the constant fear of losing loved ones in battle haunted people throughout the Union and the Confederacy**. **Lincoln occasionally ignored constitutional safeguards in order to maintain control of border states like Maryland**. Women were called to do the work of men on the home front and on the battlefield, serving as farm and factory workers as well as nurses. **Many women hoped their contributions would lead to greater rights as citizens when the war ended**.

The North flourished during the war, with a streamlined banking system, busy factories, and a Republican Congress. The South was reduced to poverty and persistent inflation, particularly after the war moved deep into southern territory.

Lincoln's Emancipation Proclamation was extended in 1865 with the Thirteenth Amendment, which abolished slavery throughout the country. **Former slaves began to flock to Union lines, offering their services to the war effort**. By 1864, General Grant had driven the war into the heart of the Confederacy, with his generals taking Atlanta and his own troops surrounding Lee and the Army of Northern Virginia. Lincoln's reelection was secured as the news from the battlefields grew more optimistic, though he faced a party of **Radical Republicans in Congress who wanted harsher punishments for the defeated South than Lincoln's proposal to reestablish the Union as quickly and painlessly as possible**. The Confederacy finally collapsed in April 1865, leaving the Union preserved but hundreds of thousands dead and half the country in ruins. Slavery was gone, but it remained to be seen what real change would come to the nation as the states struggled to regain some semblance of normality.

Chapter 14
Reconstruction, 1865–1877

Chapter 14 focuses on the period following the Civil War, as Republicans tried to restore the defeated southern states to the Union and define the status of newly emancipated African Americans. Andrew Johnson assumed the presidency after Lincoln's assassination and determined to promote a lenient model for Reconstruction. The Radical Republicans in Congress disagreed, and when southern states began to enact oppressive laws like the Black Codes, they moved to push Johnson aside and take control of Reconstruction policies. They impeached Johnson, and though they failed to remove him from office, the Republicans took over the reins of government and imposed military rule on the South. Gradually, however, the Radical Republicans' control diminished, leaving many aspects of southern politics and culture similar to that before the war.

The end of the Civil War brought immediate questions about the status of the newly freed slaves in the reunited nation. President Johnson's goal was to bring the South back into the Union quickly. The southern states, however, moved to reestablish white supremacy, passing Black Codes that restricted black rights and attempting to force freedmen into agricultural labor, often on their former plantations. Radical Republicans responded with legislation creating the Freedmen's Bureau and passing the Fourteenth Amendment to the Constitution. The amendment granted citizenship to all born in the United States, regardless of previous status as slaves. Johnson's attempts to veto the legislation passed by the Radical Republicans, who won a majority in Congress in the 1866 elections, were quickly overturned. The Reconstruction Act of 1867 placed Congress in charge of all aspects of Reconstruction. That same year, Congress passed the Tenure of Office over Johnson's veto and used his violation of the act to draw up charges of impeachment against him. Though the Senate failed to get the necessary votes to remove Johnson from office, he was rendered powerless for the remainder of his term. **Radical Reconstruction moved forward, with southern states put under military control**.

The presidential election of 1868 brought General Ulysses S. Grant into office, and the Radical Republicans continued to hold a solid majority in Congress. One of their first acts was passage of the **Fifteenth Amendment to the Constitution, which granted voting rights to all American-born men**. Many women were disappointed with this amendment, as they felt they had earned the vote as well. African American women had a hard choice to make. **While some African American women felt they too should have the vote, they wanted to support any legislation that would ensure that their men had that right**.

As freedmen began to realize the limitations of their new status, they found themselves in conflict with northerners who wanted to revive southern cotton cultivation for international markets. Many ended up working the same land they had tilled as slaves, only this time they held the status of sharecroppers, a role in many ways even more economically precarious than the plight of slaves. Sharecroppers and tenant farmers nearly always fell into debt, and often they found themselves as bound to the land by that debt as closely as they had been by the bonds of slavery. As long as congressional Reconstruction lasted, the freedmen's community had some measure of protection, but that quickly disintegrated as the white southern power elite began to regain control of state governments in the mid-1870s.

In spite of these difficulties, black communities were able to flourish in many parts of the Deep South. Local churches became community focal points, quickly followed by small schools, civic organizations, and newspapers. While many hoped for general desegregation of all public facilities and institutions, neither Congress, the courts, nor the local power structure allowed that. **Despite the Civil Rights Act of 1875 requiring full and equal access to public accommodations, no real support would come for desegregation until the 1960s**.

Radical Republican control of Congress began to unravel in the mid-1870s. A financial panic in 1873 took the country's attention away from the plight of the freedmen and focused it on their own bank accounts. The scandals of the Grant administration further discredited the congressional majority. Many began to wish for a return to stability, and white Democrat leaders in the South promised just that. **As military troops were withdrawn from southern states, "Redeemer" governments assumed power, including many leaders from the former Confederacy**. Freedmen immediately began to find their rights constrained by local laws and the illicit activities of groups like the Ku Klux Klan. **Supreme Court cases further undermined the hopes of freedmen for support from the federal court, and they found themselves locked into a political world controlled by many of their former masters**.

What followed was the long, slow decline of Radical Republican policies and power. Though the Redeemers regained power in the South, slavery was indeed gone and black communities managed to thrive in spite of long odds against them. **The Fourteenth and Fifteenth amendments were part of the Constitution, though it would take another one hundred years for these two pieces of legislation to have the impact that was intended**. The South continued to lag behind the rest of the nation in both economic development and social progress, though the seeds were planted for the civil rights revolution that came in the twentieth century.

Chapter 15
Conquering a Continent, 1860–1890

Chapter 15 examines the expansion of the United States from 1860 through 1890. During these years, the United States expanded to the Pacific Coast and linked the East and West Coasts with a transcontinental railroad. The national economy grew at an unprecedented rate with the markets created by the war, the demands from new consumers, and the help of a business-friendly Republican government. Greenbacks competed with gold as the new currency as others sought to add silver coins as well. U.S. foreign policy became more expansive through the acquisition of Alaska and **increased international trade with the Pacific, Asia, and Latin America**. Those settling on the Great Plains became integrated into the national economy at the expense of the American Indians and the great herds of buffalo. Homesteaders transformed the **western environment to the point that the federal government began to set land aside for natural preserves**, another blow to the culture of the American Indians who depended on these hunting grounds. After the end of the Civil War, President Grant sought treaties aimed at **assimilating American Indians who would cooperate and exterminating those who would not**. By the late 1880s, most tribes had faced defeat and moved to reservations, though they persisted in their efforts to maintain their tribal identity. The United States was poised to become a major player on the world stage.

The completion of the first transcontinental railroad was a political as well as a technological triumph. Republicans had exercised nearly complete domination of Congress since the southern states left the Union in 1860 and 1861, and among their goals was the railroad, a stronger protective tariff, and the growth of the nation's industrial sector through various forms of public-private partnerships. The possibilities of new riches through overseas trade had been on the Republican agenda since the 1850s when trade with Japan began. Chinese labor had already proved valuable to American industry, and these workers played a major role in the building of the transcontinental railroad. The **new railroad companies transformed American capitalism with the creation of corporations**, all under the benevolent eye of the U.S. Congress. High tariffs protected American industry well after the end of the Civil War and the return of some southern Democrats to the government. Conservative appointments to the Supreme Court ensured favorable rulings for businesses as well. The nation also prospered from the discovery of **vast mineral wealth, particularly gold and silver**. These discoveries strengthened U.S. currency in the international markets and attracted European investment.

Congress moved to open the West on a grand scale with the Homestead Act of 1862. Farmers competed with miners and cattle ranchers in their race to the riches the West offered. Women played a significant role in this settlement as well, often finding greater political power in the territories than what was offered to them back east. Many homesteaders struggled with extreme environmental conditions, inadequate homestead allotments, and backbreaking labor as they worked to carve out a living from grasslands that often defied easy settlement. Among them were **African Americans who migrated out of the South** in search of independence and land in the newly opened frontier. Range wars were common between cattlemen and the newly arriving farmers, who fought over access to grazing land and water. Miners added another layer of competition, as the mining frontier began to move from west to east, encroaching on lands claimed by both farmers and cattlemen.

Often overlooked or underestimated in this scramble for western lands were the **numerous American Indian tribes that also called the Great Plains home**. The systematic destruction of the vast buffalo herds on which Plains Indians depended for survival **led to Indian wars** and attempts by Congress at mediation that rarely favored American Indian interests. **Wars between the army and the American Indians on the Great Plains began before the Civil War ended and intensified during Reconstruction**. Reservations set aside for American Indians by the federal government proved to be woefully inadequate, with marginal land, poor supplies, and corrupt government officials who were charged with administering them, not to mention the loss of traditional ways of life for the American Indian nations.

Lulls in the conflicts were always brief, and by the 1870s, the federal government was working to **force most Plains tribes onto reservations with false promises and increasing violence**. Assimilation meant boarding schools for children, life in near poverty on reservations, and efforts by missionaries to substitute Christianity for native religions. The Dawes Act of 1887 sought to break up tribal lands into individual homesteads, **another step along the road to assimilation**. The Ghost Dance movement in the1890s was a last-ditch effort by Plains tribes to make a united stand against the U.S. military, but it was ended once and for all by the slaughter of more than one hundred Sioux at Wounded Knee, South Dakota. The world of the Plains Indians became the basis for entertainments like Buffalo Bill's Wild West Show, with rugged pioneers taking center stage and Indians and buffalo being relegated to background scenery.

Period 5 Practice Questions

Multiple-Choice Questions

Questions 1–3 refer to the excerpt below.

"We are glad at last to get a clear case, one on which no shadow of doubt can hang. This is not meddling with other people's affairs—this is other people meddling with us. This is not going crusading after slaves who it is alleged are very happy & comfortable where they are: all that amiable argument falls to the ground, but defending a human being who has taken the risks of being shot or burned alive, or cast into the sea, or starved to death or suffocated in a wooden box—taken all this risk to get away from his driver and recover the rights of man. And this man the Statute says, you men of Massachusetts shall kidnap & send back again a thousand miles across the sea to the dog-hutch he fled from. And this filthy enactment was made in the 19th century, by people who could read & write. I will not obey it, by God."

Ralph Waldo Emerson, 1851

1. The controversy Emerson eludes to in the passage above happened in which of the following historical contexts?
   (a) The debates about the constitutionality of the Louisiana Purchase
   (b) The beginning of the Market Revolution
   (c) The aftermath of the Mexican-American War
   (d) The debates over Reconstruction policies

2. Which of the following historical developments does this excerpt highlight?
   (a) Partisan debates
   (b) Regional differences
   (c) Foreign policy disputes
   (d) Laissez-Faire economics

3. The act referenced above was part of a compromise to
   (a) allow Missouri to enter the Union as a slave state.
   (b) allow a southern route for a transcontinental railroad.
   (c) allow California to enter the Union as a free state.
   (d) end the threat of southern states nullifying the protective tariff.

Questions 4–6 refer to the excerpt below.

"Hon. Horace Greeley:

"Dear Sir. . . . I would save the Union. I would save it the shortest way under the Constitution. The sooner the national authority can be restored the nearer the Union will be 'the Union as it was.' If there be those who would not save the Union unless they could at the same time save Slavery, I do not agree with them. If there be those who would not save the Union unless they could at the same time destroy Slavery, I do not agree with them. My paramount object in this struggle is to save the Union, and is not either to save or destroy Slavery. If I could save the Union without freeing any slave, I would do it, and if I could save it by freeing all the slaves, I would do it, and if I could save it by freeing some and leaving others alone, I would also do that. What I do about

Slavery and the colored race, I do because I believe it helps to save this Union, and what I forbear, I forbear because I do not believe it would help to save the Union. I shall do less whenever I shall believe what I am doing hurts the cause, and I shall do more whenever I shall believe doing more will help the cause. I shall try to correct errors when shown to be errors; and I shall adopt new views so fast as they shall appear to be true views. . . . Yours, A. Lincoln."

Abraham Lincoln to Horace Greeley, August 22, 1862

4. The above letter helps to best explain which of the following?
   (a) The Emancipation Proclamation
   (b) The ratification of the Thirteenth Amendment
   (c) The establishment of the Freedmen's Bureau
   (d) Congressional Reconstruction

5. Which of the following represents an important outcome of the ideas expressed in the letter above?
   (a) The emancipation of all enslaved people
   (b) The lack of diplomatic support from Great Britain
   (c) A rapid ending to the Civil War
   (d) Racial segregation in northern states

6. Which of the following best describes the immediate aftermath of the policy described in the letter above?
   (a) The movement to constitutionally guarantee African Americans the right to vote
   (b) The change from a war about the preservation of the Union to one that also included new freedoms for African Americans
   (c) Wartime legislation enacted by the Republican Party for transportation developments
   (d) Westward expansion and the construction of transcontinental railroads

Questions 7–9 refer to the map below.

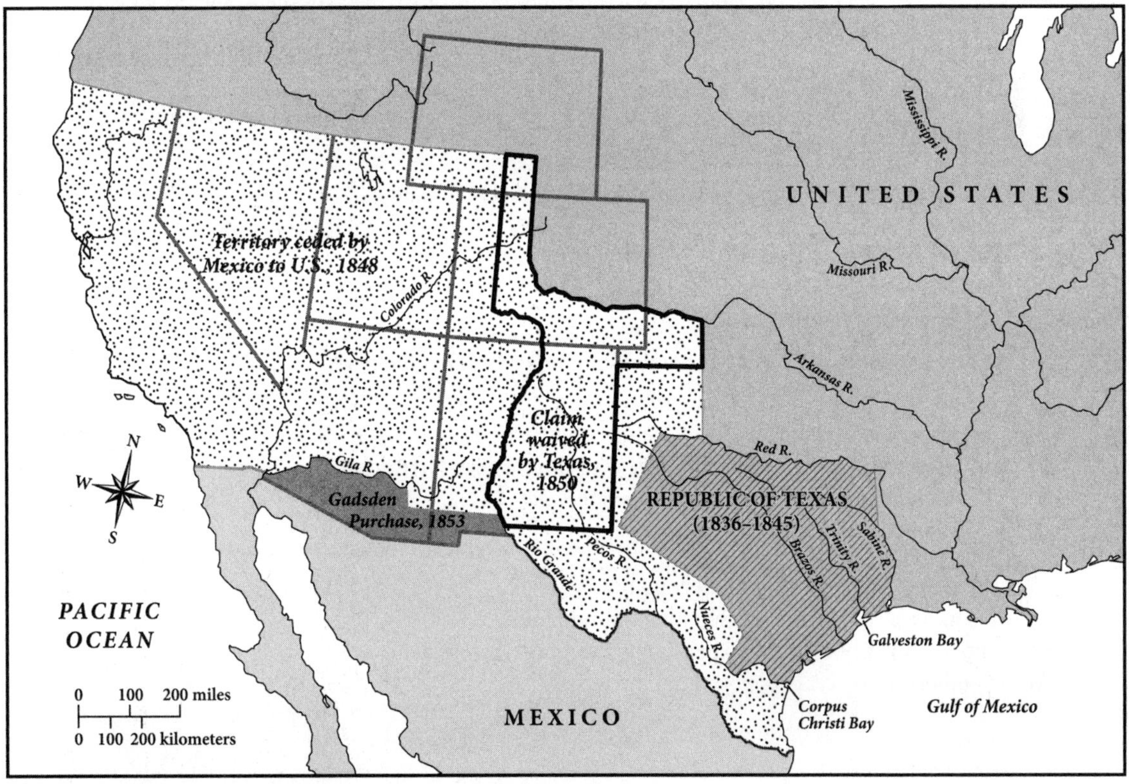

The Mexican Cession, 1848

7. The events referenced in the map above most directly led to which of the following historical developments?
   (a) Texas being annexed by the United States
   (b) The elimination of slavery west of the Mississippi
   (c) The breaking of U.S. diplomatic relations with Spain
   (d) Renewed debate over the expansion of slavery

8. Which of the following contributed most directly to the Mexican-American War?
   (a) The advocacy of utopian communities
   (b) An increase in immigration to the United States
   (c) The belief in Manifest Destiny
   (d) Commercial rivalries with the French and British

9. The Mexican-American War and its aftermath led most directly to which of the following?
   (a) A northern majority in the legislative branch
   (b) Completion of the transcontinental railroad
   (c) An easing of sectional tension
   (d) Secession of South Carolina from the Union

Questions 10–11 refer to the excerpt below.

> "11. That Kansas should, of right, be immediately admitted as a state under the Constitution recently formed and adopted by her people, and accepted by the House of Representatives.
>
> "12. That, while providing revenue for the support of the general government by duties upon imports, sound policy requires such an adjustment of these imposts as to encourage the development of the industrial interests of the whole country. . . .
>
> "13. That we protest against any sale or alienation to others of the public lands held by actual settlers . . . and we demand the passage by congress of the complete and satisfactory Homestead measure which has already passed the House.
>
> "14. That the Republican Party is opposed to any change in our Naturalization Laws, or any State legislation by which the rights of citizenship hitherto accorded by emigrants from foreign lands shall be abridged or impaired. . . .
>
> "16. That a Railroad to the Pacific Ocean is imperatively demanded by the interests of the whole country; that the Federal Government ought to render immediate and efficient aid in its construction."

Republican Party Platform, 1860

10. The Republican Party platform of 1860 was an indication that the party
    (a) supported the abolition of slavery.
    (b) sought to broaden its appeal to include southerners.
    (c) opposed the extension of enslavement to the western territories.
    (d) was moving toward a more nativist stance.

11. The Republican Party platform of 1860 attempted to broaden its appeal to include
    (a) northern manufacturing and economic interests.
    (b) a southern route for a transcontinental railroad.
    (c) support for filibustering expeditions into Latin America.
    (d) Southern Democrats opposed to new tariffs.

12. The most immediate result of Lincoln's election in 1860 was that
    (a) attempts at compromise were abandoned.
    (b) the Civil War began.
    (c) South Carolina seceded from the Union.
    (d) the Emancipation Proclamation was made public.

END OF MULTIPLE-CHOICE SECTION

Short-Answer Questions

"The South's highly evolved system and customs of leasing slaves from one farm or factory to the next, bartering for the cost of slaves, and wholesaling and retailing of slaves regenerated itself around convict leasing in the 1870s and 1880s. The brutal forms of physical punishment employed against "prisoners" in 1910 were the same as those used against "slaves" in 1840. The anger and desperation of southern whites that allowed such outrages in 1920 were rooted in the chaos and bitterness of 1866. These were the tendrils of the unilateral new racial compact that suffocated the aspirations for freedom among millions of American blacks as they approached the beginning of the twentieth century."

-Douglas A. Blackmon, *Slavery by Another Name: The Re-Enslavement of Black Americans from the Civil War to World War II,* 2009

"In fact, Reconstruction governments were ambitious. They were hated in part, because they undertook impressive reforms in public education, social services, commerce, and transportation. Like their northern allies, southern Republicans admired the economic and social transformations that had occurred in the North before the Civil War and worked energetically to import them."

Edwards et al., *Henretta's America's History,* Tenth Edition, 2021

1. Using the excerpts about Reconstruction above, answer a, b, and c.
    (a) Briefly explain ONE difference between Blackmon's and Edwards et al.'s position on Reconstruction.

    (b) Provide ONE piece of relevant historical evidence from 1865-1896 that supports Edwards et al.'s position and explain how and why it supports that position.

    (c) Provide ONE piece of relevant historical evidence from 1865-1896 that supports Blackmon's position and explain how and why it supports that position.

"But I take higher ground. I hold that, in the present state of civilization, where two races of different origin, and distinguished by color, and other physical differences, as well as intellectual, are brought together, the relation now existing in the slaveholding states between the two, is, instead of an evil, a good—a positive good. . . . I turn to the political; and here I fearlessly assert, that the existing relation between the two races in the South, against which these blind fanatics are waging war, forms the most solid and durable foundation on which to rear free and stable political institutions. . . . The condition of society in the South exempts us from the disorders and dangers resulting from this conflict; and which explains why it is that the political condition of the slaveholding states has been so much more stable and quiet than those of the North."

John C. Calhoun, Speech in the U.S. Senate, 1837

2. Using the excerpt above, answer a, b, and c.

(a) Briefly explain ONE way in which southerners defended this point of view on enslavement by Calhoun using the period from 1787 to 1848.

(b) Briefly explain ONE way in which southerners used political power to enforce the views described by Calhoun using the period from 1787 to 1848.

(c) Briefly explain ONE way in which people challenged Calhoun's argument above using the period from 1830-1860.

END OF SHORT-ANSWER SECTION

Long Essay Question

Question: Evaluate the extent to which the Civil War and Reconstruction changed the social fabric of the United States in the period from 1860 to 1877.

END OF LONG ESSAY SECTION

PERIOD 6, 1865–1898

Overview

Between 1865 and 1898, the United States was transformed from a primarily agricultural society to one dominated by urbanization and industry. This shift brought with it many environmental, cultural, political, and economic changes. The rise of major industries led to increased migration to cities, resulting in changes in all areas of life for those living in urban areas. The federal government aided the growth of big business, as changes in technology and international communication linked American producers and consumers with the rest of the world.

In the years following the Civil War, the U.S. government subsidized industries that were viewed as essential to national expansion and aided the growth of new technologies and business models. The creation of monopolies allowed a small number of businessmen to expand their companies to dominate entire segments of the economy. These companies also expected that the government would help them control overseas resources. The prevalent belief in Social Darwinism, the idea that the more talented groups and individuals would and should rise to the top, helped justify the growing divide between the few very rich and the increasing numbers of poor. This discrepancy was particularly evident in urban areas, where the lifestyles of the rich were in sharp contrast to the more numerous poorer neighborhoods.

Various groups did offer challenges to the dominance of big business leaders. Labor movements gradually gained influence, hoping for better pay, better working conditions, and limits to child labor. The South continued to be primarily agricultural rather than industrial, with sharecropping and tenant farming replacing the old plantation system in what was called the "New South."

Westward migration continued to lead to conflicts about the management of natural resources. Some progress was made during this era in the establishment of the first national parks, though conservationists had an uphill battle. More efficient farming technology meant greater demands for land and more reliance on railroads to get farm goods to regional and national markets. Government favoritism toward business, coupled with unpredictable farming conditions, led to the creation of the people's (Populist) Party to represent the political and economic interests of farmers and other workers.

Immigrants, minorities, and women faced both progress and challenges during these years. America's cities became destinations for growing numbers of immigrants from Southern and Eastern Europe, as well as African Americans who sought better situations than they could find in the Deep South. They did find economic opportunities, but they also were relegated to poorer neighborhoods, often divided by race and class. Urban areas were often dominated by political machines that preyed on the needs of poorer classes, though some private efforts, such as the settlement house movement, sought to provide some relief to the working poor. Women's clubs worked to offer opportunities for middle-class women to become involved in civic and political issues.

The completion of the transcontinental railroad and the resulting flood of new settlers to the Great Plains and the West hastened the demise of independent American Indian tribes. Those who survived military action were decimated by the loss of the buffalo on which their culture depended. Reservations replaced tribal homelands in a misguided effort to force assimilation. Additional conflicts arose in the Southwest between settlers and Mexican Americans.

The rapid growth of big business during the Gilded Age was characterized by widespread corruption in both industry and government. Soon reformers were calling for changes, but they met stiff resistance from the powers in Congress, the Supreme Court, and the monopolists. Racism and nativism were reinforced with Supreme Court rulings like *Plessy v. Ferguson*. Even so, not all industrial leaders were Social Darwinists. A few suggested that the wealthy and successful did have an obligation to help the poor. Many reformers took up the goals of reform under the banner of the Social Gospel. Others directed their efforts at specific groups, especially African Americans and women.

Key Terms

Be sure that you understand the meaning of these terms and their relevance in U.S. history. Page numbers from the textbook are provided.

Gilded Age (447, 607, 610, 611)
Transcontinental railroad (480, 482)
American bison (357, 365, 367,490)
Dawes Severalty Act (504)
New South (526)
Plessey v Ferguson (558, 625, 643)
Trusts (485, 518–519, 612, 622, 632)
Vertical integration (517–518)
Horizontal integration (517–518)
Social Darwinism (519, 547–549, 643)
Jane Addams (596–599)
Settlement houses (596–599, 602)
Gospel of Wealth (519)
Social Gospel (553)
Laissez-faire (304, 310, 470, 483, 610, 717)
People's Party (Populists) (539, 613, 628)
Interstate Commerce Act (539-540, 611, 622)
Sherman Anti-trust Act (612, 622, 632)

Focus Questions

As you study Period 6, keep the following questions in mind.

American and National Identity

- How did ethnic and regional identities help shape Americans' views of progress during the late nineteenth century?
- In what ways did westward expansion transform Americans' national identity?
- Why and in what ways did white Americans attempt to influence American Indians to adopt white customs and behaviors?
- What accounts for the emergence of the American labor movement in the Gilded Age?
- How were immigrants able to become Americanized and at the same time maintain many elements of their traditional identities?
- How did women's roles change during the Gilded Age, and what part did women play in bringing about change, especially in American cities?
- What did Elizabeth Cady Stanton mean by the "solitude of the self," and what did women and women's groups do to facilitate this "solitude"?
- What obstacles faced African Americans in the years after the Civil War, and how did they confront those obstacles?
- What economic, political, and regional obstacles did farmers face in the late nineteenth century as they attempted to counter the power of big business?

Work, Exchange, and Technology

- What role did technological advances play in propelling American migration all the way to the Pacific Ocean?
- What were the forces that transformed the American economic system in the last half of the nineteenth century?
- How were a few industrialists able to consolidate so much production and profit in industries like steel, oil, and railroads?
- Why were tariffs such a source of passionate debate in the late 1800s?
- How did technological advances transform the lives the American farmers?

- What were the most significant obstacles faced by labor unions, and how did unions attempt to improve the lives of workers prior to 1900?
- What is a consumer culture, and how did the late-nineteenth-century consumer culture transform American life?

Geography and the Environment

- Why, and in what ways, did the federal government implement new policies on land management in the late nineteenth century?
- How did American Indians forced from their homelands adapt to their changing environment?
- Why did Americans in the late nineteenth century develop a love of the outdoors, and what resulted from this?

Migration and Settlement

- What tensions accompanied the arrival of white settlers in the trans-Mississippi West, and how did both American Indians and white Americans react?
- What obstacles confronted immigrants who arrived in the United States between 1865 and 1900, and what steps did immigrants take in order to adapt to their new home?
- How did industrialization and immigration help to transform the American city in the late nineteenth century?

Politics and Power

- How did local governments and officials in Washington address the problems that accompanied the influx of Europeans into America during the Gilded Age?
- What role did the government play in restricting the opportunities and the liberties of racial and ethnic groups?
- What was the federal government's role in supporting the economic transformation that occurred during the Gilded Age?
- To what extent did a "New South" emerge in the years following the Civil War?
- How were white southerners able to "redeem" the South in the aftermath of Reconstruction?
- Why, despite their shortcomings, were political machines able to become such a powerful force in America's cities?
- How successful were farmers in reaching their goals? What factors accounted for their successes and failures?
- Why, by the end of the nineteenth century, did the public increasingly demand political, social, and economic reform?

America in the World

- How and why did the role of the United States in the world change in the decades following the Civil War?
- How did economic changes at home affect U.S. policies abroad?

American and Regional Culture

- How did nativism help shape government policy in the late nineteenth century?
- How did late-nineteenth-century literature reflect the problems confronting urban workers and farmers in this period?
- What were some characteristics of the new popular culture, including music, theater, and sports, that emerged in American cities in the last half of the nineteenth century?

Social Structures

- What were some of the arguments that justified the rapid accumulation of wealth in the hands of a few in the late nineteenth century?
- In what ways did critics challenged the dominant "corporate ethic" of the American elites?

Thematic Timeline

TIME	Key Events
1865	

American and National Identity
- Association for the Advancement of Women founded (1873)
- Woman's Christian Temperance Union founded (1874)
- National Farmers' Alliances form (1875–early 1880s)
- San Francisco mob attacks Chinatown (1877)

Work, Exchange, and Technology
- Economic depression (1873–1879)
- First department store opens in Philadelphia (1875)
- Alexander Graham Bell invents telephone (1876)
- Great Railroad Strike (1877)
- Deskilling of labor under mass production

Geography and the Environment
- First national park created at Yellowstone (1872)
- Appalachian Mountain Club founded (1876)
- Yellow fever epidemic devastates Memphis, Tennessee (1878)
- John Wesley Powell presents *Report on . . . Arid Region of the United States* (1879)

Migration and Settlement
- Exoduster migration to Kansas (1879)

Politics and Power
- Greenback-Labor Party elects fifteen congressmen (1878)

America in the World
- Social Darwinism gains growing acceptance in Europe and the United States
- Hostility toward Chinese immigrants grows

American and Regional Culture
- Comstock Act bans circulation of most information about sex and birth control (1873)
- Baseball's National League founded (1876)

Social Structures
- Henry George publishes *Progress and Poverty* (1879)
- Salvation Army established in United States (1879)

1880

American and National Identity

- Rise of the Ghost Dance movement
- Knights of Labor peaks in membership (1884)
- Rock Springs massacre of Chinese miners (1885)
- Haymarket Square violence in Chicago (1886)
- American Federation of Labor founded (1886)
- Dawes Severalty Act (1887)

Work, Exchange, and Technology

- First vertically integrated corporations
- John D. Rockefeller creates Standard Oil trust (1882)
- First skyscraper completed in Chicago (1885)
- Knights of Labor peaks
- American Federation of Labor founded (1886)

Geography and the Environment

- Dry cycle begins on the Great Plains (1886)
- Hatch Act (1887) provides federal support for agricultural research and experiment stations
- Industrialization and urban growth cause rising pollution

Migration and Settlement

- Congress passes Chinese Exclusion Act (1882)
- Violence prompts mass immigration of Russian Jews (1880s)
- Chiricahua Apache leader Geronimo surrenders (1886)
- American Protective Association founded to oppose immigration (1887)
- Jane Addams and Ellen Gates Starr found Hull House (1889)

Politics and Power

- Pendleton Act (1883)
- Peak of Woman's Christian Temperance Union (1880s)
- Hatch Act provides federal support for farmers (1887)
- Interstate Commerce Act (1887)
- New Jersey law invites trusts to operate in the state (1889)
- Hull House settlement founded (1889)

America in the World

- Rapid industrialization draws immigrants from around the world; American cities grow rapidly
- Chinese Exclusion Act (1882–1943)

American and Regional Culture

- William Dean Howells calls for realism in literature
- Birth of American football
- Popularity of vaudeville
- Sitting Bull tours with Buffalo Bill's Wild West (1885)

Social Structures

- Increasing numbers of students attend college
- Booker T. Washington founds Tuskegee Institute (1881)

TIME	Key Events
1898	

American and National Identity
- Massacre of Sioux Ghost Dancers at Wounded Knee, South Dakota (1890)
- National American Woman Suffrage Association unites suffragists (1890)
- Lockout of workers at Carnegie plant in Homestead, Pennsylvania (1892)
- Sierra Club founded (1892)
- Booker T. Washington delivers Atlanta Compromise address (1895)
- National Association of Colored Women founded (1896)

Work, Exchange, and Technology
- Severe depression hits; causes mass unemployment and wave of corporate mergers (1893)
- J. P. Morgan arranges gold purchases to rescue U.S. Treasury (1895)
- Accelerated corporate mergers in key industries
- First subway line opens in Boston (1897)
- Birth of modern advertising

Geography and the Environment
- John Muir founds Sierra Club (1892)
- "Bicycle craze" and rise of hiking and camping get more Americans outdoors

Migration and Settlement
- New York's Ellis Island opens (1892)

Politics and Power
- Disfranchisement in South (1890–1905)
- Sherman Antitrust Act (1890)
- People's Party founded (1890)
- Coxey's Army marches (1894)
- *Plessy v. Ferguson* (1896)
- William McKinley elected president (1896)

America in the World
- Gorras Blancas confront wealthy Anglo interests in New Mexico
- Unemployed whites attack Chinese farmworkers
- Ellis Island opens (1892)
- Supreme Court upholds segregation of schools and public facilities in *Plessy v. Ferguson* (1896)

American and Regional Culture
- World's Columbian Exposition in Chicago (1893)
- Ragtime music introduced at Exposition, Chicago (1893)
- Charles Sheldon publishes *In His Steps* (1896)

Social Structures
- Jacob Riis publishes *How the Other Half Lives* (1890)

America's History Chapter Summaries

(required AP® content in bold)

Chapter 16
Industrial America: Corporations and Conflicts, 1877–1911

Chapter 16 explores the rise of the industrial United States between 1877 and 1911. Steel magnate Andrew Carnegie seemed to be a classic example of a poor immigrant who became a rags-to-riches success story through hard work and good timing. Although he knew firsthand the struggles of the laboring classes, workers at his mills felt they were not treated fairly and launched what became the Homestead Strike, an ill-fated union attempt to force concessions from management that resulted in loss of jobs and even of lives. **This era saw many such movements, most without resulting in many gains for the workers.**

Businesses boomed due to a **combination of new technology, more efficient management models, and access to seemingly unlimited resources**. The transcontinental railroad led to the rise of large industrial processing centers like Chicago and Cincinnati. Major industries were soon dominated by a **small handful of leaders who created trusts, monopolies that allowed them to control the production and sale of nearly all major commodities**. John D. Rockefeller's Standard Oil led the way in horizontal integration, which drove competitors out of business and allowed the creation of a complete monopoly in the oil industry. Other industries soon followed, and by 1900, America's largest one hundred companies controlled a third of the nation's productive capacity.

The work of these robber barons transformed the nation's economy. A **consumer culture arose**, and along with it, department stores developed. Montgomery Ward and Sears built mail-order empires, bringing merchandise to rural areas. A class of managers and salesmen arose, and women began to find jobs in corporate offices, though rarely in the areas of management. Skilled workers still had some autonomy in this new economy, but as industrialism advanced, the need for craft work began to decline. Mass production and scientific management theories valued speed and efficiency over craftsman skills. Many workers found the new factories to be dangerous and polluted places, which often operated with no concern for the surrounding environment. Child labor became common, particularly in coal mines and textile mills, and African Americans often found themselves at the bottom of most job opportunities and wage scales.

Immigrants, often willing to take jobs for **the lowest pay offered**, provided a boost to the labor force. Many native-born Americans resented them, feeling they drove down wages for everyone. **Many of those coming to America during these years were from Southern and Eastern Europe**. Many Jewish immigrants came to escape the pogroms of Russia. Chinese immigrants had been arriving on the West Coast since the 1840s, and they faced some of the harshest treatment of all. Nativist pressure forced Congress to limit Chinese immigration with the Chinese Exclusion Act of 1882, the first such act of its kind, which created the legal foundation for future exclusionary policies.

Industrial workers began to look for ways to improve their situation and turned to labor unions. The Great Railroad Strike of 1877 was the first labor action to gain real public attention, a strike that quickly turned into riots and led state governments to call out troops to restore order. Writers began to take up the cause of workers, offering both practical and utopian suggestions about how society might address the workers' complaints. Farmers also felt themselves at the mercy of corporations, particularly the banks that held their mortgages and the railroads that charged whatever rates they wanted regardless of the hardship it caused their rural customers. An early political group, the Grangers, sought relief for farmers, soon merging their efforts into the Greenback-Labor Party. Despite some early successes in regulating railroad rates, the party found it lacked real power. Even the short-lived **Populist Party** would prove to be generally ineffective.

The first major labor union, the Knights of Labor, founded in 1869, hoped to represent all workers regardless of skill level. The Knights grew rapidly and enjoyed some early successes, although the organization was sprawling and decentralized. Their downfall came in May 1886 with an attempt to hold another nationwide railroad strike that was to begin with a gigantic rally in Haymarket Square in Chicago.

A bomb blast turned the rally into a riot, and police fired into the crowd. Though no one ever knew for certain who was responsible, eight alleged anarchists were convicted of murder, and the reputation of the Knights of Labor suffered as well through guilt by association. The group never recovered its former strength and soon passed from the scene.

Farmers were attempting to organize through a series of **regional farmers' alliances**. Many had hoped to forge networks with labor groups in order to gain more national leverage. The federal government, feeling the mounting pressure of these different groups, did make some concessions in the 1880s. The Interstate Commerce Act created the Interstate Commerce Commission to investigate charges of unfair shipping rates. Though the commission looked promising on paper, there was no enforcement power built into its mandate and a **probusiness Congress and Supreme Court continued to give industrialists most of what they wanted at the expense of farmers and workers.**

The American Federation of Labor (AFL) moved in to fill the vacuum left by the end of the Knights of Labor. This group worked to serve skilled labor only, organizing individual craft unions under its umbrella of the AFL. Samuel Gompers led this organization for many years. He justified a more exclusive union on the grounds that this gave the group better bargaining power. Unskilled workers, women, tenant farmers, domestic workers, and other minorities were not allowed to become members. Although the AFL would enjoy little real success in the late nineteenth century, it was poised for better luck when new leadership came to the White House and Congress in the coming decades.

Chapter 17
Making Modern American Culture, 1880–1917

During these years explored in Chapter 18, the United States began to develop distinct working classes and a growing middle class. Global trade and mass production made consumer goods affordable, though large department stores allowed the working classes in only as clerks and cashiers. Those who could afford new electric lights and telephones installed them. The Pullman Palace Car company offered luxurious travel for those who could pay, with second-class and smoking cars for those who could not and for all minorities regardless of income. A dispute over segregated railroad cars led the **Supreme Court to affirm states' rights to impose Jim Crow laws with its decision in *Plessy v. Ferguson* in 1896**, a ruling that would stand until the 1950s.

Cities saw the growth of organizations like the Young Men's Christian Association and the popularity of sports competitions, particularly baseball. Here segregation also played a part, forcing the organization of Negro Leagues. Football began on elite college campuses and quickly gained popularity with the general public. Bicycling and camping gained devotees, with women taking part as well. Magazines began to praise the "New Woman," exemplified by the Gibson Girl, more educated, athletic, and independent than her mother or grandmother. **The establishment of national parks gained support through the work of conservationists** like John Muir, who founded the Sierra Club in 1892.

Women began to push again for political and economic rights, particularly as they began to take part in the urban reform movements that characterized this period. Families were smaller by this era, as women began to have greater access to rudimentary birth control. High school education was more readily available to boys and girls, and many schools were coeducational. Colleges moved from the traditional emphasis on Latin, Greek, and rhetoric to what was called a "liberal arts" curriculum, with many offering specific technical training in response to the needs of the job market. Booker T. Washington founded Tuskegee Institute in 1881, a school for African American youth that focused on industrial education as well as literacy and mathematics. Washington gained national fame when he spoke at the Cotton States Exposition in Atlanta in 1895, where he urged the races to work together so all could achieve economic success. **He hoped education and hard work on the part of African Americans would overcome racial prejudice**.

In spite of education and economic gains, women still found political equality elusive. **Various women's groups formed around the country**, making the argument that women should serve the community as well as the home and that such service was worthy of equal treatment under the law. Many women became involved in the temperance movement, working through organizations like the Women's Christian Temperance Union. They also organized the Daughters of the American Revolution, with southern women following up with the United Daughters of the Confederacy. Denied admission into these groups, **African American women formed the National Association of Colored Women, focusing on social initiatives as well as hoping to make a dent in racism**. Ida B. Wells-Barnett was a leader in this movement, taking up the campaign to try to get a national antilynching law. **Political rights for women were addressed by a number of groups**, including the National American Woman Suffrage Committee, though Congress still refused to entertain a constitutional amendment giving women the right to vote.

Rapid developments in science began to shake traditional religious foundations during these years. The 1893 World's Columbian Exhibition showcased scientific marvels of industry, transportation, and communication, showing the world rapidly becoming a very different place. The work of Charles Darwin challenged the Old Testament view of the world, though some felt his **theories of natural selection justified the Social Darwinist attitudes of many of the rich toward those who were worse off**. Some went even further and posed the theory of eugenics, suggesting that humans could be bred for certain traits. Such attitudes fed the nativism that plagued many new immigrants to the United States.

The world of the arts responded to a more urban America with schools of realism in art and naturalism in literature. Many writers took a fairly bleak view of the direction in which the country was headed, feeling that men had lost a measure of control over their fates. Some, like Mark Twain, thought the United States was working for progress for its own sake rather than for the sake of those whose lives would be affected by it. Religions became more diverse with the huge numbers of immigrants arriving in the last decades of the nineteenth century. Catholics, Jews, and Eastern Orthodox vied with mainline Protestants in many large cities. This was a time of a great deal of missionary work overseas by Protestant denominations, and much of this fed into a growing determination that America was to serve as the example to the less fortunate of the world. Good intentions quickly took on an air of chauvinism, and the work of Christian missionaries sometimes became a justification for imperialism.

Racist groups like the American Protective Association vied with advocates of the Social Gospel about whether immigrants should be kept out or whether those who were better off should extend a helping hand. Groups like the Salvation Army worked to offer assistance to the urban poor, though America entered the twentieth century with many of these debates unresolved.

Chapter 18
"Civilization's Inferno": The Rise and Reform of Industrial Cities, 1880–1917

The rise of the industrial city brought many changes to traditional views of urban life, from skyscrapers to subways to public parks and museums. There were neighborhoods of great wealth close to areas of grinding poverty, and these conditions led to questions about corruption, reform, and the obligations of the community to the individual.

Industrial cities combined traditional urban elements—neighborhoods, public meeting spaces, schools and churches—with centers of manufacturing, finance, and trade. Large populations and the need to move about efficiently led to the development of mass transit, cable cars, and elevated trains. Steel girders, plate glass, and elevators made skyscrapers possible. Louis Sullivan became the leader in such architecture, and he put Chicago on the map as an innovative city in urban design. Electricity made nightlife possible, opening up all sorts of evening entertainment for city dwellers.

Immigrants flocked to America's cities, often settling in ethnic neighborhoods. They organized mutual aid societies to help ease the transition from overseas to their new lives. A small number of African Americans began to move north looking for better jobs and an escape from Jim Crow, though most could find work only in the service sector. **Race riots broke out periodically in northern cities, proving that racial prejudice was not only a southern problem**.

City planners responded to the **floods of immigrants by building low-cost five- and six-story tenement apartment buildings with cramped, airless apartments that were at least affordable**. These tenement neighborhoods quickly became overcrowded and rife with disease and infant mortality. Urban reformers took on these neighborhoods as they sought to find solutions to overcrowding and sanitation issues.

Despite these drawbacks, cities proved to be exciting places to live for many. Theaters and amusement parks showcased ethnic talent and drew large appreciative audiences. Social restrictions were lax in the city, and many young people found there was less supervision from parents and older relatives. Young women often lived in boardinghouses, and many of the older generation lamented their vulnerability to prostitution. Many cities had a more or less open gay subculture, something that would have been unheard of in earlier generations. Many cities also offered excellent art museums, often funded by wealthy patrons. Libraries and opera, theater, and literary guilds abounded. The popularity of libraries was testament to the gains made in general literacy in the decades after the Civil War. The daily press flourished in cities like New York and Chicago, though there were often no requirements for verification of the truth of stories that lured in readers. This was the era of "yellow journalism," when sensationalism was valued over close attention to the truth. **Some journalists took on the social ills of the time and called for reform**. These "muckrakers" often prodded politicians to address social problems they might otherwise have ignored.

Many major cities were ruled by unscrupulous political bosses and machines. Some, like Boss Tweed and G. W. Plunkitt, became notorious for their corruption. Newly arriving immigrants were their base of support. They gained votes in exchange for help finding housing and jobs and needed public services. The problems came when political greed took over and the machines benefitted more than their constituents did. By the financial depression of the 1890s, city political machines were unable to handle the crisis of unemployment, hunger, and mobs of the homeless. Voters began to demand more efficient and transparent government, and reform-minded politicians began to win elections. The era of Progressive reform was about to debut.

Progressivism was an urban movement first, an attempt to address the plight of those living in substandard housing, facing dangerous work for low wages, and dealing with hunger, poor sanitation, and infant mortality at home. Journalists used the newly available art of photography to graphically illustrate the poverty they sought to end. Public health moved to the forefront of reform when a number of epidemics broke out in northern cities. The "City Beautiful" movement sought to develop more urban park space for the relief of those living in overcrowded tenements. Social reformers sought to close down prostitution districts, though often no one bothered to look into the conditions that led many of these women to such a life.

The settlement house movement created community welfare centers in major cities, modeled on the first, Hull House, founded by Jane Addams in a working-class section of Chicago. **Settlement work led to other projects—health issues, calls for better schools, easier access to health services for women.** Margaret Sanger led the call for more open access to birth control. Reform did not come quickly or easily, but many middle-class women found fulfillment in this work. Women headed the National Consumers' League and the Women's Trade Union League. The call for safer working conditions became national news with the Triangle Shirtwaist Company fire in 1911. Over one hundred women died because there was no access to fire escapes in their New York building.

Progressive reform was just beginning at the dawn of the twentieth century. Over the next two decades, the crusade to improve the lives of those living in the nation's major cities would become a significant part of the national agenda.

Chapter 19
Whose Government? Politics, Populists, and Progressives, 1880–1917

From the end of the Civil War to the beginning of World War I, reformers in the United States concentrated on four areas: cleaning up political corruption, limiting the power of big business, reducing poverty, and working for social justice. **These years were known as the Progressive Era, and there were many reformers and reform agendas**.

The decades immediately after Reconstruction, known as the **Gilded Age, were years of political corruption and enormous industrial profits, while underlying it all were rising poverty, environmental pollution, and little attention paid to workers' rights**. A few reforms managed to win congressional approval: the Pendleton Act, which established the Civil Service Commission; the Interstate Commerce Act, which created the Interstate Commerce Commission; and the Sherman Antitrust Act, which was designed to identify and restrict monopolies. All of these pieces of legislation looked good on the surface but in fact lacked any enforcement power.

Frustration with the government to initiate any real reform led to the creation of the Populist Party, an attempt by farmers to force monetary and political reform. Their Omaha Platform in 1892 spelled out an agenda for regulation of monopolies, rate setting for railroads, more popular participation in choosing members of Congress, and currency based on silver rather than gold. The economic depression of 1893 led to the formation of Coxey's Army, hundreds of unemployed men who marched on Washington demanding government action to create jobs and provide relief. Republicans managed to retain power in the upcoming elections, but the problems facing the nation were not solved. The South was a stronghold for the Democrats, although they did not support the Populists because southerners felt that party did not support segregation and Jim Crow. The "Solid South" would remain until well into the next century.

Nationally the Democrats tried to make some gains from the Populists' positions and chose William Jennings Bryan as their presidential candidate in 1896. His positions mirrored many of those held by the Populists, including a call for bimetalism, or the use of silver coins as well as gold. The Democrats were not able to muster the votes to deny William McKinley, a Republican, the presidency, and over the next few years, the Populists began to fade from the political scene.

The Supreme Court was also a bastion of conservatism and generally hostile to attempts at political reform. The Court rejected attempts to limit workers' hours, **approved "separate but equal" facilities and schools for blacks and whites**, and endorsed monopolies. President McKinley was no friend of reform either, but his life was cut short by an assassin's bullet in 1901. Teddy Roosevelt proved to be a very different kind of president. Roosevelt was a supporter of private enterprise and big business, but he made a distinction between those who operated with the public good in mind and those who did not. He decided cases on their merits rather than simply siding with management. His administration supported the first trust-busting cases in the courts, and he signed the Hepburn Act into law, putting teeth into the Interstate Commerce Commission. He was also a **supporter of conservation, working with John Muir and Gifford Pinchot to identify potential national forest and parkland and creating irrigation projects that changed the face of the American West**. His successor, William Howard Taft, had neither Roosevelt's energy nor his devotion to reform, so he spent his one term in office trying to balance Roosevelt's expectations with his own less determined approach to progressive reform.

Many of the Populist ideals finally became law during the Progressive Era: initiative, recall, and referendum are a few. Changes in the Supreme Court led to decisions favoring limits to working hours, though only for women. Men did benefit from workmen's compensation laws. Little progress was made in the area of child labor, however.

The roots of the modern civil rights movement lay in the Progressive Era. African Americans found themselves divided by the pragmatic, industrial education approach of Booker T. Washington and the call for immediate equality and access to higher education coming from W.E.B. Du Bois. Du Bois would be a member of the Niagara Movement, a gathering that led to the creation of the National Association for the Advancement of Colored people (NAACP), which called for a more activist approach to make the promises of the Fourteenth and Fifteenth amendments a reality for African Americans.

Labor movements were still dominated by the American Federation of Labor, though this group was challenged by the new Industrial Workers of the World, a Marxist group that urged more strikes and activism on the part of workers.

The presidential election of 1912 saw the Republicans self-destruct with wrangling between their nominee, Taft, and Teddy Roosevelt, who launched a third-party "Bull Moose" candidacy. There was yet another candidate, Eugene V. Debs, who ran as a Socialist from a prison cell in Atlanta, Georgia, and polled almost 1 million votes. The Republican squabbles paved the way for the Democratic candidate, Woodrow Wilson, to come into office advocating his own brand of progressivism that he called the "New Nationalism." Wilson had the support of labor and farmers, but he did not draw many votes from African Americans. It would be during his term of office that the Great Migration of African Americans out of the South for urban areas in the North, Midwest, and West Coast began in earnest. Progressive promises had failed to make life under Jim Crow much easier, and millions decided to look for better opportunities on their own.

Wilson did initiate a number of landmark economic reforms. The progressive income tax became part of the Constitution with the Federal Reserve Act. The Federal Reserve System was organized. Monopolies were further regulated by the Clayton Antitrust Act in 1914. Wilson did not offer much to the African American community, and even went so far as to offer praise for the movie *Birth of a Nation*, which had a heroic depiction of the Ku Klux Klan.

While progressivism did not accomplish everything its reformers hoped to, there were tremendous economic and administrative improvements. Monopolies were brought under some control, women began to have more of a presence in public life, environmental gains were made with the creation of national parks and forests, conservation efforts were successful, and the lives of millions in the country's growing cities were made more comfortable. All of these reforms would be expanded in the coming decades.

Period 6 Practice Questions

Multiple-Choice Questions

Questions 1–3 refer to the image below.

Killing the Bison, 1870s

1. The expansion of railroads to the West Coast led to the
   (a) destruction of American Indian habitats.
   (b) first American Industrial Revolution in the Northeast.
   (c) realization that private funding alone should build America's railroads.
   (d) admission of California as a free state.

2. Which of the following best explains an immediate cause for the expansion of railroads in the west?
   (a) An increase in the number of independent farmers
   (b) An increase in the number of international immigrants
   (c) Government policies promoting economic development
   (d) The development of industry on the east coast

3. The completion of the transcontinental railroad led to
   (a) increased sectional tension.
   (b) assimilation of Mexican Americans into society as equals.
   (c) hostility between the government and big business.
   (d) economic growth and the expansion of Asian markets.

Questions 4–6 refer to the excerpt below.

"We consider the underlying fallacy of the plaintiff's argument to consist in the assumption that the enforced separation of the two races stamps the colored race with a badge of inferiority. If this be so, it is not by reason of anything found in the act, but solely because the colored race chooses to put that construction upon it. . . . The argument also assumes that social prejudice may be overcome by legislation, and that equal rights cannot be secured except by an enforced commingling of the two races. . . . If the civil and political rights of both races be equal, one cannot be inferior to the other civilly or politically. If one race be inferior to the other socially, the Constitution of the United States cannot put them upon the same plane."

U.S. Supreme Court, majority opinion, *Plessy v. Ferguson*, 1896

4. *Plessy v. Ferguson* resulted in which of the following?
   (a) Integration of public schools
   (b) Violent riots that swept through major northern cities in the 1890s
   (c) Ratification of the Fifteenth Amendment by southern states that had been holding out
   (d) Racial segregation in public and private facilities

5. In the period immediately before *Plessy v. Ferguson* to the start of World War I, most African Americans in the post-Reconstruction South
   (a) migrated north and took jobs in industrial cities.
   (b) became sharecroppers or tenant farmers.
   (c) migrated west to take advantage of free homesteads.
   (d) left the United States and emigrated to Africa.

6. Which of the following was the most widely used response to *Plessy v. Ferguson* by African-Americans?
   (a) Violent protests
   (b) Nonviolent civil disobedience
   (c) A "back-to-Africa" movement
   (d) Gradual accommodation

Questions 7–9 refer to the excerpt below.

"The eighth wonder of the world is this: two pounds of iron stone purchased on the shores of Lake Superior and transported to Pittsburgh, two pounds of coal mined in Connellsville and manufactured into one and one-fourth pounds of coke and brought to Pittsburgh, one-half pound of limestone mined east of the Alleghenies and brought to Pittsburgh, a little manganese ore, mined in Virginia and brought to Pittsburgh, and these four and one-half pounds of material manufactured into one pound of solid steel and sold for 1 cent. That's all that need be said about the steel business."

Andrew Carnegie, *Ode to Steelmaking*, c. 1900

7. Andrew Carnegie reflects which of the following business models of the Gilded Age in the above quote?
   (a) Conspicuous consumption
   (b) Social Darwinism
   (c) Laissez-faire economics
   (d) Vertical integration

8. The rise of big business was fostered by all of the following during the Gilded Age EXCEPT
   (a) improved transportation systems that opened new resources and market.
   (b) peaceful cooperation between labor and management.
   (c) plentiful natural resources.
   (d) a growing immigrant labor force.

9. Which of the following best describes the beliefs of the rise of Industrial Capitalism?
   (a) Welcomed competition as a motivator to improve the quality of products
   (b) Rejected overseas markets as unfeasible due to high transportation costs
   (c) Endorsed the corporate model of the trust
   (d) Rejected the notion of conspicuous consumption

Questions 10–12 are based on the map below.

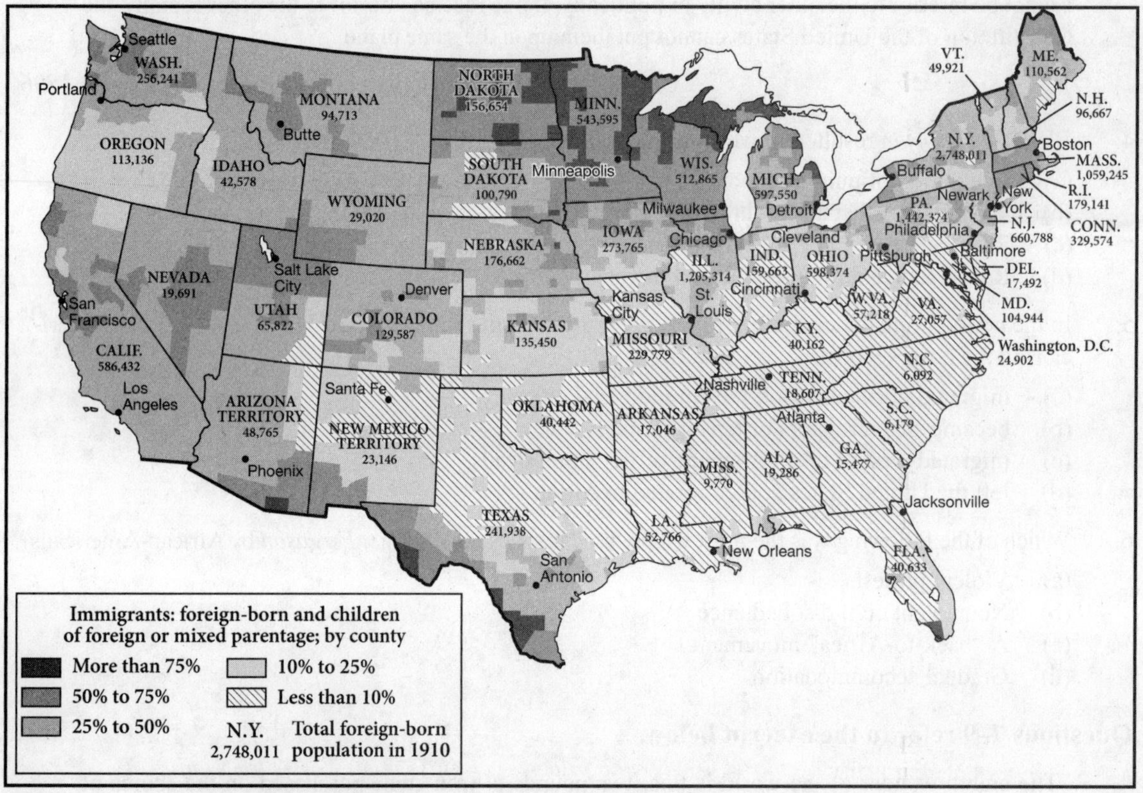

The Impact of Immigration, to 1910

10. According to the map, most immigrant populations settled
   (a) in coastal cities in the South.
   (b) in rural areas of the North.
   (c) on the West Coast.
   (d) in industrial cities.

11. The rapid increase in urban populations, referenced in the map above, best explains which of the following trends?
    (a) Neighborhoods composed of mixed classes where the rich mingled with the poor
    (b) The rich tending to move to the center city
    (c) Immigrants moving to the city periphery because of easy access to streetcars
    (d) Ethnic and racial enclaves that offered cultural opportunities

12. The rapid increase in the pace of immigration referenced in the map most directly led to
    (a) increased nativist sentiment.
    (b) the resurrection of the Know-Nothings as a major third party in presidential elections.
    (c) massive deportations of Catholics and Jews.
    (d) the voluntary return of a majority of immigrants to their country of origin.

END OF MULTIPLE-CHOICE SECTION

Short-Answer Questions

"You come to us and tell us that the great cities are in favor of the gold standard. I tell you that the great cities rest upon these broad and fertile prairies. Burn down your cities and leave our farms, and your cities will spring up again as if by magic. But destroy our farms and the grass will grow in the streets of every city in this country. . . .

"Having behind us the commercial interests and the laboring interests and all the toiling masses, we shall answer their demands for a gold standard by saying to them, you shall not press down upon the brow of labor this crown of thorns. You shall not crucify mankind upon a cross of gold."

William Jennings Bryan, Cross of Gold Speech, July 8, 1896

1. Using the excerpt above, answer a, b, and c..
    (a) Briefly explain ONE historical reason why some people supported the ideas expressed by William Jennings Bryan in the period 1870-1900.

    (b) Briefly explain ONE historical reason why some people opposed the ideas expressed by William Jennings Bryan in the excerpt above in the period 1870-1900.

    (c) Briefly explain ONE historical consequence of the ideas expressed by William Jennings Bryan in the period from 1900-1914.

Setting the Ball A-Rolling

2. Using the political cartoon above, answer a, b, and c.

   (a) Briefly explain ONE economic reform in America from 1877-1896.

   (b) Briefly explain ONE political reform in America from 1877-1896.

   (c) Briefly explain ONE group of people who challenged the reform explained in EITHER (a) OR (b).

END OF SHORT-ANSWER SECTION

Document-Based Question

Directions: The following question is based on the accompanying documents. The documents have been edited for this exercise. Spend approximately 15 minutes planning and 45 minutes writing your answer. Write an essay that does the following:

- States an appropriate thesis that directly addresses all parts of the question.
- Supports the thesis or argument with evidence from all or all but one of the documents AND your knowledge of U.S. history beyond the documents.
- Analyzes all or all but one of the documents.
- Explain the significance of the author's point of view, author's purpose, historical context, and/or audience for at least three documents.
- Uses historical evidence beyond the documents to support your argument.
- Places the argument in the context of broader regional, national, or global processes.
- Incorporates all of the elements above into a convincing essay.

Question: Evaluate the extent laborers changed ideas about Industrial Capitalism in the period from 1865 to 1900.

Document 1

Source: Gift for the Grangers, 1873

Library of Congress

Document 2

Source: I. G. Blanchard, "The Eight Hour Day," *Boston Daily Voice*, 1886

We mean to make things over,
We're tired of toil for naught,
With bare enough to live upon,
And never an hour for thought;
We want to feel the sunshine,
And we want to smell the flowers,
We're sure that God has willed it,
And we mean to have Eight Hours.
We're summoning our forces
From shipyard, shop, and mill;
Eight hours for work, eight hours for rest,
Eight hours for what we will!

Document 3

Source: The Haymarket Riot, *Harper's Weekly*, May 15, 1886

Document 4

Source: National people's Party Platform, 1892

1. We demand free and unlimited coinage of silver and gold at the present legal ratio of l6 to 1.
2. We demand that the amount of circulating medium be speedily increased to not less than $50 per capita.
3. We demand a graduated income tax.
4. We believe that the money of the country should be kept as much as possible in the hands of the people, and hence we demand that all State and national revenues shall be limited to the necessary expenses . . .

TRANSPORTATION.—Transportation being a means of exchange and a public necessity, the government should own and operate the railroads in the interest of the people. The telegraph, telephone, like the post-office system, being a necessity for the transmission of news, should be owned and operated by the government in the interest of the people.

LAND.—The land, including all the natural sources of wealth, is the heritage of the people, and should not be monopolized for speculative purposes, and alien ownership of land should be prohibited. All land now held by railroads and other corporations in excess of their actual needs, and all lands now owned by aliens should be reclaimed by the government and held for actual settlers only.

Document 5

Source: Jacob Coxey, 1894

Up these steps the lobbyists of trusts and corporations have passed unchallenged on their way to committee rooms, access to which we, the representatives of the toiling wealth-producers, have been denied. We stand here to-day in behalf of millions of toilers whose petitions have been buried in committee rooms, whose prayers have been unresponded to, and whose opportunities for honest, remunerative, productive labor have been taken from them by unjust legislation, which protects idlers, speculators, and gamblers: we come to remind the Congress here assembled of the declaration of a United States Senator, "that for a quarter of a century the rich have been growing richer, the poor poorer, and that by the close of the present century the middle class will have disappeared as the struggle for existence becomes fierce and and relentless."

We have come to the only source which is competent to aid the people in their day of dire distress. We are here to tell our Representatives, who hold their seats by grace of our ballots, that the struggle for existence has become too fierce and relentless. We come and throw up our defenseless hands, and say, help, or we and our loved ones must perish. We are engaged in a bitter and cruel war with the enemies of all mankind—a war with hunger, wretchedness, and despair, and we ask Congress to heed our petitions and issue for the nation's good a sufficient volume of the same kind of money which carried the country through one awful war and saved the life of the nation.

Document 6

Source: Royal Melendy, "The Saloon in Chicago," 1900

In many of these discussions, to which I have listened and in which I have joined, there has been revealed a deeper insight into the real cause of present evils than is often manifested from lecture platforms, but their remedies are wide of the mark, each bringing forward a theory which is the panacea for all social ills. The names of Karl Marx and leaders of political and social thought are often heard here. This is the workingman's school. He is both scholar and teacher. . . . Many as patriotic men as our country produces learn here their lessons in patriotism and brotherhood. Here the masses receive their lessons in civil government, learning less of our ideals, but more of the practical workings than the public schools teach. It is the most cosmopolitan institution in the most cosmopolitan of cities. One saloon advertises its cosmopolitanism by this title, "Everybody's Exchange." Men of all nationalities meet and mingle, and by the interchange of views and opinions their own are modified. Nothing short of travel could exert so broadening an influence upon these men. It does much to assimilate the heterogeneous crowds that are constantly pouring into our city from foreign shores. But here, too, they learn their lessons in corruption and vice. It is their school for good and evil.

Document 7

Source: Jane Addams, *Twenty Years at Hull House,* 1912

Halsted Street is thirty-two miles long, and one of the great thoroughfares of Chicago. . . . Between Halsted Street and the river live about ten thousand Italians—Neapolitans, Sicilians, and Calabrians, with an occasional Lombard or Venetian. To the south on Twelfth Street are many Germans, and side streets are given over almost entirely to Polish and Russian Jews. Still farther south, these Jewish colonies merge into a huge Bohemian colony, so vast that Chicago ranks as the third Bohemian city in the world. To the northwest are many Canadian-French, clannish in spite of their long residence in America, and to the north are Irish and first-generation Americans. . . .

The policy of the public authorities of never taking an initiative, and always waiting to be urged to do their duty, is obviously fatal in a neighborhood where there is little initiative among the citizens. The idea underlying our self-government breaks down in such a ward. The streets are inexpressibly dirty, the number of schools inadequate, sanitary legislation unenforced, the street lighting bad, the paving miserable and altogether lacking in the alleys and smaller streets, and the stables foul beyond description. Hundreds of houses are unconnected with the street sewer.

END OF DOCUMENT-BASED SECTION

PERIOD 7, 1890–1945

Overview

Between 1890 and 1945, the United States became an international power, while at home issues surrounding industrialization, urbanization, and the demands of an increasingly diverse society came to the fore. As the U.S. economy became more dependent on large corporations and the production of consumer goods, people increasingly moved from rural areas to urban centers where jobs were available. Although these new jobs offered opportunities to many who had been underemployed, cycles of boom and bust created periodic instability. The Great Depression was the most dramatic of these economic downturns, leading to calls for more regulation of the national economy.

Progressive reformers began to call for government intervention in the economy to relieve the suffering of the urban working classes, who faced the greatest hardships. These reformers, often urban middle-class women, targeted reform of both social and political institutions. Another groups worked in the area of conservation of natural resources. National, state, and local leaders responded to this call for reform, particularly after the trauma of the Great Depression, and the result was the transformation of the government into a limited welfare state.

Franklin Roosevelt's New Deal built on many of the ideas of earlier Progressive reformers and created government programs to aid the poor and reshape the American economy. Roosevelt faced conservative opposition in Congress and from the Supreme Court, yet he was able to introduce reforms that made many feel more secure. His programs were identified with the Democratic Party and led a number of racial and ethnic groups to switch loyalties from the Republicans.

The years from 1890 to 1945 saw the introduction of many new forms of technology and communication. Although these advances helped many improve their standard of living, others felt their traditional ways of life were being threatened. These years were a time of traumatic change for many, with economic instability, world wars, and the stresses associated with migration. Conflicts emerged on a number of fronts: social, political, economic, and religious.

The xenophobia caused by World War I led the United States to enact a series of restrictive immigration laws in the 1920s. Fears of the spread of socialism and communism also inspired Congress to pass laws restricting citizens' civil liberties, all in the name of national security. A rash of labor strikes fed the fear of a "Red Scare," (called this because red was associated with the new Soviet Union), leading to even stricter overseas immigration controls. The nation opened borders within the Western Hemisphere, however, to allow in a steady supply of cheap labor. Although Mexicans were welcomed in the 1920s, they faced uncertain futures as migrant workers in the 1930s and 1940s.

African Americans also began to move out of the South in significant numbers to urban centers in the North, Midwest, and West Coast, seeking jobs and an escape from Jim Crow. This "Great Migration" had an impact throughout the country, particularly in New York City in the form of the Harlem Renaissance, a rich contribution to the national culture.

At the beginning of this time period, the United States took its first steps into the international arena. There was much disagreement within the United States as to whether such a move was in keeping with America's traditional position. The War of 1898, or the Spanish-American War, left the country with island territories as well as military and economic interests to defend in the Caribbean and the Pacific. Debates over whether the United States should rightly be an imperialist power would continue for the rest of this century and beyond, although clearly the country was now an international presence.

World War I effectively ended the United States's long-term position as a neutral and isolated power, though debates over the U.S. role in international affairs continued in the 1920s and 1930s. The American Expeditionary Force entered in the last years of the war, which allowed Woodrow Wilson to play a role at the postwar negotiations at Versailles. The resulting Treaty of Versailles and Wilson's League of Nations proved unpopular in the United States, and the country spent the next two decades trying to follow a unilateral foreign policy and retreat back into isolationism, an ultimately unsuccessful effort.

The attack on Pearl Harbor in 1941 ended U.S. isolationism overnight and launched the country into World War II and a position of international political and military prominence that would not change with the end of the war. The mass mobilization required for the war effort effectively ended what was left of the Great Depression. Women and minorities benefitted from these jobs as well. American values came under scrutiny during the course of the war with the Japanese internment, the ongoing civil rights struggle, and the moral and ethical questions surrounding the decision to use atomic weapons on Japan. The United States and the Allies defeated the Axis powers through their combined military, economic, and technological strength. The United States emerged from World War II as the most powerful nation on earth.

Key Terms

Be sure that you understand the meaning of these terms and their relevance in U.S. history. Page numbers from the textbook are provided.

Imperialism (640, 642–643)
Anti-Imperialism (646, 648–649)
Spanish American War (643–646)
Philippines (640, 648–649)
Progressivism (623–626)
Conservationists/Preservationist (563, 727–730)
American Expeditionary Force (655)
Woodrow Wilson (627, 630, 635)
Treaty of Versailles (640, 664—668)
League of Nations (665, 667, 680, 737)
Red Scare (637, 672–674)
Great Migration (660–661, 676–677)
Assembly Line (517)
National Origins Act (691–692)
Harlem Renaissance (689, 693–697)
Great Depression (702–732)
Franklin Roosevelt (706–708)
New Deal (707–732)
Pearl Harbor (741–742)
Japanese interment (755–757)
Holocaust (760–761)
Island hopping (761–763)
D-Day (759–760)
Atomic bomb (764–766, 783)

Focus Questions

As you study Period 7, keep the following thematic questions in mind.

American and National Identity

1890–1917

- What accounted for increased ethnic and racial tensions in American cities in the early years of the twentieth century?
- What arguments were voiced by both black and white leaders about the rights and the roles of African Americans in the years leading to World War I?
- Why and how did the relationships between men and women change between 1890 and 1920?
- Why were women often in the forefront of Progressive reforms?
- Why did gay subcultures emerge in American cities in the early twentieth century?

1917–1929

- How was the United States able to mobilize for war so quickly?
- What contributions did African Americans, Native Americans, and women make to the war effort?
- How did World War I influence the debates over the role of women in the decade after this war?
- Shortly after World War I ended, a journalist said, "The World War has accentuated all our differences." In what ways was this true in postwar America?

1929–1945

- How did the depression exacerbate the struggles that Mexican Americans and Native Americans confronted?
- Despite the fact that women and minorities gained relatively little from New Deal programs, many women and African Americans became part of the Roosevelt coalition. Why did this happen?
- Wartime work for women "combined new opportunities with old constraints." What new opportunities did the war bring for women, and in what ways were they still constrained?
- How did World War II influence debates about race and ethnicity during and after the war?

Work, Exchange, and Technology

1890–1917

- Why was the coinage issue so controversial in the years leading to the twentieth century and even beyond, into the 1930s?
- How were class differences reflected in the use of new technologies in the years prior to World War I?
- What were the milestones in the struggle between American corporations and American workers in the years before World War I?
- What role did Progressive presidents play in reforming the American economic system?
- Progressive reforms that protected workers often turned out to be a double-edged sword. Why?
- In what ways was the Triangle Shirtwaist Company fire a watershed event in American history?
- What were the successes and failures of the American labor movement in the years prior to World War I? Account for these.

1917–1929

- Why was the automobile such a significant technological development?
- What were the most important characteristics of the consumer culture that emerged in the 1920s? Account for the emergence of consumerism in the 1920s, and explain how it differed from the consumer culture of the late nineteenth century.

1929–1945

- How did urban workers and farmers respond to the challenges they faced after the collapse of the stock market in 1929?
- How did economic forces affect the American political landscape in the years between the two world wars?
- What steps did Franklin Roosevelt's administration take to improve the American economy and the lives of workers?
- How did the American workplace change when the United States went to war in 1941?
- What impact did the development of the atomic bomb by the United States have on the American economy and on American culture in the decades following World War II?

Geography and the Environment

- How did urban reforms change the landscape of American cities in the years prior to World War I?
- What milestones in the environmental movement were due to the actions of Progressives?
- What environmental and geographic features contributed to the demographic changes of the World War II years?

Migration and Settlement

- As cities grew in the late nineteenth and early twentieth centuries, what new forms of amusement appeared? What functions did these new activities serve?
- What efforts were made to help the poor as they became increasingly visible in American cities?
- What demographic changes occurred in the United States as a result of American entry into each of the world wars? How did these demographic shifts affect the economic, political, and social fabric of the nation?

Politics and Power

1890–1917

- What did the Populists demand of government, and how responsive was government to the needs of rural Americans?
- Why was it that the Populists garnered so much support in the 1890s only to fade from the national political landscape a decade later?
- In what ways did the Populist movement of the late nineteenth century pave the way for the Progressive Era of the early twentieth century?
- What new challenges did American cities face at the turn of the century, and how did government address these problems?
- Many scholars argue that progressivism was largely a middle-class movement. Do you agree with this assessment? Why or why not?
- Government intervention was not the only approach used to combat the problems facing urban America. How successful were private individuals and organizations in effecting change in American cities?
- Your text argues that a major shift in Republican policy occurred when Theodore Roosevelt was in the White House. To what degree were Roosevelt's policies a major departure from those of his nineteenth-century Gilded Age predecessors?
- In what ways were the policies and actions of Theodore Roosevelt and Woodrow Wilson similar? Which president better deserves to be called "progressive"?
- Despite restrictions on the voting rights of blacks and immigrants, government actions in the early twentieth century gave more power to some voters. What changes strengthened democracy in the years prior to World War I?

1917–1929

- What were the most persuasive arguments in support of and in opposition to women's suffrage?
- What arguments were made in support of limited government in the 1920s? What specific government actions supported limited government, and which increased the scope of government?
- In what ways were the presidencies of Harding, Coolidge, and Hoover different from those of Roosevelt, Taft, and Wilson? Account for the changes that occurred in the role of the presidency in the years from 1900 to 1929.
- How did the United States justify limitations placed on individual liberty during World War I?
- Why did so many Americans oppose President Wilson's plans for the postwar world?

1929–1945

- What does your textbook present as the two competing visions of government? Compare these visions, and analyze how the battle between them shaped American politics from the 1930s to the present.
- What personal beliefs were at the heart of Herbert Hoover's response to the Great Depression? Why was his response to the problems confronting the nation considered inadequate?

- In what ways did the depression and the New Deal alter the structure and power of the federal government?
- What groups joined the Roosevelt coalition, and why did they feel that their interests were served by the Roosevelt presidency?
- What new challenges to his leadership did Roosevelt face in his second administration? How did he confront these challenges?
- How effectively did Franklin Roosevelt and Congress address the crises brought about by the Great Depression?
- In what ways did the Great Depression and New Deal contribute to a realignment of American political parties?
- What were the characteristics of the American welfare state that was established during the 1930s, and why was this development so significant?

America in the World

1890–1917

- What caused Americans to embrace imperialism in the late nineteenth century, only to reject it in the early twentieth century and into the 1930s?
- Why did the United States go to war against Spain in 1898?
- How wise do you think it was for the United States to intervene in Cuba and the Philippines?
- How did Theodore Roosevelt's foreign policy reflect the assertion of masculinity that was so prevalent in American culture?
- We often think of American intervention in other nations to be primarily military in nature. In what other ways did the United States involve itself in the political and economic life of other countries, especially in the Western Hemisphere, in the years before World War I?

1917–1929

- How was President Wilson able to reconcile his idealism with his decision to take the United States into war in 1917?
- To what extent were Wilson's Fourteen Points both idealistic and a reflection of global political and economic realities?
- How was the United States able to quickly mobilize for war in the years just prior to 1917 and 1941?
- In what ways did World War I set the stage for the outbreak of war only two decades later, in 1939?

1929–1939

- Despite the growing threat of fascism, why were so many Americans opposed to intervention in Europe? How did President Roosevelt overcome that opposition?
- What wartime strategies were most effective in achieving victory for the United States and its allies?
- In what ways was World War II also fought on the home front?
- In what ways were both World War I and World War II turning points in American history?
- In what ways did World War II hasten "profound social change" and expand the scope and authority of the federal government?
- Despite having other options, why did Harry Truman opt to use the atomic bomb on Hiroshima and Nagasaki?
- How did actions taken during World War II lay the groundwork for the Cold War?

American and Regional Culture

1890–1917

- In the late nineteenth and early twentieth centuries, America was becoming "modern." What did it mean to become modern, and in what ways did science, religion, literature, art, consumerism, popular culture, and feminism embrace modernity?
- How did the realist and naturalist writers at the turn of the century portray life in America? What accounts for this change in focus from previous literary portrayals of America?
- How did the new music of the turn of the century, ragtime and blues, both reflect and shape American culture?
- What is the difference between popular culture and high culture, and how did urban life in the early twentieth century reflect these differences?
- How did the emergence of mass culture affect the delivery of the news to Americans in the late nineteenth and early twentieth centuries?

1917–1929

- What were the battlefields of the "culture wars" of the 1920s? How were these conflicts fought, and to what extent were they resolved?
- The conflicts of the 1920s can also be viewed through the lens of the tension between tradition and change. What caused this tension, and what were some examples?
- What accounted for the burst of creativity we call the Harlem Renaissance?

1929–1945

- In what ways did New Deal programs facilitate "art for the millions"?

Social Structures

1890–1917

- How were the tensions between science and faith manifested in this period, and how did Americans attempt to reconcile "fact worship" and traditional religious beliefs?
- How do you define progressivism, and why were Progressives such an important force in the early twentieth century?

1917–1929

- What are some examples of the ways that critics of modern society in the 1920s challenged the prevailing views of war, technology, corporate power, and conformity?

1929–1945

- How did beliefs held by many Americans before and during World War II influence policies toward Jews in Europe and Japanese Americans in the United States?

Thematic Timeline

TIME	Key Events
1890	

American and National Identity
- "American exceptionalism" and rise of imperialism
- Alfred Mahan, *The Influence of Sea Power upon History* (1890)

Work, Exchange, and Technology
- Depression of 1890s increases pressure to secure foreign markets
- Central Labor Union protests in Cleveland (1899)

Geography and the Environment
- Americans debate overseas expansion and empire
- Teller Amendment (1898)

Migration and Settlement
- Josiah Strong encourages overseas Christian missionaries

Politics and Power
- Republicans sweep congressional elections after severe depression (1894)
- Republican William McKinley elected president (1896)
- National Consumers' League founded (1899)

America in the World
- Congress funds construction of modern battleships
- U.S.-backed planters overthrow Hawaii's queen (1892)
- U.S. wins War of 1898 against Spain; claims Hawaii, Puerto Rico, Guam, and Philippines
- John Hay proclaims "open door" policy in China

American and Regional Culture
- "Remember the *Maine*" campaign fuels surge in nationalism

Social Structures
- Settlement house movement

1900

American and National Identity
- *Insular Cases* establish noncitizenship status for new territories (1901)
- California, Washington, and Hawaii limit rights for Asian immigrants
- Women's Trade Union League founded (1903)
- Industrial Workers of the World founded (1905)
- National Association for the Advancement of Colored People founded (1909)

Work, Exchange, and Technology
- J. P. Morgan creates U.S. Steel (1901)
- Women's Trade Union League founded (1903)
- Industrial Workers of the World founded (1905)
- *Muller v. Oregon* (1908)
- Root-Takahira Agreement affirms free oceanic commerce (1908)
- Ford Motor Company introduces Model T

TIME	Key Events

Geography and the Environment
- Congress authorizes funds to purchase land in Colombia for future canal
- Lacey Act protects wildlife (1900)
- Antiquities Act (1906)
- National Audubon Society forms (1901)
- Newlands Reclamation Act (1902)
- U.S. Forest Service created (1905)

Migration and Settlement
- Rising immigration from Southern and Eastern Europe
- Migration of African Americans to northern cities increases
- New York passes Tenement House Law (1901)
- Robert Hunter publishes *Poverty* (1904)
- Gentleman's agreement bars Japanese immigration (1907)

Politics and Power
- McKinley reelected on pro-imperialist platform (1900)
- McKinley assassinated; Theodore Roosevelt becomes president (1901)
- Food and Drug Administration established (1906)
- Hepburn Act (1906)

America in the World
- U.S. war against Philippine revolutionaries (1899–1902)
- Rising immigration from Eastern and Southern Europe
- Height of eugenics (1900s–1920s)
- Increasing numbers of blacks move to cities; responses include "race riots" by whites
- Platt Amendment (1902)
- Roosevelt Corollary to Monroe Doctrine (1904)
- United States helps crush Boxer Rebellion in China (1900)

American and Regional Culture
- Social Darwinism used to justify U.S. imperialism (1898–1910s)
- First World Series (1903)
- Upton Sinclair's *The Jungle* published (1906)

Social Structures
- Robert Hunter publishes *Poverty* (1904)
- Walter Dill Scott publishes *The Psychology of Advertising* (1908)

1910

American and National Identity
- New Ku Klux Klan founded (1915)
- Post–World War I race riots
- Wartime pressure for "100 percent loyalty"; dissent suppressed

Work, Exchange, and Technology
- Assembly-line production of automobiles begins
- U.S. Army Corps employs tens of thousands of workers to build Panama Canal
- Triangle Fire at Triangle Shirtwaist Company, New York (1911)
- Supreme Court orders Standard Oil divided to lessen its monopoly power (1911)

Geography and the Environment
- Panama Canal construction
- Panama Canal opens (1914) and links Atlantic and Pacific Oceans
- National Park Service created (1916)

Migration and Settlement
- Great Migration brings African Americans to northern cities
- St. Louis (1917) and Chicago (1919) race riots
- Mexican Revolution causes surge in immigration from Mexico

Politics and Power
- Woodrow Wilson elected president (1912)
- Sixteenth and Seventeenth Amendments to the Constitution (1913)
- Federal Reserve created (1913)
- Clayton Antitrust Act (1914)
- Red Scare (1919)
- Wilson issues Fourteen Points (1919)
- U.S. Senate rejects Treaty of Versailles (1919, 1920)

America in the World
- Wilson intervenes in Mexico (1914)
- Panama Canal opens (1914)
- Peak of foreign missions activity by American Protestant churches (1915)
- United States enters World War I (1917)
- War ends; Wilson seeks to influence peace-treaty negotiations (1918)

American and Regional Culture
- Moviemaking industry moves to southern California
- Armory Show of modern art held in New York City (1913)
- Radio Corporation of America created (1919)

Social Structures
- *Birth of a Nation* glorifies the Reconstruction-era Klan (1915)

1920

American and National Identity
- Harlem Renaissance artists emphasize black pride
- National Origins Act limits immigration (1924)

Work, Exchange, and Technology
- Economic prosperity (1922–1929)
- Labor gains rolled back
- Era of welfare capitalism
- Rise of automobile loans and consumer credit

Geography and the Environment
- Suburban housing boom
- Popularity of automobile spurs highway construction, financed by state gasoline taxes
- First suburban shopping center opens outside Kansas City, Missouri (1924)

Migration and Settlement
- Rise of nativism
- National Origins Act (1924) imposes immigration restriction
- Marcus Garvey's Universal Negro Improvement Association (UNIA) advocates return to Africa for African Americans

TIME	Key Events
	Politics and Power • Nineteenth Amendment grants women's suffrage (1920) • Sheppard-Towner Federal Maternity and Infancy Act (1921) • Prohibition (1920–1933) • Teapot Dome scandal (1923) • Republican "associated state," probusiness policies (1920–1932) **America in the World** • Rise of "dollar diplomacy" • U.S. occupation of Haiti and other Caribbean and Central American nations **American and Regional Culture** • Rise of Hollywood • Harlem Renaissance • Popularity of jazz music **Social Structures** • Scopes "monkey trial" (1925)
1930	
	American and National Identity • Bonus Army (1932) • Indian Reorganization Act (1934) • Social Security created (1935) **Work, Exchange, and Technology** • Great Depression (1929–1941) • Rise of CIO and organized labor **Geography and the Environment** • "Dust Bowl" drought strikes Midwest (1930–1941) • Civilian Conservation Corps constructs trails, roads, parks (1933–1942) • Tennessee Valley Authority (TVA) creates flood control, dams, electricity • Works Progress Administration builds parks, zoos, trails (1935–1943) **Migration and Settlement** • Migrants ("Okies") leave drought-struck Midwest for California • U.S. deports Mexican immigrants and Mexican Americans **Politics and Power** • Franklin Roosevelt elected president (1932) • First New Deal (1933) • Second New Deal (1935) • Roosevelt attempts to reform Supreme Court (1937) **America in the World** • Rise of European fascist powers • Japan invades China (1937) **American and Regional Culture** • Documentary impulse in arts • WPA assists artists • Federal Writers' Project established (1935) **Social Structures** • Unemployment increases dramatically

1945

American and National Identity
- Internment of Japanese Americans (1942)
- Segregation in armed services until 1948

Work, Exchange, and Technology
- Bretton Woods system established: World Bank, International Monetary Fund (1944)
- War spending ends depression
- Rationing curbs consumer spending
- Married women take war jobs

Geography and the Environment
- Temporary encampments imprison Japanese and Japanese Americans in inland states (1942)

Migration and Settlement
- War production leads to migration to California and major cities
- Bracero program increases immigration from Mexico

Politics and Power
- Roosevelt elected to fourth term (1944)
- GI Bill (1944)
- Roosevelt dies (1945)
- Harry Truman becomes president (1945)

America in the World
- United States enters World War II (1941)
- Atomic bombing of Japan and end of World War II (1945)
- United Nations founded (1945)

American and Regional Culture
- Film industry aids war effort

Social Structures
- Double V campaign

America's History Chapter Summaries

(required AP® content in bold)

Chapter 20
An Emerging World Power, 1890–1918

Chapter 20 explores the emergence of the United States as a world power and as a participant in world imperialism. The United States had long claimed to be uninterested in overseas expansion, even as the country expanded across the continent with little regard for the American Indians and other inhabitants who were already there. Earlier presidential administrations had seen access to global markets as a key to power, and **now expansionists added the concept of "American exceptionalism" to the argument, the idea that the United States had an obligation to foster democracy and higher civilization around the world**. Social Darwinism further fueled this belief.

Victory in the War of 1898 left the United States with new overseas possessions in both the Caribbean and the Pacific, touching off arguments about how the country should deal with these territories. Some favored independence; **others hoped for annexation or at least military and economic control**. The reelection of President McKinley in 1900 suggested that most of the country was comfortable with overseas acquisitions, though **debates over expansion and annexation would continue in Congress and the Supreme Court for years to come**. The United States also began to play a larger role in international diplomacy, negotiating the Open Door Note concerning China in 1899. Negotiations with Japan over that country's war with Russia further centered the United States on the world stage.

President Theodore Roosevelt also turned his attention to American relations with Latin America, as he thought the time to negotiate a Central American canal had arrived. Through a combination of diplomacy and devious tactics, he was able to secure rights to a canal and set in motion many years of U.S. involvement in Latin American affairs.

When World War I broke out in Europe, the United States hoped to remain neutral, though American businesses hoped to benefit from trade with the warring nations. Unfortunately American shipping and passenger lines came under attack, particularly from German U-boats. The Germans made the claim that anyone who traded with a country involved in the war was, in fact, no longer neutral. **President Woodrow Wilson spent his first term keeping the country out of the war, but soon after his reelection in 1916, a combination of unwarranted attacks on U.S. ships and angry diplomatic communications led him to ask Congress for a declaration of war on Germany and the Central Powers**.

Many Americans eagerly went to war, hoping their efforts would "make the world safe for democracy." General John Pershing led the American Expeditionary Force, which arrived at the Western Front in Europe in early 1918. America sent a multinational force that reflected the country's population, though African Americans served in segregated units. American Indians served in integrated units, but they were often given extremely hazardous jobs as scouts and snipers. American troops missed the misery of that war's prolonged trench warfare, but they still suffered from the war's efficient mechanized slaughter, as well as the great flu pandemic of 1918. Most on the home front supported the war, answering the call to ration, economize, and sacrifice consumer goods for the war effort. Labor unions agreed to postpone strikes, and housewives collected scrap metal and followed government requests to give up certain foods on certain days in order to send more supplies to the troops at the front. The government sought to stifle any criticism of the war effort through the work of the Committee on Public Information, a propaganda agency whose charge was to stir up patriotism. Congress went further, passing the Sedition Act of 1918, which **prohibited anything that would discourage dedication to the government and the war**.

Many African Americans took advantage of wartime jobs opening up in northern and midwestern cities and began to leave the Deep South and its Jim Crow system of segregation. **This movement became known as the Great Migration**, and even though African Americans often encountered discrimination in other parts of the country, most felt they had made progress for themselves and their families. **Mexicans were also encouraged to take vacant jobs, particularly as farmworkers.** Though some found a better chance here, many still faced harsh discrimination.

Women found many wartime job opportunities, working in both the service and industrial sectors of the economy. Though most realized their jobs would evaporate when the war ended and the men returned, they were glad to have the chance to work outside the home, and many felt their contribution might aid the cause of women's suffrage. The National American Women's Suffrage Association (NAWSA) wholeheartedly supported the war effort, volunteering for relief organizations and encouraging women to take industrial jobs. The National Women's Party (NWP), led by Alice Paul, was more confrontational, picketing the White House and demanding that women's efforts for the war should be translated into political equality. Some were arrested and treated badly in prison when they staged hunger strikes. President Wilson, perhaps in response to the publicity these women were generating, announced in January 1918 that he would support women's suffrage as a "war measure." In fewer than two years, the Constitution included the Nineteenth Amendment, guaranteeing women the vote.

The end of the war in Europe brought President Wilson to the peace conference held at the palace of Versailles outside Paris. **He arrived with his idealistic blueprint of the postwar world, the Fourteen**

Points, unaware that his partners in peace—Lloyd George of Great Britain, Clemenceau of France, and Orlando of Italy—already had plans for a more punitive treaty. He saw many of his proposals collapse, but he held out for the creation of a League of Nations, an organization he felt would maintain world peace in the future through collective security. The Allies' determination to punish the Germans for the war, and the haphazard way they carved up the Ottoman Empire to satisfy their own imperialist aims, set the stage for the next war that would come in two more decades. **Wilson, however, remained optimistic that his cherished League would provide a way to sort out future conflicts without bloodshed.**

Wilson was disillusioned to find strong congressional opposition to both the treaty and his League when he returned to the United States. Many worried that the United States would be drawn into wars that were not in the country's best interests if they accepted membership in the League of Nations. Others simply did not want to be involved with the rest of the world on any terms other than trade. Wilson rejected all attempts to amend the treaty, and ultimately Congress rejected both the treaty and the League. Wilson suffered a stroke during his tireless campaigns to win the American people over to his plans for the postwar world, and he never fully recovered. The country quickly forgot about European problems as the 1920s ushered in an era of apparent prosperity and exuberant consumerism.

Chapter 21
Unsettled Property: From War to Depression, 1919–1932

Chapter 21 explores the 1920s and the early years of the Great Depression. The 1920s saw both expanding prosperity and growing cultural divides, as the country juggled the security of traditionalism with the allure and demands of modernism. The so-called Roaring Twenties came to a screeching halt with the onset of the Great Depression in 1929. The work of the earlier Progressives seemed to have evaporated.

Americans emerged from World War I to find a very different world. African Americans were no longer content to live under the Jim Crow system. **Those who left the South during the Great Migration found jobs in other parts of the country** but not the acceptance as equal citizens that they wanted. Race riots occurred in many parts of the country, showing racial prejudice to be a national problem rather than one limited to the South. Labor unions were also criticized for striking for higher pay at the war's end, but they received little sympathy from either the government or the courts. A few companies, including Ford, General Electric, and U.S. Steel, did offer workers' benefits, a form of welfare capitalism, but most workers had no safety net.

Tensions were also increased by the coming of a national "Red Scare," a fear of immigrants who might bring ideas of anarchy or communism (because the Bolsheviks, the leaders of the Russian Revolution, were known as "Reds"). The government authorized the attorney general, A. Mitchell Palmer, to investigate and arrest anyone under suspicion of sedition. The infamous Palmer raids led to the arrest and detainment of many innocent people. Suspicion of foreigners played a role in many arrests, even for offenses that did not pose issues of national security.

Republicans regained control of the White House in the 1920s, in part by arguing that strong businesses would guarantee the nation could remain secure. Women played a greater role in politics beginning in this decade, as they now had the vote and more experience working outside the home. Republican president Warren Harding personified the emphasis on business skills that many felt the country needed. Unfortunately, his proved to be a corrupt and ineffective term of office, and he was replaced at his death by Vice President Calvin Coolidge. Coolidge believed the "the business of America is business," and he supported bills that gave industries a freer hand. Foreign policy also reflected business interests during these years, with "dollar diplomacy" being the slogan of the day. Government policies were expected to support U.S. access to foreign resources and markets, even if they meant occasional military deployments. This policy lost steam with the coming of the Great Depression, as the "dollars" began to dry up.

The 1920s was also a decade of intense culture wars. Prohibition of alcohol was put in place by the Eighteenth Amendment at the end of the war. Organized crime flourished through black market sales of alcohol, while state and federal governments lost tax revenue. Public schools argued over Darwin's theory of evolution, with some feeling that science was launching an attack on Christian beliefs. **The government**

moved to limit foreign immigration even more with a series of acts designed to reduce the number of immigrants allowed into this country to a tiny fraction of what it had been in the 1890s. Such measures were supported by nativist groups like the Ku Klux Klan, which saw a resurgence in the 1920s, picking up members throughout the nation rather than just in the South.

New York's Harlem proved to be a magnet for African Americans escaping life in the segregated South. **The flowering of art, music, and literature there in the 1920s became known as the Harlem Renaissance**. The jazz musicians showcased there influenced the development of music throughout the country. Marcus Garvey introduced pan-Africanism to American culture, an idea that would continue to resonate in the mid-twentieth century.

Many American writers took issue with what they saw as the superficiality of life in the United States in the 1920s. Some left for Europe, gaining the name the "Lost Generation." **Others stayed and wrote about what they saw as the narrowness and hypocrisy of small town and rural life**. Still others criticized what they felt was a slavish devotion to pleasure and material wealth.

Although the American economy seemed to be wildly successful in the 1920s, ominous signs were already visible in the agriculture sector. American farmers flooded the world markets with agricultural products, causing prices to drop. Those living in towns and cities, oblivious to the plight of farmers, rushed to buy consumer goods on readily available credit. Automobiles, also available on credit, became common. Movies reinforced longing for the luxurious life, and Hollywood introduced the figure of the "flapper" to young women. The flapper represented sexual and social emancipation, something that worried the older generation.

The party came to an end in October 1929, when the stock market dropped, taking most segments of the American economy with it. Unemployment meant a drop in consumer spending, bank failures, slowing industrial production—in short, tighter times for all and devastation for many. The destitute had to depend on family members and local private charities for what help there was. Those who looked to the federal government for relief found nothing. President Hoover and the Republican government hoped the market would correct itself if given sufficient time, but the American people were not willing to wait, and in 1932 they voted in Franklin D. Roosevelt, a Democrat who seemed to offer hope for a recovery.

Chapter 22
Managing the Great Depression, Forging the New Deal, 1929–1938

Chapter 22 focuses on the attempts of the United States to bring the country out of the Great Depression. In his first inaugural address in March 1933, **President Franklin Roosevelt pledged to ask Congress for the power to make war on the Great Depression**. The New Deal, as it was called, was a program of federal activism unprecedented in American history. FDR's brand of liberalism saw government as the guarantor of economic security for its citizens, something conservatives decried as a dangerous role for "big government." The American depression was part of an economic downturn that affected the entire world. Herbert Hoover had hoped to let it run its course and self-correct. His approach was to urge belt tightening and stick to traditional ways of operating, including continuing to tie the nation's currency to gold even when some European countries chose otherwise. High tariffs hindered international trade, something that might have helped the economy recover. The depression's grip on the United States remained strong, and Hoover became increasingly unpopular. The "Bonus Army" of unemployed veterans marched on Washington in the summer of 1932, demanding some sort of government relief. Fearing an outbreak of disease in their sprawling camp on the National Mall, Hoover had the men evicted using troops and tear gas, actions that proved to be a public relations nightmare. Franklin Roosevelt defeated him easily in the 1932 presidential election.

Roosevelt brought personal charm, political savvy, and willingness to experiment to the White House, all assets Hoover was lacking. He gained the confidence of the nation by holding weekly radio addresses, "fireside chats," which made people feel they were a part of solving the nation's problems. He greatly expanded presidential power, something a Democratic Congress was willing to let him do. His first "Hundred Days" in office saw fifteen sweeping **bills designed to focus on banking failures, farm overproduction,**

failing businesses, and rampant unemployment. If he took liberties with the powers of his office, people were willing to accept this in the hope that his programs might turn the economy around. Landmark programs reorganized the banks, placed quotas on farm production while offering government subsidies, regulated private businesses, and provided government jobs. Other programs addressed the needs for housing, the plight of the elderly, and the need for jobs for the nation's youth. Roosevelt also proposed a regulatory agency for the nation's stock market, something designed to rein in the speculation that helped lead to the 1929 crash.

Roosevelt's New Deal was not without its critics. **Some on the right accused him of being a socialist; others accused him of destroying capitalism. Most of the justices on the Supreme Court had been appointed by Republicans in the 1920s, and they overturned several of Roosevelt's landmark programs, ruling them unconstitutional.** He also had critics who thought he had not gone far enough—people who felt the country would be best served by an open redistribution of wealth.

Roosevelt took on all these critics in his run for reelection in 1936, which he won in a landslide, gaining clear majorities in both houses of Congress as well. He launched his "Second New Deal" in an effort to address the both his critics and those who hoped for even more. Labor was pleased with his support of collective bargaining. The elderly poor were guaranteed government assistance when they were no longer able to work. Roosevelt was the creator of what became known as "New Deal Liberalism," the belief that the government should play a role in preserving individual economic well-being through assistance if it was required. This belief differed from "classical liberalism," which looked for individual welfare to come as the result of free-market policies and a weak government. These two different views of the proper role of government are still at play in American politics almost a century later.

Roosevelt's second term saw more employment programs initiated. He also began to attract large numbers of **African American voters, who saw the New Deal programs as offering more to them than traditional Republican policies**. After a brief struggle to realign the Supreme Court, Roosevelt dropped that effort when he realized that time and momentum were on his side as elderly justices began to retire and he could make his own appointments. A brief return of recession in 1937–1938 led Roosevelt to authorize more government spending, a Keynesian approach to economics that seemed to have some effect.

Roosevelt's New Deal not only fundamentally changed the relationship between American citizens and the government; it also encouraged other reforms. A labor union for unskilled as well as skilled workers, the Congress of Industrial Organizations, gained great popularity and took dominance away from the more exclusive AFL. Women played a greater role in public life, inspired by the work of Eleanor Roosevelt. African Americans saw some improvement in their situation, though **segregation and Jim Crow still remained in force in many parts of the country**. American Indians saw the return of tribal ownership of land when Roosevelt signed the Indian Reorganization Act in 1934, ending many of the restrictions of the hated Dawes Act of 1887. **For Mexican Americans the New Deal was a mix of positive and negative**. Many who came during World War I as agricultural workers were deported, yet many others were able to find jobs with New Deal agencies. Immigrants from Asia did not fare as well, laboring under exclusionary legislation from earlier years.

Roosevelt also faced enormous environmental issues, primarily the development of the Dust Bowl in the Great Plains. The New Deal developed soil conservation measures, including the planting of millions of trees to act as a continental windbreak through the middle of the country. Most important was the passage of the Tennessee Valley Authority, which established a system of dams and reservoirs throughout the Tennessee River Valley. This program brought erosion control, flood protection, and inexpensive electricity to millions of people in the Southeast. Even writers and artists found work through the New Deal's Federal Writers' project.

Though Roosevelt's New Deal was criticized for doing both too much and too little, no one could deny that his programs fundamentally changed the relationship between citizens and the government.

Chapter 23
The World at War, 1937–1945

Chapter 23 explores the outbreak and course of World War II. This war was truly a world conflict in every sense, involving six continents, killing more than 50 million people, and wounding hundreds of millions more. Much of the world lay in ruins at the war's end, and all were threatened from that point on by the specter of nuclear war. **The war changed not only U.S. history but also global history and relationships**.

When the war began in Asia and Europe, the United States hoped to remain neutral, though it was clear that Roosevelt suspected the country might be drawn in despite a neutral stance. Americans watched the rise of fascism and authoritarianism in Germany, Italy, and Japan with alarm, while congressmen like Gerald Nye worked to remind Americans that Europe's troubles were not their concern. Congress responded with a series of Neutrality Acts in the mid-1930s aimed at putting the world on notice that the United States would not be drawn into their war as had happened in World War I. Other groups felt the United States needed to be involved, particularly during the Spanish Civil War in the late 1930s. Some went to fight against the fascists as volunteers, though the majority of the country was content to leave European disputes alone.

Roosevelt watched with concern as Britain and France failed to appease Hitler's demands for more and more of Europe, but neither Congress nor the American public was ready to become involved. Roosevelt used public speeches as opportunities to remind Americans of what freedom meant here and how those values were threatened by events abroad, but isolationism remained strong. When Britain and France became involved in war with Germany, Roosevelt looked for creative ways to aid the Allied cause, lending ships and supplies when money began to run short. Congress went along, hoping such measures would allow the United States to remain on the sidelines.

Isolationism came to an end with the Japanese attack on the American naval base and airfield at Pearl Harbor in Hawaii. Congress passed the War Powers Act in 1941 that gave Roosevelt unprecedented control over the war effort. The **U.S. economy immediately mobilized for war**, with all needed civilian production directed to supplying troops. Steel mills and shipyards turned to war production, as did many of the country's largest corporations. Tens of millions of Americans joined the armed forces or the war industries workforces, or they became part of the civilian support team. The army still operated on a segregated basis, leading some civil rights groups to call for a "Double V"—victory against the Nazis abroad and racism at home. Roosevelt was able to shape some federal legislation in ways that furthered civil rights, demanding that any company receiving a government contract had to demonstrate fairness in hiring. American Indians served as communications liaisons with troops in both Germany and the Pacific, operating radios while speaking American Indian languages that neither German nor Japanese code breakers were able to understand. **Women served in the military in the war. Though barred from combat, many served in front units as nurses, and some flew transport and resupply planes. Labor leaders pledged to hold off strikes until the war was won.**

Roosevelt won unprecedented third and fourth terms of office in 1940 and 1944. Voters preferred political continuity while the nation was involved in this world conflict. Families endured rationing, planted "victory gardens," and collected scrap metal. Hollywood produced patriotic films, and people sang patriotic songs. Once again, wartime jobs led to internal migration as people relocated to places where work was available. Racial tensions increased, with attacks on African Americans in Detroit in 1943, and the "zoot suit" riots aimed at Hispanic teenagers in Los Angeles that same year. Wartime migration gave an unexpected boost to gay and lesbian communities in a number of urban centers, though the military still tried to screen out homosexuals.

Japanese Americans received especially harsh treatment during the war. Though many had lived in the United States for generations, **entire communities were forced to relocate to detention centers for the duration of the war because of fears that they might harbor loyalties to Japan**. Many lost everything: they had to abandon their homes and businesses with mortgages and give up pets, belongings, and the treasures of a lifetime. At the end of the war, many found they had no homes to return to, and some tried to seek restitution from the courts. The case of *Korematsu v. United States* was not decided in their favor until 1988, and this restitution represented only a fraction of what was lost.

The alliance of the United States, Great Britain, Free France, and the Soviet Union gradually began to get the upper hand in both Europe and the Pacific. By 1944, the tide had turned in favor of the Allies on both fronts. With the invasion of northern France on D-Day, on June 6, 1944, the Germans began a steady retreat back toward their own borders. With the Russians closing in from the east, Hitler committed suicide in April 1945, and the war in Europe ended one week later. The liberation of Europe also uncovered the German efforts to exterminate Jews, Poles, Slavs, Gypsies, political dissidents, and other "undesirables."

The war in the Pacific took some months longer to win. Island hopping had brought the Allies back to the Philippines and islands close to the Japanese archipelago. Military plans called for an invasion of Japan, an action that might cost up to 1 million lives. President Truman, who became president on Roosevelt's death from a stroke in early January 1945, made the decision to try to force a Japanese surrender by **dropping the newly developed atomic bombs on two Japanese cities**. The bombs were the result of the supersecret Manhattan Project and had been completed only that summer. The first was dropped on Hiroshima in early August 1945 and the second on Nagasaki several days later, resulting in more than 160,000 deaths in the two cities. The Japanese offered surrender on August 10, and the formal papers were signed on September 2, 1945. World War II was at an end, and **the United States emerged as the most powerful nation on earth**.

Period 7 Practice Questions

Multiple-Choice Questions

Questions 1–3 refer to the excerpt below.

> "All that this country desires is to see the neighboring countries stable, orderly, and prosperous. Any country whose people conduct themselves well can count upon our hearty friendship. If a nation shows that it knows how to act with reasonable efficiency and decency in social and political matters, if it keeps order and pays its obligations, it need fear no interference from the United States. Chronic wrongdoing, or an impotence which results in a general loosening of the ties of civilized society, may in America, as elsewhere, ultimately require intervention by some civilized nation, and in the Western Hemisphere the adherence of the United States to the Monroe Doctrine may force the United States, however reluctantly, in flagrant cases of such wrongdoing or impotence, to the exercise of an international police power."

Theodore Roosevelt's, Roosevelt Corollary to the Monroe Doctrine,
Annual Message to Congress, December 6, 1904

1. Which of the following best represents a historical continuity to the ideas expressed in this speech?
   (a) New territories in the Pacific
   (b) An active U.S. presence in Latin American affairs
   (c) Trade agreements with China
   (d) Neutrality at the start of World War I

2. Which of the following represents an immediate consequence of the ideas expressed in the excerpt?
   (a) The acquisition of Cuba
   (b) The construction of the Panama Canal
   (c) War in the Philippines
   (d) Trade agreements with Great Britain

3. Which of the following statements best reflects the argument in the excerpt about America's role in the world?
   (a) The United States should expand its institutions around the world
   (b) The United States should retreat from Latin American countries
   (c) The United States should decrease the size of its Naval forces
   (d) The United States should not make unilateral decisions

Questions 4–6 refer to the excerpt below.

"Just as he was an Elk, a Booster, and a member of the Chamber of Commerce, just as the priests of the Presbyterian Church determined his every religious belief and the senators who controlled the Republican Party decided in little smoky rooms in Washington what he should think about disarmament, tariff, and Germany, so did the large national advertisers fix the surface of his life, fix what he believed to be his individuality. These standard advertised wares—toothpastes, socks, tires, cameras, instantaneous hot-water heaters—were his symbols and proofs of excellence; at first the signs, then the substitutes, for joy and passion and wisdom."

Sinclair Lewis, *Babbitt*, 1922

4. Which of the following most clearly represents the subject of this excerpt?
   (a) Debates over science
   (b) Debates over religion
   (c) Debates over financial regulatory systems
   (d) Debates over modernism

5. The societal debates described in this excerpt continued in which of the following decades?
   (a) 1930s
   (b) 1940s
   (c) 1950s
   (d) 1960s

6. The excerpt above best illustrates which of the following historical trends?
   (a) The rejection of new mediums of entertainment
   (b) Production of new consumer goods
   (c) Cultural controversies
   (d) New forms of mass media

Questions 7–9 are based on the excerpt below.

"Until four-thirty this morning I had hoped against hope that some miracle would prevent a devastating war in Europe and bring to an end the invasion of Poland by Germany.

"For four long years a succession of actual wars and constant crises have shaken the entire world and have threatened in each case to bring on the gigantic conflict which is today unhappily a fact. . . .

"It is easy for you and for me to shrug our shoulders and to say that conflicts taking place thousands of miles from the continental United States . . . do not seriously affect the Americas-and that all the United States has to do is to ignore them and go about its own business. . . . .

"This nation will remain a neutral nation, but I cannot ask that every American remain neutral in thought as well. Even a neutral has a right to take account of facts. Even a neutral cannot be asked to close his mind or his conscience. I have said not once, but many times, that I have seen war and that I hate war. I say that again and again."

Franklin Roosevelt, Fireside Chat, September 3, 1939

7. President Roosevelt's claims about neutrality best reflect which of the following beliefs in the 1930s?
   (a) Most Americans wanted to declare war against Nazi Germany
   (b) The unwavering insistence on isolationism
   (c) An opposition to direct military confrontation against Nazi Germany
   (d) The desire for an international collective security organizatoin

8. The foreign policy statements of President Roosevelt in the late 1930s best reflect which of the following changes from the foreign policy of the 1920s?
   (a) A return to the isolationism of the Gilded Age
   (b) A call for increased military invention in Latin America
   (c) More aggressive confrontation with the Soviet Union
   (d) Greater involvement in world affairs

9. By the time of U.S. entry into World War II in December 1941, the United States had done all of the following EXCEPT
   (a) provide the Allies with much-needed supplies.
   (b) move Japanese Americans to internment camps.
   (c) institute the first peacetime draft in U.S. history.
   (d) meet with Allied leaders to agree on war aims.

Question 10–12 refer to the graph below.

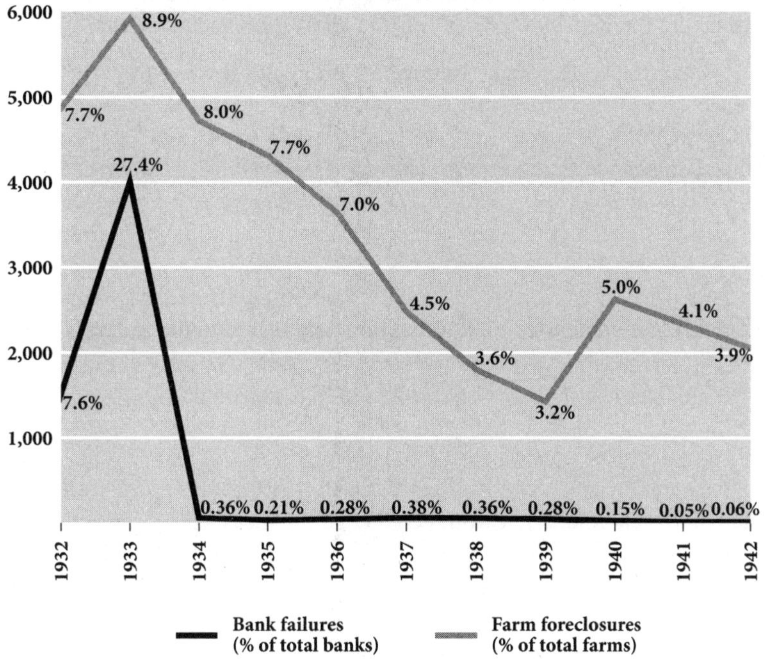

Bank Failures and Farm Foreclosures, 1932–1942

10. Which of the following statements is best supported by the graph above?
    (a) Farm foreclosures remained the same throughout the New Deal.
    (b) The rates at which banks failed and farms were foreclosed were about the same.
    (c) Banks recovered quickly in the early years of the New Deal.
    (d) Farm foreclosures went down steadily throughout the New Deal.

11. Which of the following reflects the greatest change in government policy ushered in by the New Deal?
    (a) The government was more responsible for the economic well-being of the country
    (b) The government should steadfastly retain a laissez-faire approach to economic recessions
    (c) The government's primary role should be to defend the United States from foreign invasion
    (d) Quack remedies would not put an end to the Great Depression

12. Which of the following best reflects the causes of the Great Depression as seen in the graph above?
    (a) An industrial economy
    (b) Market instability
    (c) Stratification of wealth
    (d) Underconsumption

END OF MULTIPLE-CHOICE SECTION

Short-Answer Questions

"America's present need is not heroics, but healing; not nostrums, but normalcy; not revolution, but restoration; not agitation, but adjustment; not surgery, but serenity; not the dramatic, but the dispassionate; not experiment, but equipoise; not submergence in internationality, but sustainment in triumphant nationality. It is one thing to battle successfully against world domination by military autocracy, because the infinite God never intended such a program, but it is quite another thing to revise human nature and suspend the fundamental laws of life and all of life's acquirements."

Warren G. Harding, "Return to Normalcy," Boston, May 14, 1920

1. Using the above excerpt, answer a, b, and c.
    (a) Briefly explain ONE of the claims made in the excerpt above.

    (b) Briefly explain ONE historical development that led to the ideas expressed in the excerpt above.

    (c) Briefly explain ONE historical development that would challenge the ideas expressed in the excerpt above.

2. Based on the graph on the following page, answer a, b, and c.
    (a) Briefly explain ONE specific historical event or development that caused an immigration trend illustrated in the graph.

    (b) Briefly explain ANOTHER specific historical event or development that caused an immigration trend illustrated in the graph.

(c) Briefly explain ONE specific historical result of an immigration trend illustrated in the graph.

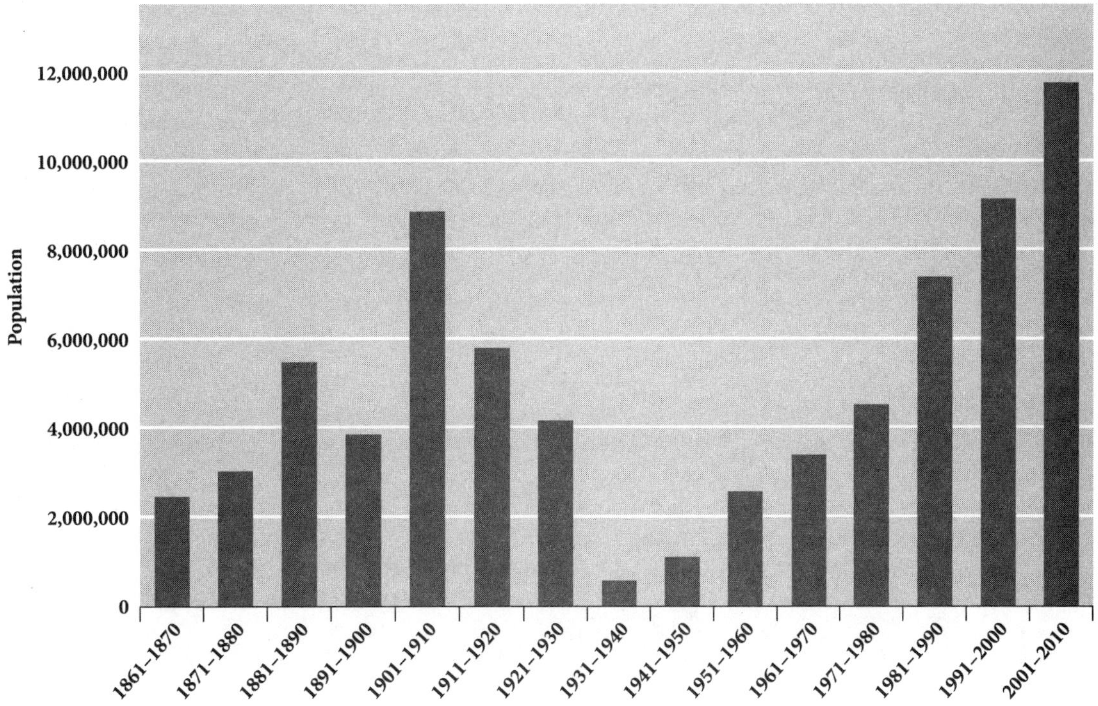

Immigration into the United States, 1861–2010

END OF SHORT-ANSWER SECTION

Long Essay Question

Question: Evaluate the extent to which the Progressive Era changed American society in the period from 1880 to 1920.

END OF LONG ESSAY SECTION

NOTES:

PERIOD 8, 1945–1980

Overview

The United States entered the post–World War II era as the most powerful country in the world. Among the challenges the country faced were the spread and containment of communism, leadership in the global economy, and maintenance of security both at home and abroad. The containment of communism during these years led to a number of "brushfire" engagements in other parts of the world, including Korea and Vietnam. The United States entered into a period of Cold War, with periodic crises followed by years of quiet coexistence.

The end of colonialism at the close of World War II opened the way for nationalist movements in Asia, Africa, and the Middle East, efforts complicated by the demands of the United States and the Soviet bloc that new countries choose sides in the Cold War. The United States also worked to ensure that friendly governments would emerge from newly created Latin American countries. Diplomatic relations with the Middle East were complicated by that region's vast oil supplies and the U.S. economy's dependence on that fuel source.

Fear of spreading communism played a significant role in domestic politics in the United States. While both political parties supported limiting communism's influence, there were disagreements about how this should be accomplished. The war in Korea resulted in some domestic protest; however, the war in Vietnam led to national, often violent, antiwar protests. Other issues were the proliferation of nuclear weapons, the influence of the military in domestic politics, and the proper role of presidential power in making foreign and military policy.

The 1950s and 1960s saw a rejuvenated civil rights movement challenging Jim Crow and segregation in the courts and in the streets. Landmark decisions resulted in the desegregation of the military, the end of separate but equal with the *Brown v. Board of Education of Topeka, Kansas* decision, and the sweeping Civil Rights Act of 1964. White segregationists continued to resist government attempts to end segregation, and civil rights activists themselves debated the best strategies to follow in the mid-1960s.

Calls for the end to segregation and Jim Crow led to calls for equal treatment from other minority groups, particularly women and gays and lesbians. Latinos, American Indians, and Asian Americans soon followed with demands of their own. Others spoke up for the poor, asking how a country known for its affluence could still have communities living in significant poverty.

President Lyndon Johnson's liberal domestic program, the Great Society, attempted to address many of these issues. His programs were supported by the Supreme Court, yet opponents of his approach began to gather strength as well. A new conservative movement began to question Johnson's vision of the scope of state and federal authority. His programs also came under fire from those on the far left who felt the government was not doing enough and who opposed America's foreign involvement in what they felt were local nationalist struggles.

The decades following World War II were a time of great economic growth and prosperity. Parents of baby boomers flocked to the suburbs in the 1950s and 1960s, demanding better schools, better infrastructure, and more opportunity for the growing middle class. Others saw the nation moving into conformity and spoke out against what they saw as a homogeneous mass culture. Conservatives worried that traditional values would be lost as urban and suburban areas grew further apart.

The United States continued to be the destination of choice for immigrants from around the world, especially after President Johnson liberalized immigration laws in 1965. Others focused on the growing awareness of the need to curb environmental pollution and begin to work more effectively at conserving natural resources.

As this time period drew to a close, new issues began to take over national debate. The traditional nuclear family was less in evidence as more women worked outside the home and divorce and single-parent households became more acceptable. The youth counterculture movement of the 1960s led to the rejection of the values of earlier generations, ushering in a sexual revolution and a much more informal culture.

Conservatives and liberals debated these social changes as well as issues about the proper role of the federal government and ways to offer greater protection of individual rights.

Key Terms

Be sure that you understand the meaning of these terms and their relevance in U.S. history. Page numbers from the textbook are provided.

Cold War (772–802)
Korea (768, 786)
Containment (769, 778–787)
Red Scare (787–791)
Baby Boom (813, 818)
Sun Belt (828–829)
Rust Belt (912)
Mass culture (769)
Brown v Board of Education (847–848)
Military-Industrial complex (807–808)
Decolonization (861)
Vietnam (884–889)
Lyndon Johnson (873–877)
Great Society (875-877)
Immigration Act of 1965 (979)
Martin Luther King Jr. (852–853)
Non-violent civil disobedience (849–851)
Civil Rights Act of 1964 (855, 874, 878)
Counterculture (888–889)
Arab Oil Embargo (906–907)
Environmental Protection Agency (910, 951)
Watergate Affair (916–918)

Focus Questions

As you study Period 8, keep the following thematic questions in mind.

American and National Identity

- What did the American middle class want in the years after World War II? Account for the expansion of the middle class in postwar America.
- What caused the social tensions that the nation faced after World War II, and how were these tensions manifested?
- Why was it that the 1950s produced the phenomenon of the American teen culture?
- Despite significant changes in gender roles, marriage, and the family, why did paternalism remain an important force?
- How did middle-class assumptions reflect the tensions between the traditional role of women and the forces promoting change?
- Why did some women reject feminism, and to what extent were conservative groups successful in thwarting the goals of the feminist movement?
- Besides women, what other groups challenged traditional authority? How effective were these groups in achieving their goals?
- What forces led to a significant change in Americans' views on racial equality in the two decades after World War II?
- Why were the Fourteenth and Fifteenth amendments, ratified one hundred years earlier, so central to African Americans' efforts to achieve civil rights in the 1950s and 1960s?
- What were some of the goals and strategies that black civil rights organizations used? To what extent were these different strategies successful?
- How and in what ways did student involvement help change the direction of the civil rights movement?
- What rifts threatened the black civil rights movement in the 1960s, and to what degree were differences in goals, methods, and leadership resolved?
- What challenges did Mexican Americans and Japanese Americans face during and after World War II, and how did they confront these challenges?

- How did the goals, issues, leadership, and methods of Chicano and Native American groups compare to those of African Americans?
- In what ways did "the new generation of Americans" that President Kennedy referred to in his inaugural address alter the political and social landscape of the 1960s and 1970s?
- What were the many constituencies of the antiwar movement of the 1960s and 1970s? How were the concerns of these disparate groups crystallized by the war in Southeast Asia?
- What did affirmative action programs attempt to do, and why were they so controversial?
- Despite the nation's move to the right in the 1970s, how were women, gays, and other groups able to sustain their efforts to expand civil rights?

Work, Exchange, and Technology

- In what ways were the rights of workers affected by the Cold War?
- Despite many achievements, labor unions remained vulnerable. What progress did unions make, and what storm clouds were on the horizon for American workers?
- In what ways did the divide between the rich and the poor increase in the 1970s? Why did this occur?
- In what ways did television play an important role in American politics and government?
- Why was Eisenhower so concerned about the "military-industrial complex"?
- What was the impact of the space race on science, education, and foreign policy?
- How did television transform American life?
- Why were the media able to have such an important role in shaping American opposition to the war in Vietnam?
- What factors accounted for limited economic growth in the 1970s?
- What effect did the gas crisis of the 1970s have on American assumptions and attitudes?
- What accounted for the transition from an industrial to a service economy?

Geography and the Environment

- What were the historical precedents for the environmental activism of the 1970s?
- How did Richard Nixon's policies on environmental issues contribute to his reputation as a transitional president?

Migration and Settlement

- Why did the United States become a suburban nation? What were the characteristics of this demographic change, and how did government policy, technology, and economic forces contribute to it?
- What groups made up the "other America" that Michael Harrington described? What efforts were made to address his concerns?
- In what ways was segregation in the North similar to southern segregation? How was it different?
- In what ways did the report of the Kerner Commission send a wakeup call to urban America and to those who governed American cities?
- What problems were specific to American cities in the 1970s, and how successfully did government address these problems?
- What were the effects of the changes made to U.S. immigration law in 1965?

Politics and Power

- What was "Cold War liberalism"?
- In what ways did President Truman alter FDR's vision of America?
- In what ways did American domestic policies reflect the tensions of the Cold War?
- To what extent do you feel that actions directed against communists in the United States were justified? Defend your argument.
- In what ways did American politics and policies reflect ideological differences in the Republican Party?
- How effective were President Eisenhower's policies in both combatting communism and solving problems at home?
- How successfully did President Kennedy confront the Cold War crises he faced?
- How did party politics reflect racial tensions in the decades following World War II?
- In what ways did opponents of the black civil rights movement attempt to link their opposition to the Cold War?
- What role did the courts play in formulating and enforcing policies that expanded civil rights?
- Account for the crumbling of the New Deal coalition in the 1970s and 1980s. How did the elections of Richard Nixon and Ronald Reagan reflect that realignment?
- What led to the decline of liberalism in the 1970s?
- Why did liberals and conservatives view government so differently?
- What were the contradictions that were characteristic of John Kennedy's life and presidency?
- What were Lyndon Johnson's goals as he assumed the presidency in 1963? How did his successes and failures reflect these goals?
- To what extent were the reforms of the New Deal and Johnson's Great Society similar?
- In what ways was the Great Society a manifestation of the centuries-old debate over the proper role of government?
- Richard Nixon is often considered a transitional figure. Why?
- Why did some Americans believe that the courts went too far in furthering the interests of the left?
- Why did the Nixon White House engage in such widespread abuse of power, and how did Nixon's actions change the nation?
- Is there a constitutional guarantee of privacy? If so, where in the Constitution is it found? Why has the right to privacy mattered so much in the years since World War II?

America in the World

- In what ways did World War II set the stage for the Cold War?
- Why did opposition to communism become such a key component of American foreign policy after World War II?
- What specific actions did the U.S. government take to combat communism?
- In what ways did actions taken by both the United States and the Soviet Union exacerbate the tensions between the two powers?
- As the Cold War escalated, the United States turned to two former enemies—Japan and West Germany—for support. Why?
- To what extent was containment an effective tool of U.S. foreign policy?
- In what ways was NSC-68 a turning point in the Cold War?

- How did the memory of Munich inform American foreign policy after World War II?
- In what important ways had the world changed by 1964, and how did these changes force a change in U.S. foreign policy?
- What was more important in shaping American foreign policy in this period: the preservation and expansion of democracy or the search for stability?
- The textbook asserts that with regard to Vietnam, "the elemental paradox remained unchanged." What was this paradox, and what events supported this argument?
- Why did events in Vietnam escalate into a protracted and costly conflict?
- What factors led to American involvement in the Caribbean, the Middle East, and Africa?
- The Eisenhower Doctrine became yet another extension of Monroe's famous 1823 assertion of American foreign policy. What are the similarities and differences among these statements of American foreign policy: the Monroe Doctrine, the Roosevelt Corollary, the Truman Doctrine, the Eisenhower Doctrine, and the Nixon Doctrine?
- Many reform movements sprang from what the textbook calls "the progressive spirit" of the 1960s. How did these movements compare in their goals, methods, and leadership?
- What was the impact of the Vietnam War on U.S. politics, economy, and social movements?
- In what ways did world events in the 1970s change the lives of everyday Americans?

American and Regional Culture

- The textbook argues that the Cold War "compromised, as much as supported, stated American principles." What evidence supports this statement?
- In what ways were the 1920s and the 1950s alike? How did they differ?
- What aspects of postwar culture were most targeted by intellectuals, writers, and other critics? Why did these critics believe that American society was in crisis?
- To what extent was the hippie culture of the 1960s similar to the culture of the Beats of the 1950s and the Lost Generation of the 1920s?
- Though many critics were pessimistic about America's future, many did not share their concerns. What gave Americans reason to be optimistic?
- How did music define the youth culture and reflect tensions in American society?
- Account for the rise of cultural conservatism. What factors supported the status quo, and which encouraged change in the decades after World War II?
- How has postwar popular culture reflected tensions in the family and in the workplace?
- What accounted for the sexual revolution of the 1960s and 1970s, and what was its impact?
- How was the sexual revolution portrayed in popular culture, and in what ways did popular culture serve to promote changes in sexual mores and behavior?
- What were the characteristics of the Fourth Great Awakening of the late twentieth century, and how did this religious movement compare to those that preceded it?
- In what ways did evangelical Christianity and its adherents craft and spread a message that appealed to many Americans?

Social Structures

- Changes in language often reflect and shape social change. In what ways was this true in the decades after World War II?
- In the years since World War II, what forces have promoted change in the nature and function of the American family? In what ways has the American family changed?

Thematic Timeline

TIME	Key Events
1945	
	American and National Identity • "To Secure These Rights" (1947) • Desegregation of armed services (1948) • *Shelley v. Kraemer* (1948)
	Work, Exchange, and Technology • Baby boom establishes new consumer generation
	Geography and the Environment • Continued South-North migration of African Americans • First Levittown opens (1947) • FHA and VA subsidize suburbanization
	Migration and Settlement • War production and expansion of military reshape the Sunbelt • Wartime southern migration (black and white) to northern and western cities • First Levittown opens (1947)
	Politics and Power • Loyalty-Security Program (1947) • Taft-Hartley Act (1947) • Truman reelected (1948) • Truman's Fair Deal (1949)
	America in the World • Truman Doctrine • Israel created (1947) • Marshall Plan (1948) • Containment strategy emerges • NATO created; West Germany created (1949)
	American and Regional Culture • World War II migrations produce vibrant, diverse cities • Bebop jazz • Advent of television changes entertainment (1940s–1950s)
	Social Structures • Red Scare and anticommunism suppress dissent (1947–1950s)
1950	
	American and National Identity • *Brown v. Board of Education* (1954) • Montgomery Bus Boycott (1955) • Little Rock Central High School desegregation battle (1957) • Southern Christian Leadership Conference founded (1957)
	Work, Exchange, and Technology • Labor-Management Accord struck in major industries (1950s) • Military-industrial complex begins to rise • National Defense Education Act (1958) spurs development of technology

Geography and the Environment
- National Interstate and Defense Highways Act (1956)
- Growth of suburbia and Sunbelt
- Atomic bomb testing in Nevada and Pacific Ocean

Migration and Settlement
- Bracero program revived (1951)
- Surging middle-class migration to suburbs
- Patterns of racial segregation in cities and suburbs reinforced
- Migration to Sunbelt (1950s–1970s)
- McCarran-Walter Act (1952)
- Puerto Rican "great migration" to New York

Politics and Power
- Cold War liberalism
- McCarthyism and Red Scare
- Eisenhower's presidency (1953–1961)

America in the World
- Permanent mobilization as a result of NSC-68
- Korean War (1950–1953)
- Geneva Accords regarding Vietnam (1954)

American and Regional Culture
- Emergence of rock 'n' roll and youth culture
- Disneyland opens (1955)
- McDonald's restaurants lead emergence of fast food
- Beat culture flourishes in New York and San Francisco

1960

American and National Identity
- Greensboro sit-ins (1960)
- *The Feminine Mystique* (1963)
- Civil Rights and Voting Rights Acts (1964–1965)
- National Organization for Women founded (1966)
- Alcatraz occupation (1969)
- Black Power (1966)
- Student and antiwar activism

Work, Exchange, and Technology
- Economic boom
- Government spending on Vietnam and Great Society
- Medicare and Medicaid created (1965)

Geography and the Environment
- Great Society environmental initiatives
- Urban riots (1964–1968)
- Kerner Commission Report (1968)

Migration and Settlement
- Immigration and Nationality Act of 1965
- Reflecting the new law, immigration from Asia, Latin America, and Africa increases (1960s–1990s)
- Rustbelt begins to lose population

TIME	Key Events

Key Events

Politics and Power
- John F. Kennedy's New Frontier
- John F. Kennedy assassinated (1963)
- Lyndon B. Johnson's landslide victory (1964)
- War on Poverty; Great Society
- Riots at Democratic National Convention (1968)

America in the World
- Cuban missile crisis (1962)
- Gulf of Tonkin Resolution (1964)
- Johnson sends ground troops to Vietnam; war escalates (1965)
- Tet offensive (1968); peace talks begin

American and Regional Culture
- Major antiwar protests (1965–1969)
- Counterculture
- Black Arts movement

Social Structures
- Civil rights movement merges protest and gospel music
- Stonewall Inn riot (1969)

1970

American and National Identity
- Equal Rights Amendment (1972)
- *Roe v. Wade* (1973)
- Siege at Wounded Knee (1973)
- *Bakke v. University of California* (1978)
- Harvey Milk assassinated (1978)

Work, Exchange, and Technology
- Energy crisis (1973)
- Inflation surges, while economy stagnates (stagflation)
- Deindustrialization
- Tax revolt in California (1978)

Geography and the Environment
- First Earth Day (1970)
- Environmental Protection Agency established (1970)
- Endangered Species Act (1973)
- Three Mile Island accident (1979)

Migration and Settlement
- After 1975, Vietnamese refugees fleeing communist regime arrive in U.S.
- Rustbelt population decline and Sunbelt population growth produce regional realignment in congressional power (1970s–1990s)

Politics and Power
- Richard Nixon's landslide victory (1972)
- Watergate scandal; Nixon resigns (1974)
- Jimmy Carter elected president (1976)
- Moral Majority founded (1979)

America in the World

- Nixon invades Cambodia (1970)
- Paris Accords end Vietnam War (1973)
- Camp David Accords between Egypt and Israel (1978)
- Iranian Revolution (1979) and hostage crisis (1979–1981)

American and Regional Culture

- Women's and gay rights movements flourish
- Evangelical Christian resurgence

Social Structures

- Cultural and political conflict over the nuclear family

America's History Chapter Summaries

(required AP® content in bold)

Chapter 24
The Cold War Dawns, 1945-1963

Chapter 24 examines the tensions that led to and maintained the era of the Cold War up to 1963. The end of World War II set the stage for the beginning of the Cold War, a time of tense relations and world competition of the United States and its Western allies with the Soviet Union and its client states. The Yalta agreements in the final months of the war, in addition to establishing the United Nations, allowed the Soviet Union to occupy and control most of Eastern Europe. At the Potsdam Conference in the summer of 1945, Stalin refused to compromise with Truman and refused to hold open elections in areas he controlled, thus maintaining Soviet power. Germany remained divided as it had been at the end of the war, with the West becoming a democracy and the East remaining under Soviet communist rule. Britain's Winston Churchill described Eastern Europe as trapped behind an "iron curtain" of Soviet rule, a term that became a watchword of the era.

The United States responded with a strategy that was dubbed **"containment," the determination to stop the spread of communist influence and control wherever it threatened to surface in the world**. Turkey, Greece, and Yugoslavia became early centers of this struggle. George Kennan, an advisor to the president, believed the Soviet system was unstable and would eventually collapse. He urged the United States to adopt the policy. President Truman took this advice and provided U.S. aid to Greece when that country was threatened with a communist uprising in 1947. At the same time, he issued the Truman Doctrine, outlining the policy of containment.

In response to the need to bolster the shattered economies of Western Europe—and also as part of a plan to bolster up noncommunist nations—the United States developed the Marshall Plan, which provided financial aid to any country in Europe that could demonstrate that it had a freely elected government. Western Europe's recovery quickly outstripped that of the East, which remained under Soviet control. In 1948, Stalin made an attempt to at least push Western powers out of the old German capital of Berlin by blockading the city. Truman responded with the Berlin Airlift, an around-the-clock stream of supply planes that brought supplies into the city for more than a year. Stalin finally abandoned the blockade, but Germany remained divided. Western powers formed the North Atlantic Treaty Organization (NATO) to deal with similar situations in the future.

Since the use of the atomic bomb during the war, many in the U.S. government worried about the inevitable proliferation of nuclear weapons, and in 1949. the Soviets detonated a bomb of their own. Congress passed the National Security Act in 1947, which created the National Security Council. That body's report in 1950, known as **NSC68, called for a massive buildup of the American military, the development of a hydrogen bomb, and whatever else it took to surpass the military power of the Soviet Union**.

China proved to be another theater of the Cold War. Civil war had been raging between the Western-backed Nationalists of Jiang Jieshi (Chiang Kai-shek) and the Communists under Mao Zedong. Mao triumphed and established the people's Republic of China in 1949, as the Nationalists fled to the island of Taiwan. The United States refused to recognize Communist China as the legitimate China.

In 1950, **Communist-backed North Korea launched a surprise attack on South Korea, an ally of the United States**. The United Nations came to the defense of South Korea, relying heavily on American troops under the leadership of General Douglas MacArthur. MacArthur's determination to press the war into China led President Truman to relieve him of command, and the Korean War settled into a stalemate that became an issue in the presidential election of 1952. Republican candidate Dwight Eisenhower was able to turn this stalemate to his advantage in the presidential campaign.

The Democratic Party also suffered from the loss of labor support by 1952. A backlash against unions resulted in Congress's passing the Taft-Hartley Act in 1947 that weakened collective bargaining and initiated right-to-work laws prohibiting union shops. Truman had managed to win reelection in 1948 by a narrow margin, though his version of Roosevelt's domestic program, his Fair Deal, struggled with a Congress that did not often support him.

Fear of the spread of communism engulfed the country in the late 1940s and early 1950s. Congressional committees like the House Un-American Activities Committee were already calling suspect organizations and individuals to task. This committee was led by a freshman congressman from California, Richard Nixon, who made a special project of tracking down and working to convict Alger Hiss, a member of Roosevelt's inner circle, as a communist sympathizer. Senator Joseph McCarthy organized a Senate committee to investigate suspicious activities that quickly turned into a national witch hunt. In 1954, he was undone by making baseless accusations against the army and by being exposed as a bully and a fraud on national television. He died in disgrace several years later, though not before he had ruined many lives with his accusations.

Eisenhower won the presidential election of 1952, chosen because many hoped he would be a conservative alternative to the legacy of Franklin Roosevelt. In fact, Eisenhower proved to be a largely middle-of-the-road Republican who supported some New Deal programs while reining in others. **He was clearly a Cold Warrior, but one dedicated to containment rather than confrontation. The arms race accelerated, and Eisenhower appointed as secretary of state John Foster Dulles, who threatened those who disturbed international peace with "massive retaliation."** The newly created Central Intelligence Agency (CIA) intervened in the domestic politics of Iran, Central America, and Vietnam. Eisenhower and Dulles were **determined to intervene in Vietnam when the French decided to end their efforts to prevent a communist government from taking over in their former colony**. The United States picked up the support of the South Vietnamese forces at the Geneva Conference in 1954 as the French were pulling out. The goal was to install a Western-friendly regime there that would be a counter to the communist government of Ho Chi Minh in North Vietnam.

More controversy awaited in the Middle East, with the continuing conflict between the Israelis and the Palestinians, and now with the addition of a crisis involving Egypt and the Suez Canal. Egyptian support of the Palestinians led to a British and French attack on the Suez Canal, resulting in a stalemate that the United Nations had to sort out. The United States issued the Eisenhower Doctrine, reemphasizing American "support for any nation facing the threat of International Communism."

The year 1960 saw the election of Democrat John F. Kennedy, a Cold Warrior yet one who had the advantage of youth and charisma. In his inaugural address, Kennedy promised America a "New Frontier," and he brought in a cadre of young, highly educated advisors to make up his cabinet and staff. His administration immediately faced crises in Cuba and Berlin. **The ill-fated Bay of Pigs invasion was a disaster for the young president**, and many felt Kennedy's indecision emboldened Khrushchev to authorize the building of the Berlin Wall in August 1961. Kennedy redeemed himself by standing up to Khrushchev during the **Cuban missile crisis in October 1962, forcing the Russians to dismantle missile bases in Cuba under the threat of nuclear retaliation**. Under President Kennedy, the United States became even more mired in Vietnam. Kennedy authorized the use of military advisors and Special Forces, "Green Berets," whose specialty was unconventional warfare. American officials in Vietnam were dismayed at local protests against the government the United States supported, particularly Buddhist monks who chose to publicly burn themselves alive rather than endorse the government supported by the United States. The South Vietnamese government sponsored by the United States collapsed in a coup in November 1963, resulting in the assassination of Ngo Dinh Diem, the South Vietnamese president. South Vietnam was left without a popularly supported leader, but American foreign policy insisted that the North's Ho Chi Minh could not be considered a legitimate replacement. Vietnam remained a foreign policy problem for the United States. President Kennedy was assassinated a few weeks after the Vietnamese coup, and the question of what to do in Vietnam passed on to President Lyndon Johnson.

Chapter 25
Triumph of the Middle Class, 1945–1963

Chapter 25 examines the expansion of the middle class in the post–World War II decades. **One of the greatest social phenomena of the postwar period was the growth of the American middle class**. America dominated the global economy and had the highest standard of living in the world. The growth of the suburbs did not come without a dark side, however. Urban areas declined and racial segregation was on the rise. **Many on the margins of society, such as immigrants, minorities, the elderly, and the working poor, were not included in this prosperity**.

With Germany and Japan in shambles at the end of the war, **the United States entered a postwar economic boom in both internal and international marketplaces that would last for three decades**. The United States played a preeminent position in the creation of the World Bank and the International Monetary Fund, making the American dollar a currency valued worldwide. The General Agreement on Tariffs and Trades (GATT) fit America's vision of an open-market global economy as well. The Defense Department continued to offer enormous government contracts to private industries in the name of national security. The Soviet launch of *Sputnik* in 1957 led to the investment of even more millions in these programs under the National Defense Education Act (NDEA), as the United States was determined to keep pace with and then surpass the Soviet Union. Science, industry, and the military became so intertwined that Eisenhower, on leaving office, warned of the **potential dangers of what he termed the "military industrial complex."**

Corporate power characterized American capitalism during these years, employing huge numbers of white-collar workers. Some felt the working world in these corporations often stifled creativity, valuing "organization men" rather than original thinkers. Automation increasingly replaced blue-collar workers with machines, something that would have long-term effects on the economy by the end of the century. **While many enjoyed unprecedented prosperity, tenacious poverty lurked among those at the bottom of the economic ladder in both urban and rural areas**.

Prosperity meant seemingly endless waves of consumer goods. Returning GIs were able to take advantage of government programs to attend college in record numbers and to buy homes with low-interest loans. Workers rejoined trade unions on returning to work, though unions met with resistance in Congress, which passed legislation curbing some union powers. Management hoped to loosen the grip of unions in the decades to come. Americans bought homes, cars, and household appliances in record numbers. Their children, the "baby boom" generation, grew up as the focus of both their parents' attention and that of the advertising world. As they grew older, the marketing focus changed from games and television to music and the other interests of teenagers. Television became an essential part of nearly every American home, reinforcing the images of a good life through consumption of the latest goods and services. Television shows glorified the perfect suburban family, something that often fell short of the reality. Theirs was a vision of white middle-class tastes and values with little effort to add any nuance to the picture.

The teen culture of the 1950s and 1960s was also a new phenomenon. Elvis Presley provided the cross-over music that linked African American rhythm and blues to a young white audience. Youth rebellion became big business, with music, poets, writers, and artists providing the **younger generation with a rich alternative to their parents' predictable suburban lifestyle**. Church membership soared during the 1950s, in part because many felt **religion was an antidote to the threat of atheistic communism. In the 1950s the phrase "one nation under God" was added to the Pledge of Allegiance and "In God we trust" was added to the nation's coins**.

The baby boom lasted until about 1964 when birthrates began to decline. The boomers have given their generation a significant impact on the past six decades of American history because there are so many of them. They have enjoyed the best health care in history, have been generally well educated, and in many cases were indulged by parents who remembered the Great Depression and wanted to "give them the best." Many of their mothers stayed home because it was expected of them. Women who did work were usually relegated to "pink-collar" jobs as secretaries, nurses, or waitresses, to name a few. Most women also received less pay than men did for the same work. Many women had no choice but to work so that their families could pay their bills. The domestic ideal of the nuclear family with the father as the breadwinner was already crumbling around the edges.

The 1960s saw the coming of the sexual revolution. People began to talk about and acknowledge such topics as sex outside marriage and gay and lesbian relationships, and they began to have frank and open discussions of sexual matters that were previously kept out of public discourse. The baby boomers would be the first generation in history to have access to reliable birth control, another factor that would revolutionize sexual mores.

The growth of the suburbs was accelerated by the development of Eisenhower's Interstate Highway Act, a network of roads that made access to suburbs even easier. The subdivisions built by men like William Levitt became the young family's opportunity for independence, although minorities were not allowed to buy into them. Fast food outlets and shopping malls made life in the suburbs even more attractive. National demographics began to change as well, as plentiful jobs and pleasant weather led thousands to flock to the Sunbelt states of the South and Southwest. By the end of the 1960s, the nation was almost evenly divided between the urban and the suburban, with cities increasingly characterized by racial segregation, higher crime, poverty, and unemployment. Those in the suburbs felt protected from these woes by distance and wealth. Attempts at urban renewal met with limited success during these years. Immigrants often made their way to urban areas in search of inexpensive housing and what jobs they could get. The contradictory visions of America held by those in the cities and those in the suburbs would become a major part of the protest movements that characterized the 1960s.

Chapter 26
The Civil Rights Movement, 1941–1973

Chapter 26 explores the era of modern civil rights that began during World War II and continued throughout the 1950s and 1960s. The modern civil rights movement began to emerge during World War II and the early Cold War era, with both grassroots efforts by churches and organizations like the Congress of Racial Equality (CORE) and **work through the courts to enforce the equal rights guaranteed in the Constitution to all American citizens**. Jim Crow had been a reality for African Americans living in the South since the days of Reconstruction, limiting both social equality and political participation. The North was only marginally better, with de facto rather than de jure segregation—low-paying jobs and separate neighborhoods with poor city services. Segregation and racial discrimination were a national rather than a regional problem.

The National Association for the Advancement of Colored People (NAACP) had been challenging racial segregation in a series of court cases since the group was formed in 1909. Marcus Garvey's United Negro Improvement Association attracted some attention in the 1920s. It was not until the emergence of a strong black middle class in the 1940s that progress began to seem possible. Churches and college students would provide the vanguard for the 1950s and 1960s.

A. Philip Randolph, head of the Brotherhood of Sleeping Car Porters, urged President Franklin Roosevelt to make racial fairness part of his wartime effort. Roosevelt signed into law Executive Order 8802, prohibiting racial discrimination in defense industries. This was followed by the Fair Employment Practices Commission, a weak body but a precedent nevertheless. Randolph also launched the "Double V" campaign, calling for victory over the Axis powers and over racism at home as well.

After the war, Jackie Robinson broke the color line in Major League Baseball, and President Truman appointed the Presidential Committee on Civil Rights and announced the desegregation of the armed forces. Truman's actions earned him enemies among southern politicians. In 1948, he faced a challenge from the States' Rights Democratic Party, the short-lived Dixiecrats, an early warning of the divisions that would face the Democratic Party in the years to come.

Other minorities endured discrimination as well. Mexican Americans in the Southwest faced a caste system similar to that of Jim Crow, including job discrimination and segregation in schools. Japanese Americans struggled to regain property lost during their forced internment during the war years.

The NAACP continued to look for the landmark court case that would turn segregation on its head. **Thurgood Marshall led the legal team that brought the case of *Brown v. Board of Education of Topeka, Kansas*, to the Supreme Court in 1954**. The Court ruled that segregation violated the principle of equal protection under the law, a clear breach of the guarantees of the Fourteenth Amendment. The South struck back, with 101 **southern political leaders signing the "Southern Manifesto," declaring that they would defy the Court's decision**. Only after President Eisenhower sent federal troops into Little Rock, Arkansas, to enforce desegregation did southern states begin to move grudgingly in the direction of compliance. The murder of a young black teen, Emmett Till, by Klansmen in Mississippi, resulted in a not-guilty verdict by a local court. That miscarriage of justice galvanized a generation of young African Americans to join the protest movements.

Desegregation of public facilities beyond schools was the next step, and Rosa Parks's arrest for refusing to give up her seat to a white passenger on a Montgomery, Alabama, bus provided the cause. The resulting bus boycott brought Martin Luther King Jr., a young Montgomery minister, to national attention. His advocacy of nonviolence changed the face of the civil rights movement and won respect for the protesters all over the world. He founded the Southern Christian Leadership Conference (SCLC) to organize protests and demonstrations, always with nonviolence as the watchword. Sit-ins by students in Greensboro, North Carolina, led to the creation of the Student Non-Violent Coordinating Committee (SNCC) to work with the SCLC. They staged Freedom Rides in an effort to desegregate interstate bus services, a tactic that resulted in serious injuries when the buses they rode were attacked by Klansmen in Alabama and other southern states.

The city of Birmingham, Alabama, became the scene of shocking violence when the local sheriff authorized the use of police dogs and fire hoses to break up civil rights demonstrations. King was arrested there and wrote his famous "Letter from a Birmingham Jail" to those who criticized his involvement in protests that were sure to turn violent. King was determined to see the passage of a national civil rights law that was before Congress in fall 1963. To lobby national support for the bill, he helped organize a march on Washington, D.C., in August that year to show Congress how much public support of it there was. Hundreds of thousands of people, black and white, converged on the nation's capital and heard King's famous "I Have a Dream" speech. Even so, it was not enough to get the necessary votes in Congress, and the bill was defeated that fall. **Lyndon Johnson would get Civil Rights Act passed the following year in 1964**.

The summer of 1964 saw SNCC's voter registration project, "Freedom Summer," begin in Mississippi. The students who participated were often naive about what they were facing, and three young workers were killed. An attempt to challenge Mississippi's segregated delegation to the Democratic National Convention that summer also failed, and many of the young SNCC members began to feel disillusioned. Even so, they had made gains: Congress passed the Voting Rights Act of 1965, and this bill, along with the Twenty-Fourth Amendment, which outlawed poll taxes, enabled thousands of blacks to vote for the first time since Reconstruction.

The mid-1960s saw the rise of more activist civil rights group. Stokely Carmichael and others who left SNCC began to look for more concrete ways to attack the problems they felt faced minority communities. He advocated what he called "Black Power," black self-reliance in attacking poverty and injustice. A new generation of black nationalists looked to the earlier example of Marcus Garvey for inspiration. The Nation of Islam, the Black Muslims, gained popularity among African Americans, mainly in northern cities. Malcolm X, a leader of the Nation of Islam, broke with that group in 1964 and sought to work for civil rights through a broader Muslim organization that did not focus so much on the racial exclusiveness of Black Muslims. A much more militant approach was advocated by the Black Panthers, a radical nationalist group founded in Oakland, California, by Huey Newton and Bobby Seale. They also opposed the Vietnam War as a white man's war. Following this lead, the Puerto Rican community saw the organization of the Young Lords, a group calling for self-determination for Puerto Ricans.

Many young black politicians began to work within the system and win elective offices in major cities around the country. They even organized the National Black Political Convention that met in Gary, Indiana, in 1972, hoping to produce an agenda that would have an impact on the national Democratic Party meeting later that year to choose a presidential candidate. They were not successful, but black politicians continued to win elective office in the decades that followed.

The year 1965 saw the beginnings of violence and rioting in inner cities throughout the country. The riots in the Watts neighborhood of Los Angeles that summer were the first of many "long hot summers" for people living in urban ghettos. It became clear that poverty and racism were national problems rather than just southern issues. King hoped to expand his work to include issues of poverty and opposition to the Vietnam War as well as racism, but he was assassinated in April 1968. His civil rights work became fragmented with the loss of his leadership, as the leaders who followed did not have the charisma to replace him. The battle for equal rights now became tied to the antiwar movement as the decade of the 1960s drew to a close.

The nation also saw an organized Chicano movement emerge, under the leadership of Cesar Chavez, a champion for the rights of migrant workers and leader of the United Farm Workers (UFW). Young Mexican Americans, wanting a more activist approach, formed the Brown Berets, a group modeled after the Black Panthers, and organized a political party, La Raza Unida (The United Race), to promote Chicano interests. **The American Indian Movement (AIM) formed to work for better conditions on American Indian reservations.** A takeover of the federal facilities at Wounded Knee, South Dakota, drew national attention to their cause.

The experience of African American civil rights advocates served as a model for similar civil rights movements among other minorities in the United States. All of these groups worked to achieve inclusion in mainstream American society, but each found themselves also including more nationalist celebrations of their own ethnic heritages as their movements developed and matured.

Chapter 27
Liberal Crisis and Conservative Rebirth, 1961–1972

Chapter 27 charts the progress of liberalism and the resurgence of conservatism in the 1960s and early 1970s. **The liberal movements of the 1960s soon came under assault from a number of directions, from young people frustrated with the slow process of change and from conservatives who felt that change was coming too fast and that the size of government was getting out of control**. By the end of the decade, the political pendulum began to move away from the reform-minded toward the more traditional.

When Lyndon Johnson came into office after the assassination of John Kennedy, he hoped to create a domestic agenda that would finish the job the New Deal began. He called his program the "Great Society," and he immediately began to push for civil rights legislation as well as a full slate of other programs designed to alleviate the condition of the poor and marginalized. He spoke of a "War on Poverty," with the federal government leading the way.

Johnson won a term on his own in 1964, defeating the conservative Barry Goldwater. He also carried both houses of Congress, giving him a clear path for his legislative agenda. Among his first bills were Medicare and Medicaid, guaranteeing health care to, respectively, the elderly and the poor. The programs that followed, including environmental protection, education reform, aid to cities for transportation and housing, and even the arts, touched almost every segment of society. **Johnson proposed a significant change in immigration, replacing old quotas with numeric limits that were less discriminatory**.

While poverty rates did drop, not everyone was pleased with the impact of the Great Society vision. **Conservatives felt the programs were too expensive and argued that improvements would have come anyway with a stronger economy**. **Others pointed out that many problems remained, among them entrenched poverty and racial segregation.**

A number of groups did see progress, however. **The women's movement was revitalized as more women moved into the workplace and demanded equal pay for equal work**. Betty Friedan, author of the *Feminine Mystique,* was one of the founders of the National Organization for Women, a group dedicated to lobbying for equal treatment of women in the job and as citizens.

Hovering over the Johnson administration, however, was the growing war in Vietnam. As Kennedy had inherited this war from Eisenhower, so Johnson inherited the conflict from Kennedy. He saw South Vietnam as a vital outpost in the war to contain communism, so he was determined to prevent Southeast Asia "from going the way China went." Johnson used an alleged incident involving a U.S. destroyer in the Gulf of Tonkin in the summer of 1964 to get authorization from Congress for widening the war. The Gulf of Tonkin Resolution gave Johnson a free hand and led to a massive **escalation of U.S. involvement in Vietnam**, both through increases in ground troops and bombing raids on North Vietnam. As the casualties mounted, Johnson found American public opinion shifting against the war. Nightly television coverage showed the carnage, and the public began to doubt the rosy predictions of easy victory that came in a steady stream from the White House. Fueled by college students, many of whom had been involved in the civil rights movement, **antiwar sentiment began to grow and become more organized**. The Selective Service System became an early target of the antiwar effort as young people resisted the draft or applied for conscientious objector status. Antiwar demonstrations grew in numbers and strength through the Johnson years, while **young supporters of the war countered with the creation of the conservative Young Americans for Freedom**. The new counterculture, a movement rebelling against middle-class values and authority in general, blended antiwar energy with rock music, recreational drugs, and an open attitude toward sex that startled the older generations.

The year 1968 proved to be a watershed year of sorts, with protests against the war escalating as the military faced the Tet Offensive, an offensive by the North Vietnamese (at the time of the Vietnamese holiday of Tet) that showed U.S. gains in the South to be more at risk than the public had been led to believe. Johnson was discredited in the public eye, and many were no longer willing to believe his positive pronouncements on the progress of the war. Political assassinations rocked the country. Martin Luther King Jr. was killed in April, and Robert Kennedy, front-runner for the Democratic presidential nomination, was assassinated in June. The summer found the Democratic Party in disarray, holding a chaotic political convention in Chicago and choosing Vice President Hubert Humphrey as a less-than-inspiring candidate for the fall election. The Republicans took advantage of the Democrats' problems and nominated Richard Nixon as their conservative alternative, a man who promised to restore law and order to the country. Many voters, tired of the antiwar movement, the counterculture, and urban rioting, began to drift away from the Democratic Party. A third-party candidate, segregationist George Wallace of Alabama, offered an alternative to southern voters, another group that felt they no longer had a political home with the Democrats. Nixon lured southern voters himself by downplaying his commitment to aggressively enforcing civil rights laws. Nixon won a narrow victory, and the country began a slow turn to the political right.

The struggle for civil rights continued, though some groups also took up the antiwar cause. **The women's liberation movement broadened its goals to support equal treatment of women in all areas of society**, and more women were elected to public office. A riot at the Stonewall Inn in New York focused **national attention on the issue of gay rights, and the Gay National Task Force was formed to organize lobbying efforts for nondiscrimination laws**.

President Nixon continued to insist that most Americans agreed with his basically centrist policies; he called them the "silent majority," as distinct from those who took to the streets in protest. He hoped to ease the country out of the war through what he called a process of "Vietnamization," letting the South Vietnamese gradually take over the war effort as America withdrew.

Nixon was determined to find a way out that would provide "peace with honor." As he approached the presidential election of 1972, he announced progress in the long-stalled peace talks with the North Vietnamese that had met sporadically in Paris for several years. In early 1973, he announced that the North and South Vietnamese had agreed to a Paris Peace Accord that would slowly allow the United States to withdraw, turning the war over to the South Vietnamese. When the United States did bring the troops home, the South Vietnamese government was not able to hold out on its own. In April 1975, the North Vietnamese defeated the South Vietnamese, and the country of Vietnam was unified under a communist government much like it might have been had they been allowed self-determination in 1954 when the French withdrew.

President Nixon was also able to change the direction of the Supreme Court, a body that had been predictably liberal for several decades. After his landslide reelection victory in 1972, he had the opportunity to make several Court appointments that began to shift the Court in a more conservative direction.

Chapter 28
The Search for Order in an Era of Limits, 1973–1980

Chapter 28 examines the crises of the 1970s. The early 1970s saw a growing backlash in the United States to the social and political upheavals of the 1960s. In addition, an international oil embargo in 1973 caused the economy to experience runaway inflation and the deepest economic slump since the Great Depression. United States support for Israel in the 1973 Yom Kippur War led the Arab members of the Organization of Petroleum Exporting

Countries (OPEC) to support raising the price of oil in retaliation. The nation put conservation measures into place, such as lower speed limits, but prices on just about everything began to rise at alarming rates.

President Nixon introduced a number of environmental measures during his presidency. He had been impressed with Rachel Carson's book *Silent Spring*, which documented the effects of the overuse of pesticides on the environment. He signed into law a number of bills designed to protect the environment, including one that created the Environmental Protection Agency. The leak of radioactive material at the Three Mile Island reactor in Pennsylvania also brought the dangers of nuclear power to the forefront of public debate, slowing the development of nuclear power sources for decades.

The U.S. economy suffered under high unemployment, stagnant consumer demand, and inflation in the 1970s, a combination known as "stagflation." There was little that any presidential administration or Congress could do to improve the situation as long as oil prices remained high. Many American industries saw overseas competition cut into profits, leading to downsizing, automation, and attempts to invest in new technologies. Parts of the Northeast and Midwest that had been industrial centers declined and became known as the "Rust Belt." Deindustrialization also hurt labor unions as cheap overseas labor drew away jobs. Labor union membership declined to the lowest levels since the 1920s.

The growth of the suburbs contributed to a corresponding decline of urban areas. Suburban residents resented paying taxes to support government services and schools that they felt did not benefit them. **California led the way in the movement known as the "tax revolt," refusing to approve new taxes to fund services that taxpayers felt they did not need**. The generous spirit of the New Deal was unraveling.

Nixon was distracted from many of these problems by difficulties of his own. The Watergate scandal was threatening to consume his presidency. For a while, he successfully dodged questions about his involvement in the efforts to cover up the break-in at the Democratic National Committee headquarters in a Washington hotel during the 1972 presidential campaign. The story was doggedly pursued by reporters from the *Washington Post*, who eventually uncovered information that pointed directly at White House involvement. Nixon ultimately had to resign to avoid impeachment on charges of obstruction of justice. While dealing with this scandal, the president also found his power in foreign policy limited by the War Powers Act, which required congressional approval to deploy U.S. troops in anything less than an emergency.

The electorate viewed many veteran politicians poorly after the Watergate scandals and President Gerald Ford's decision to pardon Richard Nixon. The elections of 1974 and 1976 brought many new faces to Congress, though government did not become much more efficient. The old Democratic coalition continued to crumble, though new alignments would not be evident for a few more years. The election of Democrat Jimmy Carter in 1976 was seen as the triumph of an outsider who was not involved in Washington's "business as usual." Despite his good intentions, Carter was not able to bring about much improvement in the economy, as gas prices stayed high. He was hurt as well by his inability to do much to protect American interests in the Iranian Revolution, failing to gain the release of hostages taken at the American embassy in Tehran.

Civil rights continued to be a major issue on the political agenda throughout these years. **The affirmative action policies of the 1960s faced new challenges by whites who saw such practices as reverse discrimination**. The Supreme Court **moved away from solid support for affirmative action in 1978 with the *Bakke* decision**, which rejected the use of quotas to ensure diversity in college admissions. Women's rights efforts were also curtailed by the states' rejection of the Equal Rights Amendment (ERA) in 1982. **A number of conservative women's groups joined the fight to stop ERA, and they were ultimately successful. Women did win the right to legal abortion with the *Roe v. Wade* decision in 1973, though controversy over that ruling continues today. Gay rights activists continued their work as well, though not without controversy and push-back from the conservative community**.

Nixon appointed Warren Burger as chief justice of the Supreme Court, thus beginning a shift toward greater conservatism within that body. Viewed in retrospect, many of the Burger Court decisions seem more centrist than conservative, but they were still a significant change from the liberal years of Chief Justice Earl Warren.

Many Americans worried over how life in the late twentieth century was changing traditional values. Single-parent households were on the rise, more women were moving into the workplace, and union workers were not able to depend on collective bargaining to advance their causes. Some popular culture centered on the lives of blue-collar workers. Rap and hip-hop spoke of the lives of working-class blacks in the deindustrialized urban city. **Access to birth control pills gave women control over reproduction, changing in many ways the traditional relationships between men and women. Sexuality and social problems became the focus of Hollywood. Many feared that traditional middle-class marriage would become a thing of the past.**

Churches responded with what some have called another "Great Awakening." Evangelical Protestantism gained popularity, using the medium of television to reach immense audiences. They sought to translate their "Christian family values" into a political agenda that would have a tremendous impact in the last decades of the twentieth century.

Period 8 Practice Questions

Multiple-Choice Questions

Questions 1–3 refer to the excerpt below.

> "The Great Society rests on abundance and liberty for all. It demands an end to poverty and racial injustice, to which we are totally committed in our time. But that is just the beginning.
>
> "The Great Society is a place where every child can find knowledge to enrich his mind and to enlarge his talents. It is a place where leisure is a welcome chance to build and reflect, not a feared cause of boredom and restlessness. It is a place where the city of man serves not only the needs of the body and the demands of commerce but the desire for beauty and the hunger for community.
>
> "It is a place where man can renew contact with nature. It is a place which honors creation for its own sake and for what it adds to the understanding of the race. It is a place where men are more concerned with the quality of their goals than the quantity of their goods.
>
> "But most of all, the Great Society is not a safe harbor, a resting place, a final objective, a finished work. It is a challenge constantly renewed, beckoning us toward a destiny where the meaning of our lives matches the marvelous products of our labor."

Lyndon Johnson, *The Great Society*, May 22, 1964

1. The issues described in the excerpt addressed the growing concern over which of the following post-war concerns?
   (a) The prevalence of impoverishment
   (b) Nuclear energy
   (c) Nationalist movements in Asia
   (d) Appropriate power of the executive branch

2. The implementation of Great Society legislation most directly led to which of the following ongoing debates?
   (a) The level of commitment to containing communism
   (b) The costs associated with the military-industrial complex
   (c) Generational changes in political ideologies
   (d) The use of federal power to address social issues

3. Which of the following political movements most directly challenged the ideas of the Great Society expressed in the excerpt above?
   (a) Civil Rights
   (b) Conservatism
   (c) Environmentalism
   (d) Feminism

Questions 4–6 refer to the graph below.

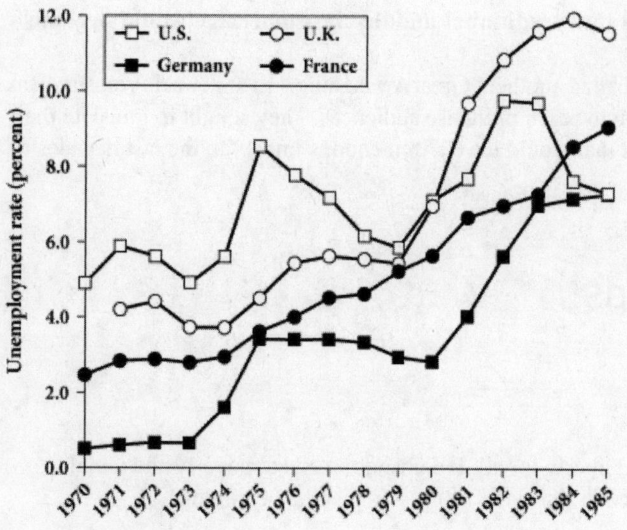

Rising Unemployment

4. Which of the following best represents a long-term historical cause of the information about U.S. unemployment in the graph above?
   (a) Energy crises due to a reliance on foreign oil
   (b) Environmental regulations established by the federal government
   (c) Postwar decolonization efforts in the Middle East
   (d) Migration patterns to the Sun Belt

5. Which of the following best represents the political response of many Americans to the information presented in the graph above?
   (a) A call for solutions from the federal government
   (b) The establishment of a national energy policy
   (c) An erosion in public confidence in the federal government
   (d) A new and more aggressive foreign policy

6. The economy of the 1970s most directly led to which of the following developments in the 1980s?
   (a) Clashes between generations over cultural values
   (b) A call for greater individual freedoms in economic choices
   (c) A demand for more economic power at the state level
   (d) An effort to limit the power of the federal government to regulate the economy

Questions 7–9 refer to the graph below.

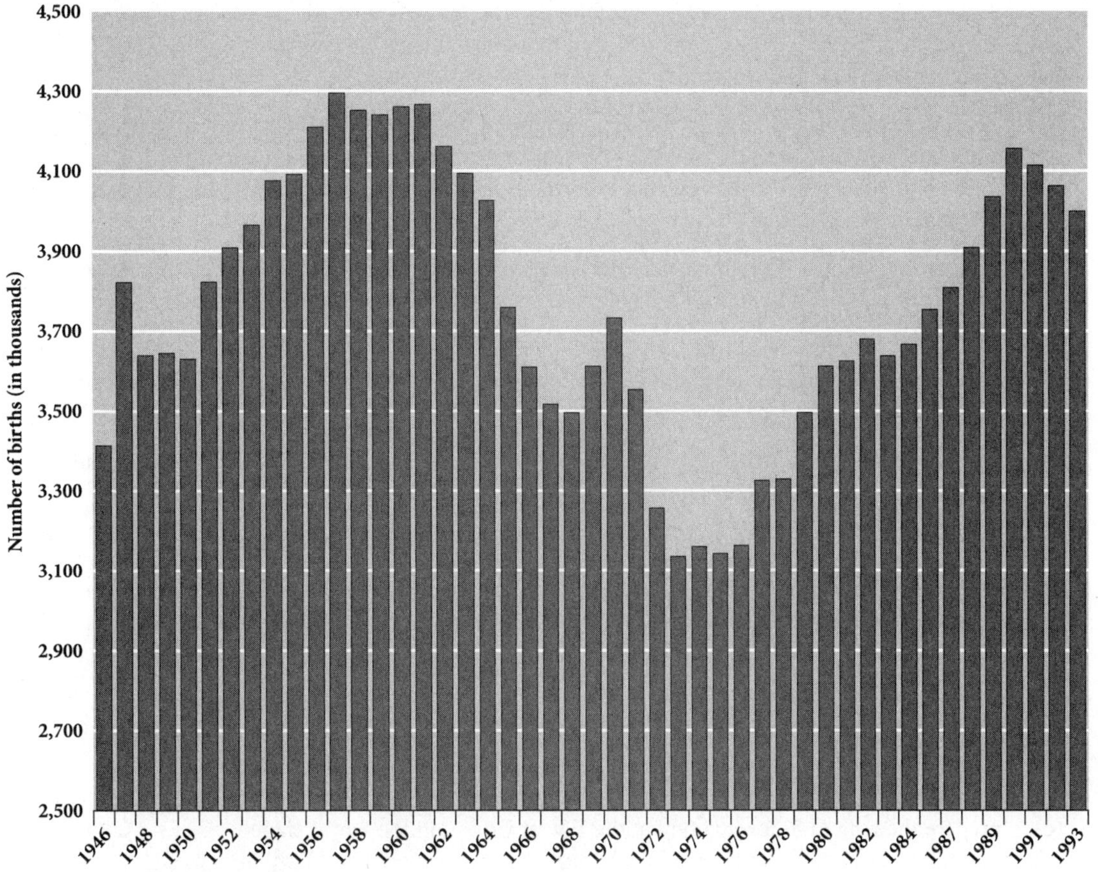

U.S. Birthrates, 1946–1993

7. Which of the following best explains the trend illustrated in the chart above from 1946-1958?
   (a) Widespread economic growth in the postwar years
   (b) New mass media in the postwar years
   (c) An increase in federal regulation of the economy in the postwar years
   (d) Global political power in the postwar years

8. The result of the increase in birthrates led to which of the following societal developments in the 1950s?
   (a) Programs to end poverty
   (b) A restriction of new mass media outlets
   (c) An increase in conformity
   (d) A decrease in internal migration patterns

9. Many children, born between 1946-1956, represented which of the following developments?
   (a) An increase in social mobility among groups migrating north
   (b) New technological developments that altered mass media
   (c) Generational disputes over political and cultural values
   (d) A belief in an aggressive foreign policy.

Questions 10–12 refer to the excerpt below.

"This bill, which I have signed today, substantially carries out most of the recommendations made by me in a speech on July 28, 1943, and more specifically in messages to the Congress dated October 27, 1943, and November 23, 1943:

"1. It gives servicemen and women the opportunity of resuming their education or technical training after discharge, or of taking a refresher or retrainer course, not only without tuition charge up to $500 per school year, but with the right to receive a monthly living allowance while pursuing their studies.

"2. It makes provision for the guarantee by the Federal Government of not to exceed 50 percent of certain loans made to veterans for the purchase or construction of homes, farms, and business properties.

"3. It provides for reasonable unemployment allowances payable each week up to a maximum period of one year, to those veterans who are unable to find a job.

"4. It establishes improved machinery for effective job counseling for veterans and for finding jobs for returning soldiers and sailors.

"5. It authorizes the construction of all necessary additional hospital facilities.

"6. It strengthens the authority of the Veterans Administration to enable it to discharge its existing and added responsibilities with promptness and efficiency."

President Franklin D. Roosevelt, Statement on Signing the GI Bill, June 22, 1944

10. The bill described above was primarily designed to
    (a) ease the adjustment of veterans into society and prevent a postwar depression.
    (b) demobilize the armed forces as quickly as possible.
    (c) prepare the United States to combat the Soviet Union on the world stage.
    (d) retain women's places in the workforce that had been necessitated by World War II.

11. Which of the following represents an immediate historical consequence of the ideas expressed in the excerpt above?
    (a) An increase in federal spending in inner cities
    (b) Challenges by artists and writers to cultural norms
    (c) Economic equality across racial lines
    (d) An increase in social mobility

12. The ideas relevant to the role of the federal government compares best to which of the following prior developments?
    (a) Jacksonian Democracy
    (b) Free Labor
    (c) Populism
    (d) New Deal Legislation

END OF MULTIPLE-CHOICE SECTION

Short-Answer Questions

"Let every nation know, whether it wishes us well or ill, that we shall pay any price, bear any burden, meet any hardship, support any friend, oppose any foe to assure the survival and the success of liberty. . . .

"But neither can two great and powerful groups of nations take comfort from our present course—both sides overburdened by the cost of modern weapons, both rightly alarmed by the steady spread of the deadly atom, yet both racing to alter that uncertain balance of terror that stays the hand of mankind's final war.

"So let us begin anew—remembering on both sides that civility is not a sign of weakness, and sincerity is always subject to proof. Let us never negotiate out of fear. But let us never fear to negotiate."

John F. Kennedy, Inaugural Address, 1961

1. Using the excerpt above, answer a, b, and c.

   (a) Briefly explain ONE historical development in the period from 1945-1960 that explains the claims made in the excerpt above?

   (b) Briefly explain ONE historical event or development in the period from 1960-1970 that resulted from the claims made in the excerpt above.

   (c) Briefly explain ANOTHER historical event or development in the period 1960-1970 that resulted from the claims made in the excerpt above.

2. Using the three maps on the following page, answer a, b, and c.

   (a) Briefly explain ONE political event or development that accounts for the change depicted in the maps.

   (b) Briefly explain ONE specific economic event or development that accounts for the change depicted in the maps.

   (c) Briefly explain ONE specific social event or development that accounts for the change depicted in the maps.

END OF SHORT-ANSWER SECTION

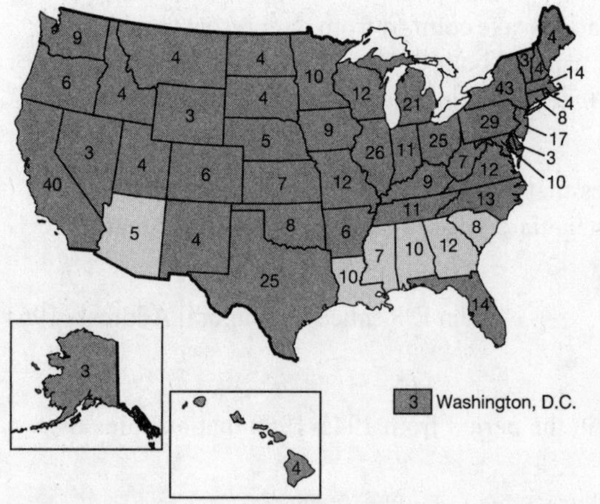

Candidate	Electoral Vote	Popular Vote	Percent of Popular Vote
Lyndon B. Johnson (Democrat)	486	43,121,085	61.1
Barry M. Goldwater (Republican)	52	27,145,161	38.5

The Presidential Election of 1964

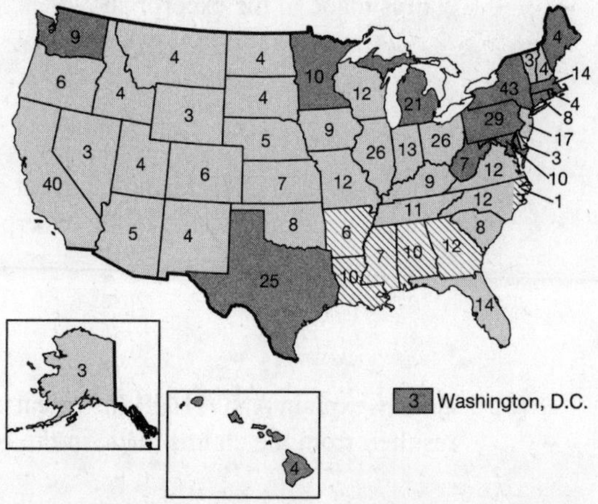

Candidate	Electoral Vote	Popular Vote	Percent of Popular Vote
Richard M. Nixon (Republican)	301	31,770,237	43.4
Hubert H. Humphrey (Democrat)	191	31,270,533	42.7
George C. Wallace (American Independent)	46	9,906,141	13.5
Minor parties	—	239,908	—

The Presidential Election of 1968

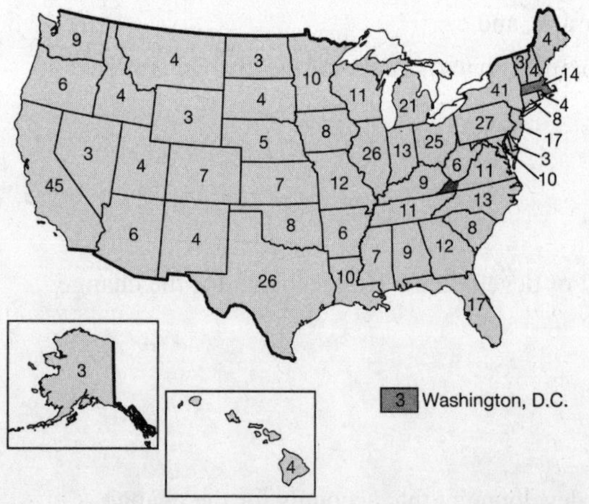

Candidate	Electoral Vote	Popular Vote	Percent of Popular Vote
Richard Nixon (Republican)	520	47,169,911	60.7
George McGovern (Democrat)	17	29,170,383	37.5
John Hospers (Libertarian)	1	3,674	0.0

The Presidential Election of 1972

Document-Based Question

Directions: The following question is based on the accompanying documents. The documents have been edited for this exercise. Spend approximately 15 minutes planning and 45 minutes writing your answer. Write an essay that does the following:

- States an appropriate thesis that directly addresses all parts of the question.
- Supports the thesis or argument with evidence from all or all but one of the documents AND your knowledge of U.S. history beyond the documents.
- Analyzes all or all but one of the documents.
- Explain the significance of the author's point of view, author's purpose, historical context, and/or audience for at least three documents.
- Uses historical evidence beyond the documents to support your argument.
- Places the argument in the context of broader regional, national, or global processes.
- Incorporates all of the elements above into a convincing essay.

Question: Evaluate the relative importance of different factors that caused foreign and domestic challenges during the period from 1968-1980.

Document 1

Source: David Falconer, U.S. National Archives, ca. 1973

David Falconer/EPA/National Archives

Document 2

Source: *New York Times*, New York Post, New York Daily News, Oct. 30, 1975

AP Photo

Document 3

Source: President Gerald R. Ford, Address to Joint Session of the Congress on U.S. Foreign Policy, April 10, 1975

The North Vietnamese, from the moment they signed the Paris accords, systematically violated the cease-fire and other provisions of the agreement. Flagrantly disregarding the ban on the infiltration of troops, the North Vietnamese illegally introduced over 350,000 men into the south. In direct violation of the agreement, they sent in the most modern equipment in massive amounts. Meanwhile, they continued to receive large quantities of supplies and arms from their friends.

In the face of this situation, the United States—torn as it was by the emotions of a decade of war—was unable to respond. We deprived ourselves by law of the ability to enforce the agreement, thus giving North Vietnam assurance that it could violate that agreement with impunity. . . . Encouraged by these developments, the North Vietnamese, in recent months, began sending even their reserve divisions into South Vietnam. Some 20 divisions, virtually their entire army, are now in South Vietnam. The Government of South Vietnam, uncertain of further American assistance, hastily ordered a strategic withdrawal to more defensible positions.

Document 4

Source: Fire on the Cuyahoga River, 1952

Bettmann/Getty Images

Document 5

Source: *Report of the President's Commission on the Accident at Three Mile Island*, October 30, 1979

At 4:00 a.m. on March 28, 1979, a serious accident occurred at the Three Mile Island 2 nuclear power plant near Middletown, Pennsylvania. The accident was initiated by mechanical malfunctions in the plant and made much worse by a combination of human errors in responding to it. . . . During the next 4 days, the extent and gravity of the accident was unclear to the managers of the plant, to federal and state officials, and to the general public. What is quite clear is that its impact, nationally and internationally, has raised serious concerns about the safety of nuclear power.

Document 6

Source: Letter from U.S. President Jimmy Carter to Ayatollah Ruhollah Khomeini of Iran, November 6, 1979

In the name of the American people, I ask that you release unharmed all Americans presently detained in Iran and those held with them and allow them to leave your country safely and without delay. I ask you to recognize the compelling humanitarian reasons, firmly based in international law, for doing so.

Document 7

Source: U.S. inflation rate, 1960–2000.

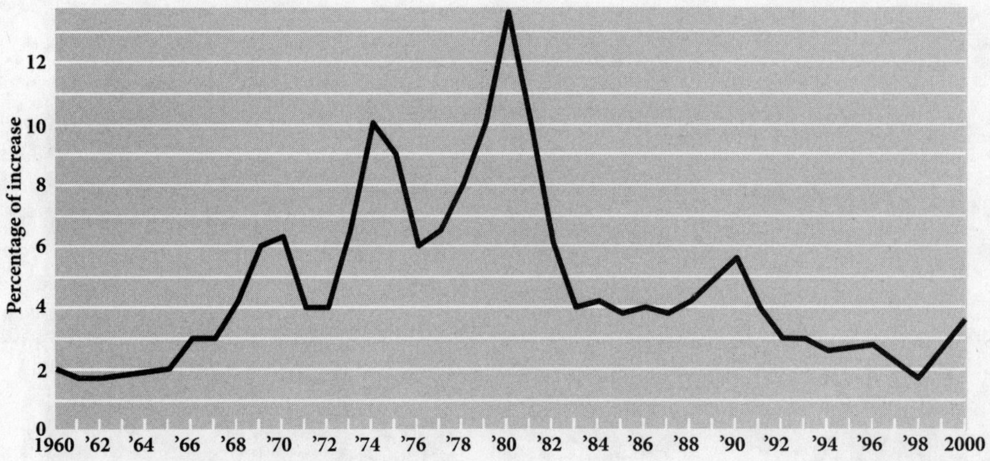

END OF DOCUMENT-BASED SECTION

PERIOD 9, 1980–PRESENT

Overview

The last decades of the twentieth century saw a resurgence of conservatism in the United States that stressed the importance of traditional values and rejected liberal views about society and the role of government. Conservatism was fuelled by a loss of faith in the ability of the government to solve problems, a growth in religious fundamentalism, economic challenges, and disillusionment with elected officials. Evangelical Christian organizations became politically active and sought to limit the influence of liberal social and political trends of earlier decades.

Conservatives found that some of the government programs they wanted to end enjoyed wide popularity with the general public. They were more successful in their efforts to limit taxes and deregulate industries than they were with their moral and social initiatives. Many "big government" programs were too popular for Republicans to cut or eliminate.

The Reagan administration made anticommunism a centerpiece of its foreign policy, though the president's cordial relations with the Soviet leader, Mikhail Gorbachev, led to productive talks and arms reductions on both sides. With the end of the Cold War, the role of the United States changed dramatically from one of the two superpowers to a nation expected to be a global peacekeeper.

The attacks on the World Trade Center and Pentagon by Al Qaeda on September 11, 2001, however, placed the Middle East and the war on terrorism at the center of U.S. concerns. U.S. policy was refocused as the United States launched military attacks on both Afghanistan and Iraq, and efforts to achieve security and safety at home raised questions about the protection of civil liberties and the safeguarding of human rights.

As the twenty-first century dawned, the United States faced significant social, economic, and demographic changes. The country was now part of the global economy, and both information technology jobs and manufacturing jobs moved overseas. Union power declined, and real wages were stalled. Politicians were unable to agree on the right course concerning free trade agreements, tariffs, and government support for domestic industries. Continuing conflict in the Middle East threatened the oil supply, and local sources were not able to meet domestic demand. Computer technology and the Internet changed the way people did business, interacted socially, and were connected to the rest of the world.

The country's population continued to move to the South and West, in search of jobs and friendlier climates. These same regions saw an influx of immigrants from Latin America and Asia, who filled entry-level jobs in those parts of the country. Issues of citizenship and illegal immigration dominated political debates. These and other demographic changes led to further discussions over issues like gender roles, family makeup, and group identity.

Key Terms

Be sure that you understand the meaning of these terms and their relevance in U.S. history. Page numbers from the textbook are provided.

New conservatism (938. 947)
Ronald Reagan (940–941)
9/11 (990–991)
War on Terror (991)
Climate change (995–996)
Moral Majority (944–945)
Supply-side economics (949–950)
Iran-Contra Affair (959–961)
Persian Gulf War (965–966)
Globalization (934)
Contract with America (987)
NAFTA (974–975)
Immigration Reform and Control Act (980)
Patriot Act (991)
Affordable Care Act (995)

Focus Questions

As you study Period 9, keep the following thematic questions in mind.

American and National Identity

- How has multiculturalism changed the American social, economic, and political landscape?
- Why has there been so much debate over immigration and multiculturalism in the past few decades?
- How does regional identity influence American politics in the twenty-first century?
- What issues have divided feminists from the Religious Right?

Work, Exchange, and Technology

- How was the Religious Right able to use the media so successfully to promote its message?
- What is supply-side economics, and why was this a central element of Ronald Reagan's economic policy?
- What were the most important achievements and the most notable shortcomings of Reagan's fiscal policies?
- What was the impact of deregulation on consumers, the federal bureaucracy, workers' rights, and the environment?
- What economic crises did Reagan face in his second term, and how did he confront them?
- How have computer technology and the omnipresence of the World Wide Web both illustrated the irony of free-market capitalism and served as a force for democratization?
- How do international organizations influence the operation of the American economy? Why are these organizations able to exert so much influence?
- What were the key aspects of President George W. Bush's economic policies, and how effective were these policies in ensuring economic progress and stability?
- What caused the Great Recession that began in 2007?
- What economic policies were implemented by Presidents Bush and Obama to help the economy recover, and how successful were these policies?

Geography and the Environment

- What actions did Reagan take that alarmed many environmentalists?
- Why has the topic of climate change stimulated so much conversation and controversy?

Migration and Settlement

- How and why have immigration patterns changed since 1965?
- How have arguments over affirmative action been linked to the debate over immigration?
- What demographic shifts have occurred since the 1980s, and what has been the impact of these changes?

Politics and Power

- Why did conservatives oppose Great Society liberalism?
- What were the three legs of the conservative movement, and how did conservatives attempt to implement their agenda?

- Why did conservative religious groups become politically active?
- In what ways did the Carter presidency make Ronald Reagan's path to the White House easier?
- Why was Reagan able to build such a disparate coalition?
- What were Reagan's domestic priorities, and to what extent did he achieve his goals?
- What are the twin dilemmas that have defined the period from the end of the Cold War to the present, and how have they influenced the American political, economic, and social landscapes?
- What was "the contradiction between New Right ideology and political reality"?
- How successful was Reagan in using the courts to further conservatism?
- During the Reagan years, why did government not shrink as much as Reagan would have liked?
- In what ways was Reagan "a master of the politics of symbolism"?
- Why was the Reagan administration slow to respond to the AIDS crisis?
- What was Bill Clinton's "third way," and to what extent was he successful in changing the American political landscape?
- Why was President Clinton impeached, and what were the consequences of his impeachment?
- Why, despite opposition to wars in Iraq and Afghanistan and concern over rising deficits at home, was President Bush reelected in 2004?
- What electoral shifts were seen in the presidential elections of 2008 and 2012?
- Often in American history, we see that unexpected events shape a presidency. What examples do you see of this in the late twentieth and early twenty-first centuries?
- What accounts for the extreme partisanship we see in American politics in the twenty-first century?
- What issues and policies have caused decreased public trust in government?
- What factors account for the emergence of the Tea Party as a force in American politics?

America in the World

- How did President Reagan's approach to dealing with the Soviets differ from that of his predecessors?
- What were the specifics of Reagan's Cold War policies?
- Despite Reagan's commitment to the expansion of democracy, why did he sometimes support authoritarian dictatorships?
- In what ways did the Iran-Contra affair threaten the Reagan presidency?
- What factors were most significant in bringing about the fall of communism in the Soviet Union and Eastern Europe?
- What was the impact of the September 11 attacks on American foreign and domestic policy?
- What issues have contributed to the continued tensions between the United States and the people and governments of the Middle East?
- What events best illustrate the difficulties the United States has had in the Middle East?
- In what ways have globalization and the end of Cold War duality shaped regional, ethnic, and religious conflict in the twenty-first century?
- What foreign policy challenges did President Obama faced, and how successfully did he address them?
- Why, after achieving military victory in Iraq, was it so difficult to end the American military presence there?

- What accounts for the continued destabilization of the Middle East?
- What do you see as the promises and the dangers of globalization?
- What twenty-first-century challenges do the expansion of the European Union and the emergence of China as an economic power present to the United States?

American and Regional Culture

- In what ways did intellectuals contribute to the conservative resurgence?
- What have been the most significant differences between liberalism and conservatism in the past thirty-five years?
- How did Americans view "the culture of success"?
- Why have Americans continued to fight about what your textbook calls "the Battles of the 60s"?

Social Structures

- What key battlegrounds have emerged in the clash over "family values"?
- In what ways has the Supreme Court been a major player in the culture wars?

Thematic Timeline

TIME	Key Events
1980	
	American and National Identity • Ronald Reagan campaigns for presidency (1980), says United States is "greatest country in the world" • Reagan campaigns for reelection (1984) with theme of "It's morning in America"
	Work, Exchange, and Technology • Recession (1981–1982) followed by strong growth (1982–1987) • Reagan tax cut (1981) • Apple IIe personal computer introduced (1983) • National debt triples (1981–1989)
	Geography and the Environment • Reagan appoints the antienvironmentalist James Watt as secretary of interior
	Migration and Settlement • Rise in Latino and Asian immigration • Californians vote to establish English as official language (1986)
	Politics and Power • New Right helps elect Ronald Reagan president • Iran-Contra scandal (1985–1987) • George H. W. Bush elected president (1988)
	America in the World • Reagan begins arms buildup • United States arms Contras in Nicaragua • Berlin Wall comes down (1989)

American and Regional Culture

- Renewed emphasis on material success and the "rich and famous"
- *Webster v. Reproductive Health Services* (1989)

Social Structures

- HIV/AIDS crisis prompts national conversation about homosexuality

1990

American and National Identity

- Americans debate multiculturalism
- World Trade Organization (WTO) protests in Seattle against globalization (1999)

Work, Exchange, and Technology

- Internet gains in popularity
- Recession (1990–1991)
- NAFTA ratified (1993)
- Debt reduction under Bill Clinton

Geography and the Environment

- New states emerge in central Asia from dissolution of Soviet Union (1989–1991)
- Oil at center of Gulf War
- European Union created (1992)

Migration and Settlement

- California bans bilingual education in public schools (1998)

Politics and Power

- Bill Clinton elected president (1992)
- Republican resurgence (1994)
- Welfare reform (1996)
- Clinton impeached and acquitted (1998–1999)

America in the World

- Persian Gulf War (1990–1991)
- USSR breaks apart; end of Cold War
- World Trade Center bombed (1993)
- NATO begins peacekeeping efforts in Bosnia (1995)

American and Regional Culture

- Pat Buchanan declares "culture war" (1992)
- Proposition 209 ends affirmative action in California universities (1996)

Social Structures

- Defense of Marriage Act (1998)

2000

American and National Identity

- "War on terror" becomes fixture in American discourse
- USA PATRIOT Act authorizes new domestic surveillance to combat terrorism
- Abu Ghraib (2004) revelations document U.S. torture practices

Work, Exchange, and Technology

- Great Recession (2007–2010)
- President Bush asks for and receives bank bailout from Congress (2008)
- Unemployment hits 10 percent

Geography and the Environment

- Kyoto Protocol international treaty on climate change signed by 84 nations (2005) but not by United States

TIME	Key Events
	Migration and Settlement • California, Texas, Hawaii, and New Mexico become "majority-minority" states (where the majority of the population is composed of different nonwhite groups) **Politics and Power** • George W. Bush wins presidency in contested election (2000) • USA PATRIOT Act (2001) • Barack Obama elected first African American president (2008) **America in the World** • Al Qaeda attacks World Trade Center and Pentagon (2001) • United States and allies invade Afghanistan (2002) • United States invades Iraq (2003) **American and Regional Culture** • *Lawrence v. Texas* (2003) **Social Structures** • Massachusetts becomes first state to legalize same-sex marriage (2004); nine states follow by 2012
2010	
	American and National Identity • Presidential candidates debate whether United States is declining as a nation and the role of international trade and immigration (2016) **Work, Exchange, and Technology** • Financial industry accounts for largest share of GDP among all industry sectors **Geography and the Environment** • President Obama issues Clean Power Plan through executive action (2015) • President Trump rescinds portions of the Clean Power Plan and orders reconsideration of the remainder (2017) **Migration and Settlement** • Obama's 2012 electoral coalition heavily African American, Hispanic, Asian American, female, and young • President Donald Trump bans immigrants from six majority-Muslim countries (2017) **Politics and Power** • Healthcare reform (2010) • Tea Party helps Republicans regain control of House of Representatives • Barack Obama reelected president (2012) • Donald Trump elected president (2016) **America in the World** • Arab Spring (2010–2012) • Osama bin Laden killed (2011) • Last combat troops withdrawn from Iraq (2011) • Syrian civil war and refugee crisis (2011–present) **American and Regional Culture** • *Obergefell v. Hodges* (2015) upholds same-sex marriage as legal in all states **Social Structures** • "Black Lives Matter" Movement

America's History Chapter Summaries

(required AP® content in bold)

Chapter 29
Conservative America in the Ascent, 1980–1991

Chapter 29 focuses on the ascendancy of conservatism in the 1980s. The 1970s witnessed a United States divided by the Vietnam War, worn out by social unrest, and panicked by economic uncertainty. **Many Americans developed a distrust of the liberalism of the Great Society, and the New Right took the lead in the Republican Party. Ronald Reagan was their champion, offering smaller government, deregulation of the economy, Christian morality, and a new determination to win the Cold War.**

Reagan built on the grassroots conservatism that had supported Barry Goldwater in his presidential bid in 1964. He also gained support from conservative women's organizations who did not feel comfortable with the women's liberation movements. The **new conservative movement rested on three principles: anticommunism, free-market economics, and religious moralism**. A number of journals and policy groups picked up this cause, among them William F. Buckley's *National Review* and the conservative Heritage Foundation. They were also supported by the new "Religious Right," **evangelical Protestants who opposed abortion, divorce, premarital sex, and feminism**. Their message was often spread by televangelists who sought to build a conservative coalition that would undo what they felt were the excesses of the Great Society.

This conservative coalition found a perfect target in President Jimmy Carter. Carter was elected in 1976 as a Washington outsider who had no taint attached to him of the Watergate scandal that had brought down President Richard Nixon. His outsider status proved to be his undoing, however, as many found him naive and idealistic when faced with international realities. His lasting legacy was the Camp David Accords, a "framework for peace" between the **Israelis and Palestinians in the Middle East**. Most of his other initiatives foundered: Strategic arms limitation (SALT II) was not approved by the Senate, a boycott of the 1980 Summer Olympics in Moscow was unpopular even though the Soviets had invaded Afghanistan, and the Iranian Revolution left more than fifty Americans held hostage in the Tehran Embassy for nearly a year.

In this climate of uncertainty and declining public trust, the Republicans seized their opportunity in 1980, nominating a confident and poised Ronald Reagan for the presidency. Reagan received over 50 percent of the popular vote in the election, and the New Right's bid for power was a success. Reagan had experience with the media from his years as a Hollywood actor, but he also had experience with industry and government, having worked with General Electric and served as governor of California. His core supporters were relatively affluent white Protestants who wanted balanced budgets, lower crime, and limits to social welfare. He also gained support from southern Democrats, who had been far too conservative to be comfortable with the Democratic agenda for some time. He spoke of supporting states' rights to a receptive audience. The Republicans also won the support of the Religious Right, as well as of blue-collar Catholics who shared many of their same concerns.

Reagan advocated increased defense spending to prosecute the Cold War. He advanced an economic policy that came to be known as "Reaganomics" or "supply-side economics." This approach advocated investment in production while at the same time lowering taxes on corporations and wealthy individuals, who would be expected to reinvest in the economy. Increasing supply would generate more demand, thereby energizing the economy for everyone. **Reagan supported tax cuts that benefitted primarily the wealthy, and he supported cuts in federal expenditures for a number of social programs**. Congress balked at these cuts, however. David Stockman, Reagan's budget director, began to voice some concerns about the soundness of supply-side economics, questioning the assumption that prosperity would "trickle down," as Reagan's program promised. In addition, **Reagan's increases in military spending increased the national debt, something the Republicans had promised to reduce**.

Attempts at the deregulation of federal agencies also led to unanticipated problems. Environmentalists, for example, were dismayed at attempts to undermine the Environmental Protection Agency, and eventually Reagan backed off somewhat. Reagan did have a lasting impact on the Supreme Court, appointing three Supreme Court justices with solid conservative credentials. Sandra Day O'Connor was the first woman appointed to the Supreme Court. In addition, Reagan appointed more than 350 federal court judges, most with conservative leanings. He chose William Rehnquist as chief justice of the Supreme Court, who led a Court that reversed a number of the more liberal decisions of the earlier Warren and Burger courts.

Reagan was president during the nation's first awareness of the HIV/AIDS epidemic, though it would take more than a decade for the country to see this virus as more than the "gay disease."

Reagan was easily reelected in 1984, emphasizing the economic recovery the country experienced during his first term, though some part of that was due to the OPEC decision to increase oil production and sales. **The nation's heavy industries continued to struggle with foreign competition, but service industries were growing, giving the country a sense of returning prosperity.**

The 1980s also saw the dawning computer age. The PC had arrived, thanks to the work of innovators like Bill Gates, Paul Allen, and Steve Jobs. **Computers would change the nature of both the work space and personal life in the next two decades.**

During Reagan's presidency, the Soviet Union collapsed as its leader, Mikhail Gorbachev, sought to reform Soviet society and foreign policy. **Reagan replaced a number of his hardline advisors and moved toward détente with the Soviet Union.** Soviet President Gorbachev tried *glasnost* (openness) and *perestroika* (economic restructuring) to save the Soviet system, but the Soviet Union dissolved in 1991. While many in the United States were eager to take credit for the fall of the Soviet Union, most historians agreed that it collapsed due to its own internal weaknesses. Pressure from the United States did play a role but only a secondary one.

Ronald Reagan left office with social welfare liberalism on the defensive. He had changed the political conversation in favor of increased power among conservatives. He was succeeded by his former vice president, George H. W. Bush, a former CIA director and a loyal follower of President Reagan's policies. Bush faced an early crisis in the Middle East when Saddam Hussein of Iraq launched an invasion of neighboring Kuwait in a dispute over access to oil reserves. The United States joined a United Nations-led coalition of countries to liberate Kuwait. The victory of UN troops gave the United States a new standing in the Middle East, though the end of the Soviet Union would result in a **postwar world that would make the Middle East, and the world in general, much more complex for all the players.**

Chapter 30
National and Global Dilemmas, 1989 to the Present

For Americans, the years between the end of the Cold War and the present have been defined by twin dilemmas: What is the position of the United States in the global arena, and how does the United States manage cultural conflicts and still ensure economic opportunity for all Americans?

By the end of the twentieth century, globalization saw the rapid spread of capitalism around the world, increases in trade and commerce, and the **diffusion of communications technology, including the Internet.** Some nations benefitted while others did not.

The bipolar world of two superpowers was gone, and multiple power centers began to emerge. In 1992, the nations of Western Europe created the European Union (EU), encompassing the third largest population in the world, after China and India. Their currency, the euro, rivaled the dollar and the Japanese yen for supremacy as an international currency. China became the world's fastest-growing economic power, supplying the American market with inexpensive imports. **All of these developments challenged America's global economic position.**

The United States entered a new era of global economics and policy in the 1990s. The world's leading capitalist nations formed a group known as the Group of Eight (G8—the United States, Britain, Germany, France, Italy, Japan, Canada, and Russia) to oversee major international financial organizations, including the World Bank, the International Monetary Fund (IMF), and the General Agreement on Tariffs and Trade (GATT). In 1995, the GATT evolved into the World Trade Organization (WTO), with over 150 nations participating.

The United States, Canada, and Mexico signed the North American Free Trade Agreement (NAFTA) in 1993 to create a free trade zone in North America. Other similar regional organizations were organized around the world. Multinational corporations became the norm in international trade in the search for new markets all over the globe. Financial deregulation made investment easier and in some cases led to spectacular profits. At the same time, the potential for equally spectacular loss was also a possibility, something that became clear in the financial crisis of 2008. The technology revolution fueled much of this growth. By the 1990s, personal computers and the Internet were no longer just for the few. **The World Wide Web opened the possibilities of the Internet to people around the globe**.

By the 1990s, **the United States had become an increasingly pluralistic society. Millions of new immigrants became part of the electorate, coming from East Asia as well as Latin America since the passage of the Immigration and Nationality Act in 1965**. Many immigrants were here illegally, something that increasingly became part of the national political discourse. **Conservatives and liberals argued over the question of whose values were to be the ones that characterized the American nation**. Some charged that the Great Society's welfare initiatives had weakened the traditional model of the two-parent household. **The abortion debate continued as well, with opposing sides lined up as either "prochoice" or "prolife." The gay rights movement continued to anger conservatives, now with the added push for the legal recognition of same-sex marriages. The Religious Right countered with the Defense of Marriage Act in 1998, allowing states to refuse to recognize gay marriages or civil unions as legal**.

Democrat Bill Clinton was elected to the presidency in 1992 in the midst of all this cultural wrangling. Clinton was president when the world witnessed the breakup of Yugoslavia and sectarian violence in the Balkans, an indication of the **changing nature of U.S. foreign policy**. The United States intervened as a part of a UN force to put a stop to the "ethnic cleansing" that characterized the attempts to form new states in that part of the world. The United States also faced hostility in the Middle East from Arab countries that felt that American foreign policy was too favorable toward Israel. This was also a time of the growth of radical fundamentalism in places like Saudi Arabia and Afghanistan, a movement the U.S. State Department largely underestimated, despite an attempt to bomb the World Trade Center in 1993. Clinton appointees identified a shadowy network of radical Islamists known as Al Qaeda.

The close election of 2000 brought George W. Bush into power, although it took a decision of the Supreme Court to validate the election results. The Bush administration immediately began to call for a return to the Reagan tax cuts, even though economists warned that massive tax cuts would only exacerbate federal debt. They did not heed these warnings, and as the Bush years progressed, the **national debt grew along with it**.

The bombing of the World Trade Center on September 11, 2001, shaped much of the Bush presidency. **The War on Terror, the Patriot Act, and the creation of the Department of Homeland Security were all responses of the Bush administration to the threats posed by Al Qaeda and other Islamic radicals**. The United States invaded both Afghanistan and Iraq in the name of rooting out terrorists and destroying weapons of mass destruction, though many of these justifications proved empty as time went on. The country misread the realities of the countries it had invaded, underestimating the difficulties of imposing Western values and government onto radically different cultures, and the hazards of fighting a war against unknown insurgents.

Bush was reelected in 2004, but his second term became one of crisis management. Hurricane Katrina devastated New Orleans in August 2005, and Bush was faulted for an inadequate response. The wars in Iraq and Afghanistan were increasingly unpopular. Then in 2008, the stock market crashed, taking housing prices and other major industries with it, the worst economic fall since the 1930s. This episode came to be known as the Great Recession.

The 2008 election brought Barack Obama into office, the nation's first African American president. He inherited two wars and an economic recession. He called for a "remaking of America," hoping to offer an optimistic tone to a jittery nation. Obama faced stiff opposition from many Republicans. Many of them responded with anger to his health reform proposal, the Patient Protection and Affordable Care Act. His opponents labeled it "Obamacare" and tried to stop its implementation. The bill passed and was affirmed by the Supreme Court. Obama also ended the "Don't ask, don't tell" policy in the military, and gays and lesbians were allowed to serve openly. He appointed two women to the Supreme Court.

The wars he inherited in Iraq and Afghanistan continued, with Obama determined to end the American presence in both places. The "Arab Spring," a wave of protests across the Middle East in 2011 that toppled a number of old regimes, at first held out promise for being liberating movements that might lead to greater democracy. Those hopes dimmed as many of the new regimes fell into new forms of autocracy, and most were not particularly friendly to U.S. interests. On the home front, Obama continued to try to address the issues of the national debt, immigration reform, America's new place in the global economy, increasing inequality in the United States, and the concerns over climate change. He also instituted the Patient Protection and Affordable Care Act, which was the first major reform of the national health care system since 1965.

The 2016 presidential election was one of the most surprising in more than a generation: celebrity businessman Donald Trump secured the majority of the electoral college and won the presidency. Since his inauguration, Trump has taken action to boost the economy, combat terrorism both on U.S. soil and abroad, and implement strict immigration and border protection policies.

Period 9 Practice Questions

Multiple-Choice Questions

Questions 1–4 refer to the excerpt below.

"These United States are confronted with an economic affliction of great proportions. We suffer from the longest and one of the worst sustained inflations in our national history. It distorts our economic decisions, penalizes thrift, and crushes the struggling young and the fixed-income elderly alike. It threatens to shatter the lives of millions of our people. . . .

"But great as our tax burden is, it has not kept pace with public spending. For decades, we have piled deficit upon deficit, mortgaging our future and our children's future for the temporary convenience of the present. . . .

"In this present crisis, government is not the solution to our problem. . . .

"It is my intention to curb the size and influence of the Federal establishment and to demand recognition of the distinction between the powers granted to the Federal Government and those reserved to the States or to the people. . . .

"It is no coincidence that our present troubles parallel and are proportionate to the intervention and intrusion in our lives that result from unnecessary and excessive growth of government."

Ronald Reagan, First Inaugural Address, January 20, 1981

1. Ronald Reagan's victory in the 1980 election signaled which of the following shifts in political thinking on the part of the American people?
   (a) A significant shift to the left from Americans fed up with the malaise of the 1970s
   (b) A massive growth in moderates dissatisfied with the bickering of extreme positions in the 1960s
   (c) A greater demand that government steer clear of moral issues such as abortion and prayer in schools
   (d) Movement toward greater conservatism by both major parties

2. The political climate of the 1980s led to which of the following?
   (a) Organized religion playing a greater role in politics
   (b) A major splintering of the Republican Party into liberal and conservative wings
   (c) Major growth in the Socialist Party's strength in presidential elections
   (d) Entrenchment of the Democratic Party in the "solid South"

3. Reagan was successful in all of his political aims as described in his First Inaugural Address EXCEPT

   (a) annual deficits by the federal government were eliminated and the national debt reduced.
   (b) social welfare programs were cut, leaving the poor in worse conditions than before.
   (c) environmental regulations on industry were reduced to promote productivity.
   (d) military appropriations were expanded and most Americans felt a resurgence of patriotic pride.

4. Which of the following represents an immediate consequence of the beliefs expressed by President Reagan in the excerpt above?

   (a) Elimination of Great Society legislation
   (b) Tax cuts and deregulation of industry
   (c) The ratification of the Equal Rights Amendment
   (d) An increase in social welfare programs

Questions 5–7 refer to the excerpt below.

> "A return to a missionary foreign policy was clearly evident under President Ronald Reagan. With references to the window of vulnerability and continual emphasis on the expansionist, evil empire of the Soviet Union, the Reagan Doctrine promised not only containment but also the rollback communism worldwide. It also led to a dramatic increase in defense spending and a renewed arms race with the Soviet Union. Central America and the Caribbean became the testing ground for his crusade. Yet, by Reagan's second term, it was becoming evident that this policy could not be sustained. With massive government deficits due to declining revenues and increased spending during his first term, the budget became a constraint on his activist foreign policy. Other factors, including substantive changes in the policies and governing principles of the Soviet Union under Mikhail Gorbachev, the stalemated civil wars in both El Salvador and Nicaragua despite tremendous aid from the United States, the Iran-Contra scandal, and the fact that Reagan and Gorbachev finally met one another and actually liked each other—all these led to yet another swing of the pendulum to a more pragmatic foreign policy."

Cliff Staten, *U.S. Foreign Policy since World War II*, 2005

5. How did U.S. foreign policy between 1990 and 2010 compare to that of President Reagan's described in the excerpt above?

   (a) The United States expanded its Cold War attempts to contain the spread of communism
   (b) The United States succeeded in not committing troops to European conflict
   (c) The United States successfully overthrew communist rule in Cuba
   (d) The United States expanded attempts to combat terrorism

6. The Reagan administration initially embraced which of the following attitudes toward the Soviet Union in the early 1980s?

   (a) A continuation of the détente policies of the preceding three presidential administrations
   (b) Negotiation with the Soviet Union to reduce the arms race
   (c) Confrontation designed to force the Soviet Union into economic hardship
   (d) Commitment of U.S. troops to aid Eastern European countries in their attempts to throw off Soviet domination

7. Which of the following represents an immediate consequence of the end of the Cold War during the decade following the Reagan administration?

   (a) An increase in nuclear weapons
   (b) Direct confrontation with other communist nations
   (c) Peacekeeping interventions in emerging nations
   (d) A national energy policy

Questions 8–10 refer to the two maps below.

8. Which of the following historical developments could be used as evidence to explain the political changes evident in the maps below?
   (a) The end of the Cold War
   (b) Demographic shifts as a result of migration patterns
   (c) Economic policies in the aftermath as a result of the war on terror
   (d) Debates over climate change

9. Which of the following represents an ongoing historical development relevant to the winner of each election?
   (a) Conflicts with communist nations
   (b) Conflicts in the Middle East
   (c) A decrease in immigration from Latin America
   (d) A decrease in technological innovation

10. The maps of the elections of 2000 and 2008 support which of the following conclusions?
   (a) Conservative political principles were favored by the majority of Americans
   (b) Democratic political power tended to be based in the northeastern quarter of the country and on the West Coast
   (c) Republicans controlled southern votes by increasing their appeal to African Americans
   (d) States with large rural populations tend to be more liberal than states with large urban populations

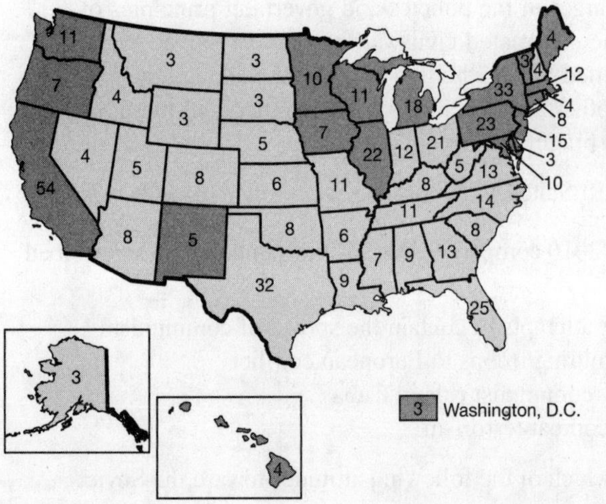

Candidate	Electoral Vote	Popular Vote	Percent of Popular Vote
George W. Bush (Republican)	271	50,456,062	47.8
Al Gore (Democrat)	267	50,996,862	48.4
Ralph Nader (Green Party)	0	2,858,843	2.7
Patrick J. Buchanan (Reform Party)	0	438,760	0.4

Election of 2000

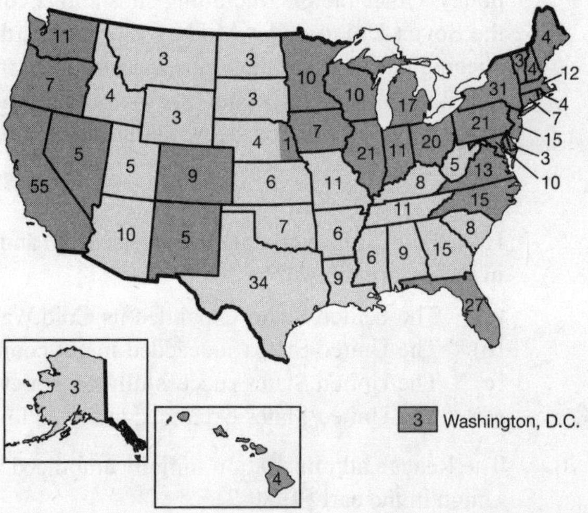

Candidate	Electoral Vote	Popular Vote	Percent of Popular Vote
Barack Obama (Democrat)	365	69,456,897	52.9
John McCain (Republican)	173	59,934,814	45.7

Election of 2008

END OF MULTIPLE-CHOICE SECTION

Short-Answer Question

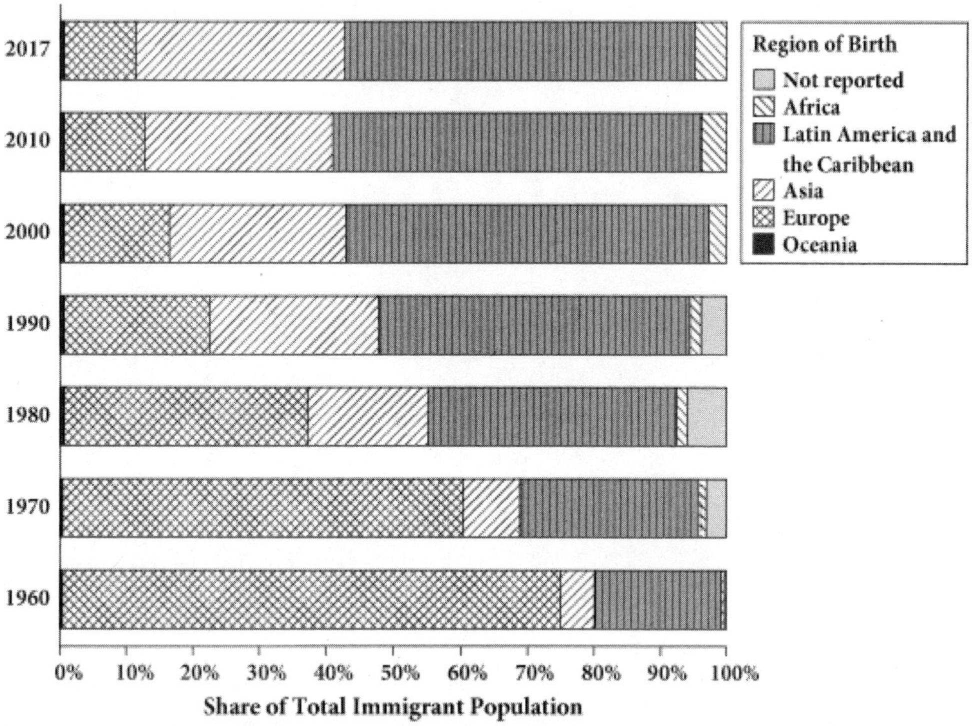

Regions of Birth for Immigrants in the United States, 1960–2017

1. Using the graph above, answer a, b, and c.

   (a) Briefly explain ONE historical factor that explains the changes in immigration illustrated in the graph above in the period between 1970 and 2000.

   (b) Briefly explain ONE historical outcome of the trends in the period from 1970 to 2000 illustrated in the graph above.

   (c) Briefly explain ONE historical factor that accounts for the increase in immigration to the United States from 1980-2000.

END OF SHORT-ANSWER SECTION

NOTES:

SECTION 2

Preparing for the AP® United States History Exam

The African American author James Baldwin once observed, "American history is longer, larger, more various, more beautiful, and more terrible than anything anyone has ever said about it." You have begun your in-depth examination of the story of the United States, and perhaps you've already discovered some beautiful and terrible truths that were new to you. You are also learning how historians examine and write about the past: you too can learn how to "do" history.

Rigorous historical study of the nation is both challenging and rewarding. The AP® Examination in May is your chance to demonstrate your mastery of U.S. history. Although the challenges of the course and test may feel overwhelming from time to time, with advance planning and consistent effort, you can enter the examination room with confidence. *Strive for a 5* will help you get there!

Registering for the Exam

Your teacher and school are probably facilitating your exam registration, but if not, make sure that you do not miss the registration deadline in the fall. If you are taking this exam without having taken the course or if your school does not offer AP® courses, or if you are unaffiliated with a school (for example, if you are home-schooled), check with the College Board to find the name of an AP® coordinator for your area. If you are anxious about other registration issues, consult the College Board's Web site (www.collegeboard.com) and locate the AP® home page.

Familiarizing Yourself with the Exam

If your teacher has not given you AP® exam questions as practice, you should examine the two practice tests in this book closely. You can also go to the AP® Web site (apcentral.collegeboard.com). Once there, search for information on the AP® U.S. History Exam. You can download the College Board's *curriculum framework,* which includes information about the exam as well as sample questions. If you are using a test-prep guide or any other resources linked to AP® U.S. History exams given before May 2019, remember that the new exam is much different.

The AP® U.S. History Exam is 3 hours 15 minutes long and consists of two sections and four parts. The first section of the exam contains multiple-choice and short-answer questions. The multiple-choice part consists of 55 questions arranged into sets of 2-5 questions that focus on a single primary source, secondary source, map, or illustration (these are known as *stimulus questions*). The multiple-choice questions test your knowledge of the key concepts and themes found in the *curriculum framework* as well as required content. You have 55 minutes to answer the multiple-choice questions.

The four short-answer questions focus on the themes and historical skills and processes required for the APUSH course. You will answer a key question in U.S. history, sometimes using stimuli such as a primary source or a secondary source. You have 40 minutes to answer three of the four short-answer questions.

The second section of the exam consists of two essay questions: a document-based question (DBQ) and a long essay question. The document-based question (60 minutes) tests your ability to analyze historical evidence and then to use that evidence to answer a historical question in a coherent, well-organized essay with a clear thesis, appropriate use of evidence, and a conclusion. You will have to analyze the evidence and support your thesis with specific, relevant historical evidence. For the long essay question (40 minutes), you have a choice between three questions. The long essay assesses your understanding of historical skills and processes and ability to analyze and synthesize significant events or issues in U.S. history. Questions are limited to the topics specifically mentioned in the curriculum framework's key concepts, but you must use historical examples to support your answer. These examples may come from the curriculum framework or from your text or your classroom discussions.

Setting Up a Review Schedule

Your teacher has factored the testing date into their course planning; they may also offer review sessions that are specifically applicable to the AP® test. Beyond what your teacher offers, be sure to set up your own review schedule, allowing time to review each of the nine parts of the textbook and nine periods of the course, take and then review the two practice tests in this *Strive for a 5,* and review any concepts that seem challenging.

The spring term at any high school can be hectic. Adding AP® exam preparation to your weekly schedule a few months prior to the exam, particularly if you are taking exams in more than one subject, is essential. Ideally, you should allow one week for reviewing each of the nine textbook parts, plus a week for taking and reviewing each of the practice tests. If you don't have time to go through the nine periods, at least take the practice tests to see what topics and skills you need to review. Cramming the night before the test is never a good idea. Your priority the evening before the test is to get a good night's sleep!

Successful Historical Writing

You will spend almost half of the time taking the AP® exam on planning and writing the two essays. Framing and responding to analytical questions is an essential part of what historians do; in fact, the poet W. H. Auden once noted, "History is, strictly speaking, the study of questions." The essay questions on the AP® exam have more than one correct approach. Whether you are writing an essay for your class or responding to the AP® exam, start by thinking about how you will frame your argument and use your time.

Effective historical writing differs from simple expression of opinion: you must use evidence to back up your generalizations and support your arguments. Good historical essay writing starts with a clearly articulated thesis and should build on a coherent organization.

What does it mean to organize your ideas effectively? Try this exercise. The following sentences are in scrambled order. Read them carefully and figure out how you can order them for maximum clarity. *Hint: Which sentence establishes an idea that unifies all of the other information? That one should come first.*

(a) The southern terrain and climate lent itself to farming large tracts of land for cash crops.
(b) Over time, southern planters came to view themselves as akin to landed gentry and shaped a patriarchal social structure that reinforced their authority.
(c) Geographic, economic, and social factors all played a part in advancing the South's dependence on slavery.
(d) The most affordable means of tending to the plantations' cash crops was using slaves.
(e) Slavery was an integral part of southern colonial society.

Write the corresponding letters for each sentence on how you think they should be ordered here:

Now that you've attempted to reorder the sentences, can you figure out what question was being asked? Here is the question: How did economic, geographic, and social factors encourage the growth of slavery as an important part of the economy of the southern colonies between 1607 and 1775? And here is how the paragraph can best be organized:

> Slavery was an integral part of southern colonial society (e). Geographic, economic, and social factors all played a part in advancing the South's dependence on slavery (c). The southern terrain and climate lent itself to farming large tracts of land for cash crops (a). The most affordable means of tending to the plantations' cash crops was using slaves (d). Over time, southern planters came to view themselves as akin to landed gentry and shaped a patriarchal social structure that reinforced their authority (b).

Note the paragraph's underlying logic: the thesis, or topic sentence, addresses the three factors that influenced the southern development of slavery. Those three factors are then addressed in the order they are first mentioned in the first sentence. Chronology is suggested in the last sentence, which begins, "Over time . . ."

Besides ordering your information thoughtfully, you should structure your response in a way that responds precisely to the question posed. After you have read a long essay or document-based question, ask yourself: "What is the question asking?" "How many paragraphs should my response have?" "What should the first paragraph include?" Be strategic. Remember how many essays the AP® exam readers have to read and evaluate in a very short period of time. Clarity and directness are essential qualities of successful responses.

First, draft your thesis. Your thesis should not be a restatement of the question; it should be your opinion *about* the question, backed up with the evidence supplied (in the case of the DBQ) and your own information. For example, if the essay is about the economy of the Chesapeake colonies in the colonial period, you will need to discuss tobacco. But the thesis would not be, "Tobacco was very important to the economy of the Chesapeake colonies." Rather, it should be something more like, "Tobacco cultivation created distinctive social, political, and cultural patterns in the Chesapeake colonies that persisted into the nineteenth century, particularly as slave labor became the primary means to grow and harvest tobacco."

Then think about how many paragraphs you will need, and sketch out an outline that includes the examples you will use as evidence to support your thesis. As you begin to write your supporting paragraphs, remember that sentences need to be clear and coherent, as do entire paragraphs. Each paragraph's topic sentence serves as the thesis for that paragraph; in addition, each paragraph should act as a building block toward proving the essay's main thesis. Keeping the essay's main thesis in mind throughout the writing process will ensure that the composition stays on topic.

Another key to excellent historical writing is narrative flow, which can be achieved by connecting each paragraph to the ones before and after by means of transitional words and phrases or a linking sentence. When you are reviewing and revising your own essays, ask yourself: "Does this paragraph logically follow from the preceding one?" "Does it add something significant to the thesis announced in the opening paragraph?" "Is the transition to the next paragraph smooth?" Paying attention to the transitions between your supporting paragraphs will set your writing apart.

Finally, an effective essay must have a conclusion that summarizes its main points and explains how those points interconnect. It is not the place to introduce new information. The conclusion should do more than merely restate the essay's original thesis; it is where you will validate your opinion. Avoid addressing the reader directly or using crutches like "in conclusion" or "in summary"; the content of the concluding paragraph alone should make its purpose clear.

NOTES:

Taking the AP® United States History Exam

This section provides an outline of the test's four parts and offers some basic strategies for tackling AP® questions successfully. All four types of questions are designed to test your mastery of both historical content and skills.

When starting the AP® U.S. History course, many students ask, "Are we going to have to memorize dates?" Here is the answer from the College Board: "Although there is little to be gained by rote memorization of names and dates in an encyclopedic manner, a student must be able to draw upon a reservoir of systematic factual knowledge in order to exercise analytic skills intelligently." In other words, you're going to have to know your material. Although you are not required to memorize specific dates, the importance of having a firm grasp of chronology and context cannot be overestimated; these are essential to understanding history.

Strategies for the Multiple-Choice Section

The multiple-choice questions on the examination require skills beyond simple recognition and recall. All of these questions include a source such as a text source, map, photograph, chart, or cartoon that you must analyze before making an answer choice. There are between two and five questions for each source. Some compare topics across time periods. All of the questions require you to make the best choice among four possible answers, several of which may be plausible but not specific enough.

The most important advice we can give you is to read the source and the possible choices extremely carefully. Some of the questions will relate directly to the source you have read, but others will require you to recall information from the course content.

Tips for Answering Multiple-Choice Questions

- Read each question carefully.
- Read all possible answers and cross out those you believe are incorrect; narrowing your choices gives you the chance to make an educated guess.
- Connect the specific information of the question to broader trends and themes.
- Assess the source carefully and eliminate answers that go beyond the bounds of the evidence given.
- Make a habit of checking your answer sheet frequently throughout the test to ensure that you are filling in the correct ovals—especially if you skip questions or leave some to come back to later.

The Short-Answer Questions

The short-answer questions focus on both historical content and skills. You will be required to answer the first two short-answer questions, then choose between questions 3 and 4. Each question will have three parts, so be sure to label your answers (a), (b), and (c). Some of the questions include a source, which might be text or a photograph or a map. Your answers must be expressed in complete sentences, not bullet points, but you do not need to write a formal essay with a thesis and conclusion. Many of the short-answer questions give you a choice of addressing differing aspects of the historical question; be sure you are not trying to answer ALL the topics when only one is required. Often the second section of the question leads from the first one, that is, you might be asked to describe an event or policy in the first part of the question and then explain why it was successful or not in the second part.

The Document-Based Question

The document-based question essay (DBQ) is the hallmark exercise of the AP® U.S. History Exam. DBQs can be drawn from any historical period between 1754–1980. The DBQ asks you to connect relevant evidence from multiple sources (generally seven documents) and use those connections to construct an analytical or interpretative essay response. In asking you to place the evidence in context and then use it to explain a cause or to substantiate a thesis, or both, the AP® Exam is, in effect, asking you to perform the central creative act of the historian's craft. Remember that each DBQ will focus on one of these historical reasoning processes: comparison, causation, and continuity and change. The DBQ will also assess your ability to demonstrate the historical thinking skills of historical argumentation and analyzing historical evidence.

When approaching the DBQ, do not immediately look at the documents. First, read the question very carefully. After making sure that you understand all of the terms in the prompt, brainstorm a list of relevant information. Try to frame an argument without using the documents, because solely relying on the documents rather than weaving both the documents and outside information into your essay can limit your score. Only after you have done this should you consider the documents and determine how you can best use them in your essay.

Frequently DBQ documents will contradict each other. This is an opportunity to begin sorting and categorizing the documents. For example, you might divide the documents into those supporting and those opposing a proposed policy. Another way to analyze documents might be by their author and his or her background, status in society, gender, job, motivation, or other factors. Is the document written by a man or a woman? By a wealthy industrialist or a factory worker? Thus, the documents themselves provide important keys needed to answer the question. You must use all or all but one of the documents to demonstrate your ability to weigh the relevance of evidence provided, sort through their complexities, and use those complexities in support of your thesis. You must examine at least three of the documents for point of view, audience, historical situation, and/or purpose. Additionally, you must explain why one of those factors is significant to your argument. For example, you might consider the intended audience of the document, its point of view, its format, and its limitations (what *doesn't* it say?).

The DBQ also requires the use of outside information that tests your ability to integrate your historical knowledge with the documents. If you can use information from the documents and connect it to your own knowledge, you will have a stronger essay.

If you have written a research paper or prepared an evidence-based essay in class, you have already practiced the process of writing a DBQ. The purpose of the essay is to support an argument using your own knowledge of history and the evidence put before you to arrive at a historical narrative or explanation.

Breaking the process down into multiple steps helps you master the process of answering DBQs. A strong DBQ response is well organized and establishes a thesis using the documents and outside information. With practice, you should be able to analyze and digest each document, determine its relevance, and use it in support of a thesis. The very best essays, like good historical writing, focus only on those elements of the documents that serve the thesis. Therefore, do not waste time and space extensively quoting or summarizing the documents.

What's the best way to cite the documents? Avoid saying "Document A says . . ." in an essay. Imagine that your essay can be read on its own, without that packet of documents attached. It's best to cite the source in the least disruptive manner possible so the essay flows well. Parenthetical citations can work, but it is smoothest to identify the quote within your own sentences, like this: "As Thomas Jefferson wrote in the Declaration of Independence in 1776, 'All men are created equal.' "

Tips for Answering Document-Based Questions

- Read the question carefully to determine exactly what is being asked of you.
- Determine how each document source relates to the question at hand.
- Find sentences in the document excerpts that contain key terms and ideas mentioned in the question.
- Determine the extent to which different document excerpts are similar or contradictory. Sort documents into several different categories to help analyze them.

- Analyze any maps or visual documents to determine their relevance to the topic.
- Be sure to include as many pertinent details as possible in support of your DBQ thesis, but don't feel compelled to include extraneous detail.
- Sophisticated essays often address ambiguities and contradictions in documents and other evidence. Don't be afraid to try to account for these contradictions.

The Long Essay Question

You will choose one of three long essay questions.Each of these essays will test the same historical thinking skill (causation, comparison, continuity and change), but for different time periods. These questions are included to measure your ability to think critically, recall pertinent information, and write a well-conceived essay that proves your thesis. As with the DBQ, you need to develop a thesis, that is, an argument *about* the topic. Because you do not have documents available, however, you need to provide the historical evidence yourself. Following the thesis, you need several paragraphs that put forward historical information to prove your point. Your conclusion should add to your original thesis and include the arguments stated in the intervening paragraphs.

Tips for Answering Long Essay Questions

- Read the three questions and determine which one you can answer more successfully.
- Sketch out a brief outline, recording facts and examples that you remember and organizing them in a sensible way. Each section of the outline should generate a supporting paragraph for your essay. Remember to use clues from the question to structure your essay when possible.
- Develop a thesis that takes a clear stand on the question posed. Be sure to state the thesis in your introductory paragraph.
- Begin each supporting paragraph with a clear topic sentence.
- Consider transitions between paragraphs.
- Conclude by restating your thesis in a fresh way, perhaps by making a connection to another moment in American history.
- Keep in mind the volume of essays the exam readers must assess. Clarity and organization are key.
- Determine what history practices and skills you must demonstrate in responding to the essay prompt.

Scoring the New AP® U.S. History Exam

The biggest change in scoring for the new APUSH exam is related to scoring the document-based question (DBQ). In the past, DBQs were graded holistically and on a 9-point scale. Now, you can earn a maximum of 7 points, each earned by satisfying a particular requirement. You can earn 1 point for your thesis, 1 point for contextualization (setting the stage for the question), a maximum of 2 points for your use of documents, and 1 point for inclusion of relevant outside examples. Finally, you can earn 2 points for demonstrating analysis and reasoning skills and sourcing (identifying audience, historical situation, point of view, and/or purpose and its significance to your argument) at least three documents. For the most up-to-date information on how the exams are scored, please visit the College Board site.

NOTES:

PRACTICE EXAMS

Practice Exam 1

SECTION I

Total time: 1 hour, 35 minutes

Part A: Multiple-Choice Questions

Time: 55 minutes

Questions 1–3 refer to the 1893 political cartoon below.

The Ohio State University Billy Ireland Cartoon Library & Museum

"Looking Backwards"

1. The political cartoon above depicts nativist reactions to immigration in which of the following historical contexts?
   - (a) The Market Revolution
   - (b) Westward Expansion
   - (c) The Industrial Revolution
   - (d) Post-World War I

2. Which of the following best represents the historical development being portrayed by the cartoonist?
   (a) Immigration restriction
   (b) Repeal of immigration quotas
   (c) Elimination of literacy tests for immigrants
   (d) A call for increased immigration

3. Which of the following was true of immigration policy during the 1920s?
   (a) The United States developed a more restrictive policy for Southern and Eastern European immigrants
   (b) The influx of massive numbers of Irish led the United States to exclude Ireland from the quota system
   (c) The United States did away with quotas for Northern and Western Europeans, but not for Southern and Eastern Europeans
   (d) Labor shortages called for the relaxation of immigration restrictions

Questions 4–6 refer to the graph below.

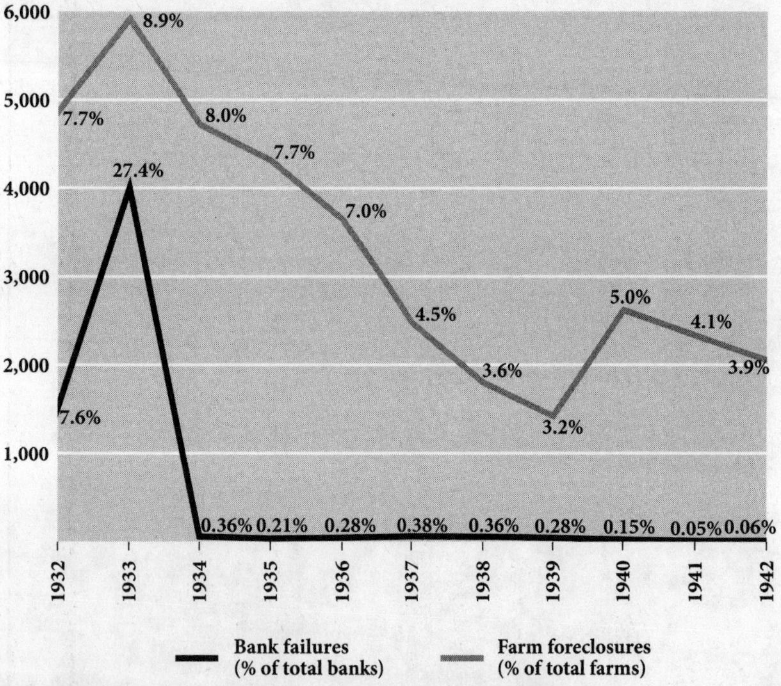

Bank Failures and Farm Foreclosures, 1932–1942

4. Which of the following statements is best supported by the graph above?
   (a) Farm foreclosures remained the same throughout the New Deal
   (b) The rates at which banks failed and farms were foreclosed were about the same
   (c) Banks recovered quickly in the early years of the New Deal
   (d) Farm foreclosures went down steadily throughout the New Deal

5. Which of the following represent the greatest change in government policy ushered in by the New Deal?
   (a) The government was responsible for the economic well-being of the country
   (b) The government should steadfastly retain a laissez-faire approach to economic recessions
   (c) The government's primary role should be to defend the United States from foreign invasion
   (d) Quack remedies would not put an end to the Great Depression

6. The Great Depression was ended by
   (a) New Deal relief programs like the Federal Emergency Relief Administration.
   (b) work programs such as the Civilian Conservation Corps and Works Progress Administration.
   (c) industrial expansion fueled by acts like the Lend-Lease Act.
   (d) the Court-packing scheme to uphold critical New Deal programs.

Questions 7–10 refer to the 1900 political cartoon below.

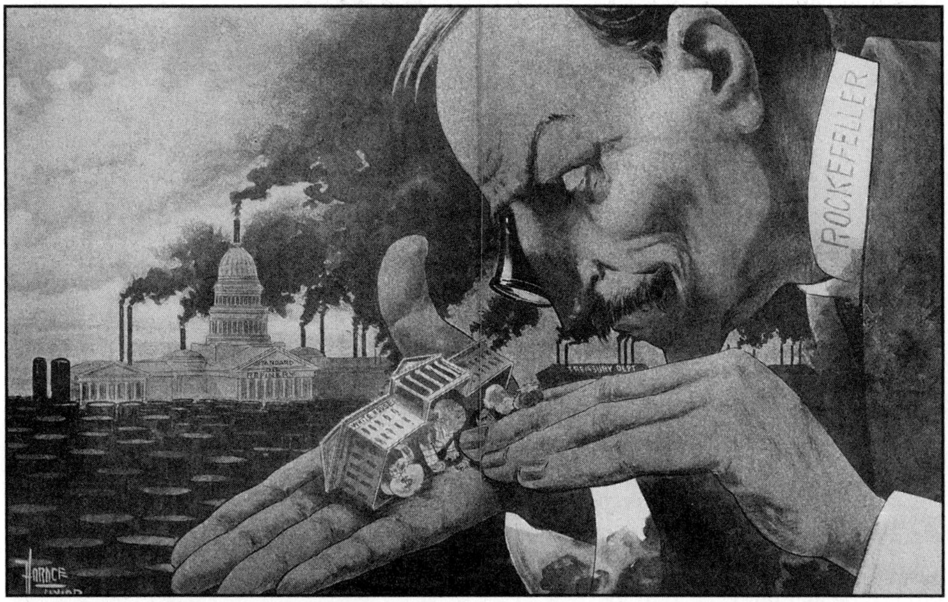

"The Trust Giant's Point of View"

7. The above cartoon best reflects a growing call for
   (a) eliminating the capitalist system.
   (b) reducing the power of the central government.
   (c) regulating big business by the federal government.
   (d) taking a more laissez-faire approach toward monopolies.

8. The supporters of which of the following concepts would be most likely to support the opinion expressed by the political cartoonist?
   (a) Believers in new imperialism
   (b) Believers in the concept of Social Darwinism
   (c) Believers in the principles of the Populist Party
   (d) Believers in the principles of boss control

9. Which of the following decades represents a break from the tone toward big business represented in the cartoon above?
   (a) 1920s
   (b) 1930s
   (c) 1940s
   (d) 1960s

10. The historical context of the cartoon above best reflects which of the following developments?
   (a) The belief in an an energetic big government
   (b) The rise of industrial capitalism
   (c) The strength of the broker state
   (d) The debates between labor and management

Questions 11–13 refer to the excerpt below.

"But what do we mean by the American Revolution? Do we mean the American war? The Revolution was effected before the war commenced. The Revolution was in the minds and hearts of the people; a change in their religious sentiments of their duties and obligations. While the king, and all in authority under him, were believed to govern in justice and mercy, according to the laws and constitution derived to them from the God of nature and transmitted to them by their ancestors, they thought themselves bound to pray for the king and queen and all the royal family, and all in authority under them, as ministers ordained of God for their good; but when they saw those powers renouncing all the principles of authority, and bent upon the destruction of all the securities of their lives, liberties, and properties, they thought it their duty to pray for the continental congress and all the thirteen State congresses."

John Adams to Hezekiah Niles, February 13, 1818

11. Which of the following best describes the claims made by Adams about British North American colonists prior to the American Revolution?
    (a) A strong desire to form an intercolonial government
    (b) An unwillingness to form any coalitions between colonies
    (c) Most continued a belief in Anglicization
    (d) Respect for the fact that resources were not renewable

12. Which of the following best explains the changes in colonial attitude described by Adams?
    (a) By 1763 a majority of Americans supported revolution
    (b) After the French and Indian War colonists developed a sense of identity
    (c) By 1776 colonists were not prepared to rebel against British authorities
    (c) By 1776 no colonial unity had developed

13. Between 1754 and 1775, the British North American colonists
    (a) formed organizational structures to combat British attempts to increase control over the colonies.
    (b) violated the provisions of the Trade and Navigation Acts for the first time.
    (c) formed alliances with European countries that sought to diminish British power.
    (d) refrained from using violent tactics against British rule.

Questions 14–16 refer to the excerpt below.

"We have become great in a material sense because of the lavish use of our resources, and we have just reason to be proud of our growth. But the time has come to inquire seriously what will happen when our forests are gone, when the coal, the iron, the oil, and the gas are exhausted, when the soils shall have been still further impoverished and washed into the streams, polluting the rivers, denuding the fields, and obstructing navigation."

Theodore Roosevelt, 1908

14. Debates over the issues referenced in the excerpt by Roosevelt led to which of the following developments?
    (a) growing concerns over the safety of nuclear power
    (b) advocacy for government involvement in environmental issues
    (c) growing concerns about the effects of pesticides on the environment
    (d) growing concern over the negative environmental impact of massive swamp drainage projects

15. By the late 1950s and 1960s, the issues described by Roosevelt changed to focus primarily about
    (a) growing concerns over the disposal of toxic wastes.
    (b) concerns over the safety of nuclear power because of the meltdown at Three Mile Island.
    (c) recognition that dwindling coal resources would eventually cripple the economy.
    (d) growing concerns about the effects of pesticides on the environment.

16. The excerpt best describes which of the following historical developments?
    (a) The establishment of national parks
    (b) Progressive control over education
    (c) Less reliance on environmental experts
    (d) Deregulation of the economy in the energy sector

Questions 17–19 refer to the excerpt below.

"There was a time in Wisconsin when the boss and representatives of the railroads nominated the candidates for both parties. How? By intervening between the voter and the nomination and 'getting' the delegates. . . .

"There was a time in Wisconsin when the railroads ruled and ruled supreme. They openly boasted of their power. For more than thirty years no law was enacted except by consent of the railroads. . . .

"La Follette secured the anti-lobby law. . . .

"La Follette secured the anti-pass law and thus did away with the common and wholesale bribery of public officials.

"La Follette secured the corrupt practices acts. . . .

"La Follette, with a clear vision, saw then what Roosevelt and Hughes see now—that the people must be freed from boss rule.

"La Follette secured the primary election law. . . .

"This great movement in Wisconsin has given Wisconsin a reputation throughout the nation. It is the Wisconsin Idea and other states are following in its wake. . . .

"But La Follette has done more than to save your dollars. He has made it possible in Wisconsin for you, the people, to rule, to govern yourselves, to be represented by men you choose."

Campaign pamphlet for Robert La Follette, candidate for U.S. Senate, 1906

17. Progressives supported legislation between 1900 and 1920 that accomplished which of the following?
    (a) An easing of racial tensions through a policy of eugenics and sterilization
    (b) Major environmental legislation such as the Clean Water Act and establishment of the Environmental Protection Agency
    (c) Elimination of the income tax, making the protective tariff the chief source of government income
    (d) Democratized the political process through initiatives such as the Seventeenth and Nineteenth amendments

18. Which of the following best represents a common goal among progressives referenced in the excerpt above?
    (a) Nationalization of the railroads
    (b) Insurance subsidies to farmers
    (c) Expansion of democratic reforms
    (d) An increase in income inequality

19. The Progressive ideals described in this excerpt continued in which of the following ways between 1960 and 1968?
    (a) A successful war that eliminated poverty in Appalachia
    (b) Eliminated conflict with the Soviet Union, ending the Cold War
    (c) A ban on the construction of nuclear power plants in light of Three Mile Island and Chernobyl
    (d) Social welfare legislation such as Medicare and Head Start designed to provide a safety net for the poor

Questions 20–22 refer to the excerpt below.

> "The recent alarming development and aggression of aggregated wealth, which . . . will inevitably lead to the pauperization and hopeless degradation of the toiling masses, render it imperative, if we desire to enjoy the blessings of the government bequeathed to us by the founders of the republic, that a check should be placed upon its power and unjust accumulation, and a system adopted which will secure to the laborer the fruits of his toil."
>
> Terence V. Powderly, *Thirty Years of Labor*, 1889

20. In the last half of the nineteenth century, which of the following contributed to the changes referenced in the excerpt above?
    (a) Large-scale growth of industrial capitalism
    (b) An active and progressive national government
    (c) Organized labor unions were outlawed by the Supreme Court
    (d) Support for labor unions from the federal government increased

21. The ideas expressed above most directly led to which of the following?
    (a) A leveling of income between laborers and management
    (b) The use of horizontal integration
    (c) Government intervention to protect labor rights
    (d) Direct confrontations between labor and management

22. In which of the following periods did the federal government show its strongest support for organized labor?
    (a) 1800–1844
    (b) 1865–1890
    (c) 1890–1945
    (d) 1980–present

Questions 23–25 refer to the map below.

Roads and Canals to 1837

23. The transportation in the map above reflects which of the following developments?
   (a) Federal government subsidies of transportation
   (b) The slow movement westward
   (c) The ongoing effects of the Market Revolution
   (d) An emphasis on overseas trading with European nations

24. The transportation revolution in the first half of the nineteenth century resulted in
   (a) suppression of western economic interests by leaving the section unconnected to eastern interests.
   (b) reduced sectional tension by tying the Northeast and Southeast together through canals and railroads.
   (c) the completion of a transcontinental railroad, opening Asian markets for eastern manufacturers.
   (d) a movement toward regional economic interdependence.

25. Which of the following is true about the development of transportation in the United States between 1800 and 1844?
    (a) A canal system was financed and built primarily by the federal government to improve coastal defenses
    (b) The first transcontinental railroads were completed by private interests with significant financial help from the federal government
    (c) The federal government financed the building of the Oregon Trail to facilitate westward expansion
    (d) The majority of transportation improvement were financed by states or private enterprise

Questions 26–28 are based on the 1786 illustration below.

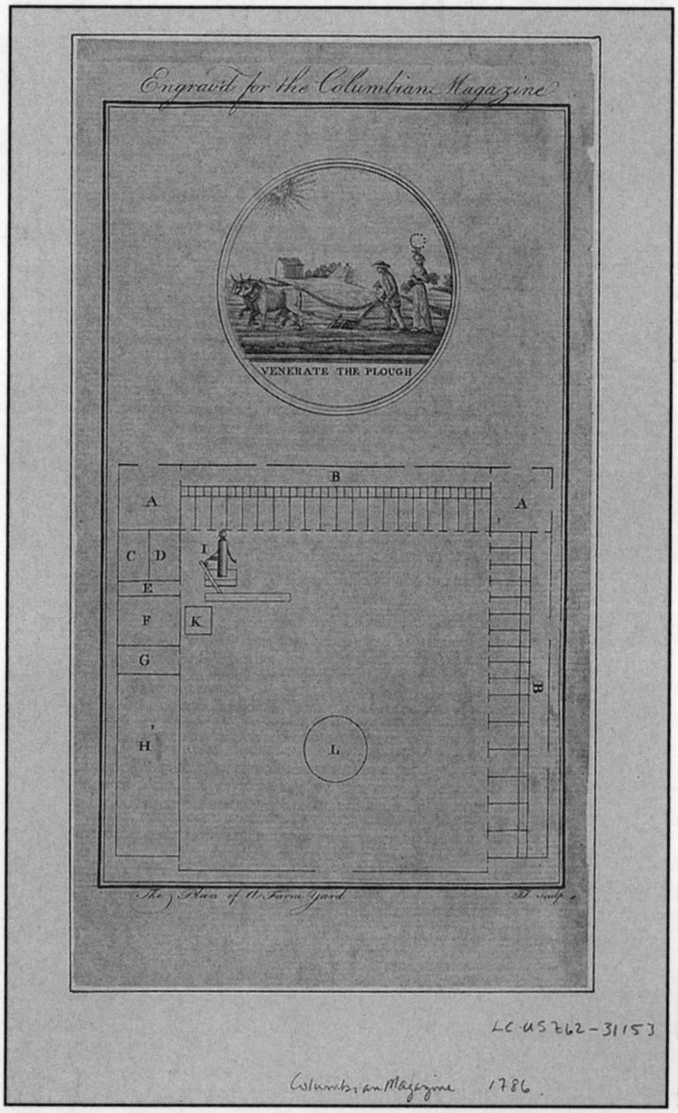

The Plan of a Farm Yard, Columbian Magazine, 1786

26. The above political cartoon best demonstrates that in the post–American Revolution time period,
    (a) the federal government discouraged westward expansion.
    (b) the role of women was significantly expanded.
    (c) an agrarian lifestyle was viewed as promoting democratic principles.
    (d) serious environmental concerns over soil depletion encouraged farmers to be more progressive in cultivation practices.

27. The continued belief in the ideals of the scene above relate to which of the following future conflicts in the United States?
    (a) The growth of industry in cities
    (b) The division of powers between state and federal governments
    (c) Encroachment on American Indian lands by the United States
    (d) The acquisition of westward territories

28. The above scene foreshadows which of the following disagreements in the new republic?
    (a) Debate over the future of the United States as an agrarian or commercial industrial nation
    (b) Debate over federal funding of internal improvements
    (c) Debate over whether future states should be added as equal states to existing states
    (d) Whether states should give up western land claims to the national government

Questions 29–31 refer to the excerpt below.

"I am tired of fighting. Our chiefs are killed. Looking-glass is dead. Too-hul-hul-suit is dead. The old men are all dead. It is the young men, now, who say yes or no. He who led on the young men is dead. It is cold, and we have no blankets. The little children are freezing to death. My people—some of them—have run away to the hills, and have no blankets, no food. No one knows where they are—perhaps freezing to death. I want to have time to look for my children, and to see how many of them I can find; may be I shall find them among the dead. Hear me, my chiefs; my heart is sick and sad. From where the sun now stands, I will fight no more forever!"

Surrender Speech by Chief Joseph of the Nez Perce, October 5, 1877

29. The above surrender speech by Chief Joseph reflects the success of which of the following government policies regarding American Indians following the Civil War?
    (a) Movement of American Indian tribes to one large reservation on the Great American Desert
    (b) Assimilation of American Indians into American culture
    (c) Movement of American Indian tribes to small, scattered reservations
    (d) The granting of 160 acres of land to every tribal member

30. Despite continued setbacks, which of the following best represents American Indians' agency in the late nineteenth century?
    (a) Preserving cultural identities
    (b) Refusing to sign all treaties about land
    (c) Successfully resisting attempts to create reservations
    (d) Promoting the idea of assimilation

31. Which of the following contributed to the decline of American Indian society?
    (a) Continued white encroachment on American Indian lands
    (b) American Indian society's treatment of women as equals
    (c) The development of unified alliances between American Indian tribes
    (d) The growth of regional trade networks among American Indian tribes

Questions 32–34 refer to the excerpt below.

"There is on the globe one single spot, the possessor of which is our natural and habitual enemy. It is New Orleans, through which the produce of three eighths of our territory must pass to market, and from its fertility it will ere long yield more than half of our whole produce and contain more than half our inhabitants. . . . Not so can it ever be in the hands of France: the impetuosity of her temper, the energy and restlessness of her character, placed in a point of eternal friction with us, . . . render it impossible that France and the U.S. can continue long friends, when they meet in so irritable a position. . . . The day that France takes possession of New Orleans . . . we must marry ourselves to the British fleet and nation."

Thomas Jefferson, 1802

32. The problem related in the above excerpt was permanently resolved through the
    (a) purchase of Florida in 1819.
    (b) formation of a perpetual alliance with Great Britain.
    (c) the Louisiana Purchase of 1803.
    (d) the Treaty of San Lorenzo granting the United States the right of deposit at New Orleans.

33. Which of the following represents an immediate consequence of the controversies referenced by Jefferson above?
    (a) Continued debates among the political parties over relations with European powers
    (b) The establishment of a national economic system
    (c) An increase in American involvement in South America
    (d) The removal of American Indians

34. The strongest support for gaining control of New Orleans came from
    (a) northeastern merchants, who wanted to gain access to new markets.
    (b) the British, who were anxious to remove the French presence from North America.
    (c) western farmers, who wanted control of New Orleans to provide an outlet for their produce.
    (d) Federalists, who saw control of New Orleans as a way to support the expansion of the power of the national government.

Questions 35–37 are based on the following Supreme Court decision.

"Prior to any questioning, the person must be warned that he has a right to remain silent, that any statement he does make may be used as evidence against him, and that he has a right to the presence of an attorney, either retained or appointed. The defendant may waive effectuation of these rights, provided the waiver is made voluntarily, knowingly and intelligently. If, however, he indicates in any manner and at any stage of the process that he wishes to consult with an attorney before speaking, there can be no questioning. Likewise, if the individual is alone and indicates in any manner that he does not wish to be interrogated, the police may not question him. The mere fact that he may have answered some questions or volunteered some statements on his own does not deprive him of the right to refrain from answering any further inquiries until he has consulted with an attorney and thereafter consents to be questioned."

U.S. Supreme Court majority opinion, *Miranda v. Arizona*, 1966

35. The excerpt above best supports which of the following trends of the Supreme Court in the 1960s?
    (a) Regulatory power of the federal government versus the private enterprise system
    (b) Power of the federal government versus the power of state government
    (c) Rights of the individual versus the regulatory power of government
    (d) The constitutionality of government regulations concerning the environment

36. Which of the following best represents a challenge to the ideas expressed in the excerpt above?

    (a) Anti-war protests in the 1960s
    (b) A burgeoning conservative movement
    (c) The liberalism of the Great Society
    (d) The environmental movement

37. Advocates of the claims in the excerpt above would have most likely also supported

    (a) Efforts to deregulate industry
    (b) Attempts to cut taxes for the wealthiest Americans
    (c) The use of federal resources to combat environmental problems
    (d) An increase in nuclear armaments as a deterrent

Questions 38–39 refer to the map below.

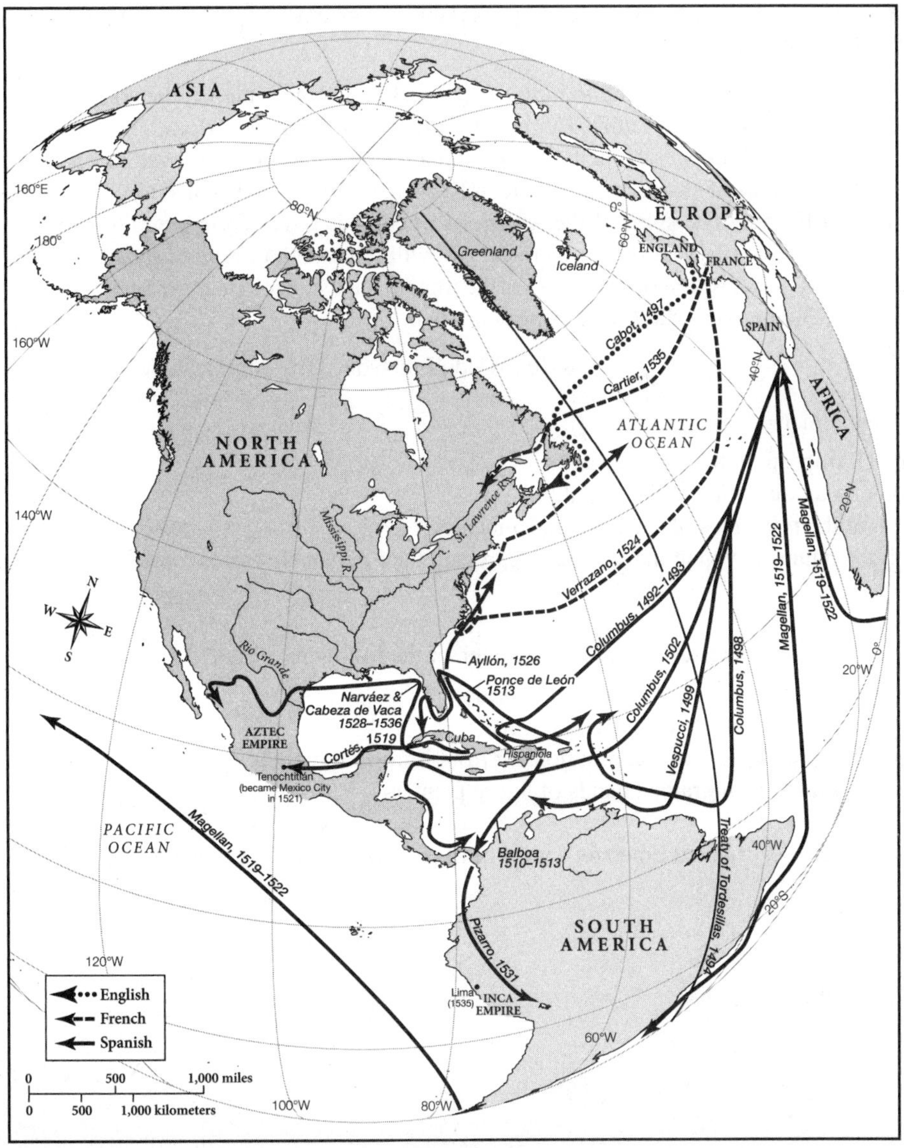

European Explorations in the Americas, 1492-1536

38. Actions such as those depicted in the image contributed to
    (a) exploration and efforts at conquest.
    (b) large mass settlements of Europeans.
    (c) political reciprocity between Europeans and American Indians.
    (d) peaceful negotiation over land disputes.

39. The most devastating effect of the Columbian Exchange on American Indians was
    (a) the introduction of horses, which destroyed the nomadic lifestyle of the Plains Indians.
    (b) superior firearms that gave the invaders a decided advantage in military struggles.
    (c) the introduction of diseases for which American Indians had little immunity.
    (d) the introduction of European crops that devastated native species and reshaped the environment.

Questions 40–43 refer to the following below.

"Another sign of our times, also marked by an analogous political movement, is the new importance given to the single person. . . .

"The scholar is that man who must take up into himself all the ability of the time, all the contributions of the past, all the hopes of the future. He must be a university of knowledges. . . . The world is nothing, the man is all; in yourself is the law of all nature, and you know not yet how a globule of sap ascends; in yourself slumbers the whole of Reason. . . . We have listened too long to the courtly muses of Europe. The spirit of the American freeman is already suspected to be timid, imitative, tame. . . . We will walk on our own feet; we will work with our own hands; we will speak our own minds. . . . A nation of men will for the first time exist, because each believes himself inspired by the Divine Soul which also inspires all men."

Ralph Waldo Emerson, "The American Scholar," 1837

40. In the above passage, Emerson is calling for
    (a) adherence to European literary standards.
    (b) the creation of a uniquely American literature.
    (c) the rejection of the principles of Jacksonian democracy.
    (d) support for communes in which individuals suppressed their personal desires for the good of the community.

41. Between 1800 and 1860, American art best reflected which of the following trends?
    (a) Glorification of nature and a sense of patriotic pride
    (b) Realism reflected in scenes of squalor and poverty
    (c) A mirroring of impressionism and expressionism from European models
    (d) Portraiture painted by the untrained hands of house painters

42. The philosophy that best encapsulated Emerson's view of the role of the individual and intuition was known as
    (a) pragmatism.
    (b) nihilism.
    (c) Social Darwinism.
    (d) transcendentalism.

43. Emerson's glorification of the individual fits most closely with which of the following political trends of the time period 1800 to 1840?
    (a) Jeffersonian democracy's belief in rule by the educated common man
    (b) Federalist notions of rule by the educated elite
    (c) Whig insistence on a powerful national government
    (d) Jacksonian democracy's belief in rule by the common man

Questions 44–46 refer to the graph below.

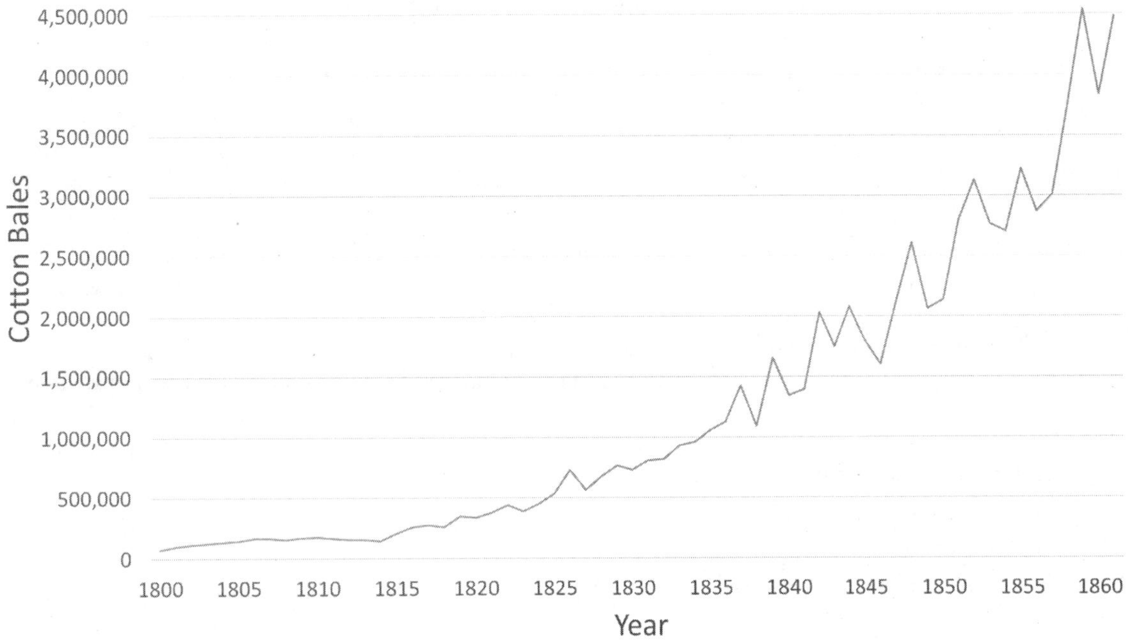

Cotton Production, 1800-1860

44. Which of the following is directly supported by the above graph?
    (a) Cotton production showed a massive decline as a result of economic depressions such as the Panics of 1837 and 1857
    (b) Cotton represented more than 50 percent of U.S. exports by 1860
    (c) The massive increase in cotton production between 1855 and 1860 was the result of the invention of the cotton gin in 1847
    (d) Cotton production continued to increase in the late 1850s despite increased sectional tension

45. The trends from the graph above most directly led to which of the following?
    (a) A decrease in the use of new lands for cotton
    (b) Political division over the status of new territories
    (c) Transportation developments in the southern region
    (d) A women's rights movement

46. Which of the following best serves as evidence of the spread of cotton production westward?
    (a) A distinctive southern identity
    (b) Unsuccessful rebellions by enslaved people
    (c) Overcultivation of lands in the Southeast
    (d) Antislavery efforts in the East

Questions 47–49 refer to the excerpt below.

"Mr. President, I wish to speak to-day, not as a Massachusetts man, nor as a northern man, but as an American, and a member of the Senate of the United States. . . . It is not to be denied that we live in the midst of strong agitations, and are surrounded by very considerable dangers to our institutions of government. . . . I speak to-day for the preservation of the Union. 'Hear me for my cause.' . . .

"Now, sir, upon the general nature, and character, and influence of slavery there exists a wide difference between the northern portion of this country and the southern. It is said, on the one side . . . that . . . slavery is a wrong; . . . The South, upon the other side, having been accustomed to this relation between two races all their lives, from their birth, having been taught, in general, to treat the subjects of this bondage with care and kindness—and I believe, in general, feeling for them great care and kindness—have not taken the view of the subject which I have mentioned."

U.S. Senator Daniel Webster, March 7, 1850

47. Between 1844 and 1860, the United States witnessed which of the following regarding the debate over the issue of slavery?
   (a) Increasingly emotionalized positions of the issue that made compromise less likely
   (b) A temporary lull in the debate as both regions savored territorial acquisition without regard to the extension of slavery
   (c) Growing recognition by the South that slavery was a "necessary evil"
   (d) Formation of the Republican Party by radical abolitionists bent on ending slavery immediately

48. Though Congress debated enslavement in the early 1850s, which of the following decisions claimed that Congress lacked the ability to determine the status of slavery in new territories?
   (a) Missouri Compromise
   (b) Kansas-Nebraska
   (c) Prigg v. Pennsylvania, 1842
   (d) Dred Scott v. Sandford, 1857

49. The debates referenced in the excerpt above led to which of the following compromise measures?
   (a) A new Fugitive Slave Law
   (b) Popular sovereignty
   (c) An end to the slave trade
   (d) Decreased support for abolitionism

Questions 50–52 refer to the excerpt below.

"We are people of this generation, bred in at least modest comfort, housed now in universities, looking uncomfortably to the world we inherit.

"The search for truly democratic alternatives to the present, and a commitment to social experimentation with them, is a worthy and fulfilling human enterprise, one which moves us and, we hope, others today."

Students for a Democratic Society, The Port Huron Statement, 1962

50. Which of the following best reflects the major reason for the discontent of out of the mainstream youth of the 1960s?
   (a) The growth of suburbs
   (b) The shallowness, superficiality, and conformity of society
   (c) The discontent of baby boomers with their lack of affluence
   (d) The failure of American education to meet the challenges of the Cold War

51. Which of the following developments most contributed to an intensification of the animus described in the excerpt?
   (a) Vietnam War
   (b) Rock 'n Roll
   (c) The Great Society
   (d) Environmentalism

52. Spurred on by challenges to the status quo by the civil rights movement's call for social justice and criticism of the regimentation of society, many other groups sought to overcome traditional obstacles to full rights in the 1960s. These groups included all of the following EXCEPT
   (a) women's rights groups that sought preserve women's role of domesticity.
   (b) migrant workers who sought to improve working conditions in factories.
   (c) the moral majority who sought to increase religious participation in politics.
   (d) gays and lesbians who sought less discrimination and a more open society.

Questions 53–55 refer to the image below.

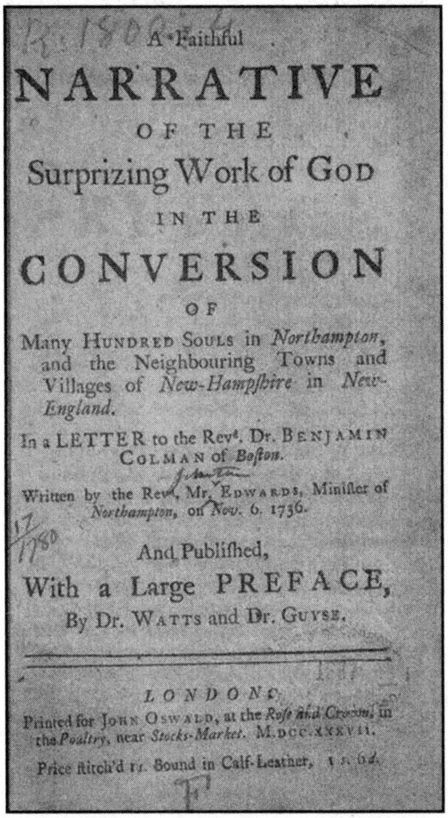
A Faithful
NARRATIVE
OF THE
Surprizing Work of GOD
IN THE
CONVERSION
OF
Many HUNDRED SOULS in *Northampton*, and the Neighbouring Towns and Villages of *New-Hampshire* in *New-England*.
In a LETTER to the Rev^{d}. Dr. BENJAMIN COLMAN of *Boston*.
Written by the Rev^{d}. Mr. EDWARDS, Minister of *Northampton*, on *Nov.* 6. 1736.
And Published,
With a Large PREFACE,
By Dr. WATTS and Dr. GUYSE.
LONDON:
Printed for JOHN OSWALD, at the *Rose and Crown*, in the *Poultry*, near *Stocks-Market*. M.DCC.XXXVII.
Price stitch'd 1 s. Bound in Calf-Leather, 1 s. 6 d.

Rare Book and Special Collections Division, Library of Congress

53. Which of the following was true of religious freedom in the British North American colonies between 1607 and 1754?
   (a) Religious freedom was promoted in Massachusetts Bay by the doctrine of intellectual freedom of the Puritan church
   (b) Religious freedom was advanced by the open immigration policy that led divergent groups to settle in the colonies
   (c) The Church of England was the dominant church in all thirteen colonies
   (d) Colonists unanimously rejected the notion of a state church supported by tax dollars

54. The diversity of religious denominations in the colonies led to
    (a) major religious wars in New England that resulted in the death of more than four thousand people.
    (b) a large amount of cultural and religious pluralism.
    (c) Parliament allowing only Anglican Englishmen to settle in the colonies after 1700.
    (d) English trade restrictions on colonial trade with Catholic nations.

55. The greatest religious diversity in the British North American colonies prior to 1754 existed in which of the following sections?
    (a) Canada
    (b) The southern colonies
    (c) The middle colonies
    (d) New England

NOTES:

Part B: Short-Answer Questions

Time: 40 minutes

Please answer the following two questions.

1. Using the excerpt below, answer a, b, and c.

> "Whoever, when the United States is at war, shall willfully make or convey false reports or false statements . . . or incite or attempt to incite, insubordination, disloyalty, mutiny, or refusal of duty, in the military or naval forces of the United States, or shall willfully obstruct . . . the recruiting or enlistment service of the United States, or . . . shall willfully utter, print, write, or publish any disloyal, profane, scurrilous, or abusive language about the form of government of the United States, or the Constitution of the United States, or the military or naval forces of the United States . . . . shall be punished by a fine of not more than $10,000 or imprisonment for not more than twenty years, or both."

Sedition Act, 1918

a) Briefly explain ONE historical development that led to the ideas in the act above.

b) Briefly explain ONE debate about the ideas in the act above in the period 1918–1924.

c) Briefly explain ONE historical change in the United States that resulted from the act above in the period 1918–1924.

2. Answer a, b, and c.

a) Identify one group or individual who was a primary focus of authorities in the first Red Scare following World War I, and explain why the group or individual was a primary focus.

b) Identify one group or individual who was a primary focus of authorities in the second Red Scare following World War II, and explain why the group or individual was a primary focus.

c) Explain ONE significant difference between the First and Second Red Scares.

Please choose between question #3 or #4 for your final SAQ question.

3. Answer a, b, and c.

a) Briefly explain ONE specific historical cause of the development of urban transportation systems in the period from 1865 to 1900.

b) Briefly explain ONE specific historical event or development that resulted from the development of urban transportation systems in the period from 1865 to 1900.

c) Briefly explain ANOTHER specific historical event or development that resulted from the development of urban transportation systems in the period from 1865 to 1900.

4. Answer a, b, and c.

a) Briefly explain ONE specific historical cause of the development of the Constitutional Convention.

b) Breifly explain ONE specific historical event or development that resulted from the development of the Constitutional Convention.

c) Briefly explain how debates over constitutional interpretation led to the development of the First American Party System.

STOP

END OF SECTION I

Section II

Total time: 1 hour, 40 minutes

Part A: Document-Based Question

Time: 60 minutes

Directions: The following question in based on the accompanying documents. The documents have been edited for this exercise. It is suggested that you spend approximately 15 minutes planning and 45 minutes writing your answer.

Write an essay that does the following:

- States an appropriate thesis that directly addresses all parts of the question.
- Supports the thesis or argument with evidence from all or all but one of the documents AND your knowledge of U.S. history beyond the documents.
- Analyzes all or all but one of the documents.
- Explain the significance of the author's point of view, author's purpose, historical context, and/or audience for at least three documents.
- Uses historical evidence beyond the documents to support your argument.
- Places the argument in the context of broader regional, national, or global processes.
- ncorporates all of the elements above into a convincing essay.

Question: Evaluate the extent to which the cultural conflicts of the 1920s changed American society in the period from 1919 to 1929.

Document 1

Source: Cartoonist Billy Ireland, 1919

The Ohio State University Billy Ireland Cartoon Library & Museum

Document 2

Source: F. Scott Fitzgerald, *This Side of Paradise*, 1920

Long after midnight the towers and spires of Princeton were visible, with here and there a late-burning light— and suddenly out of the clear darkness the sound of bells. As an endless dream it went on; the spirit of the past brooding over a new generation, the chosen youth from the muddled, unchastened world, still fed romantically on the mistakes and half-forgotten dreams of dead statesmen and poets. Here was a new generation, shouting the old cries, learning the old creeds, through a revery of long days and nights; destined finally to go out into that dirty gray turmoil to follow love and pride; a new generation dedicated more than the last to the fear of poverty and the worship of success; grown up to find all Gods dead, all wars fought, all faiths in man shaken.

Document 3

Source: H. L. Mencken, *Baltimore Sun*, July 26, 1920

When a candidate for public office faces the voters he does not face men of sense; he faces a mob of men whose chief distinguishing mark is the fact that they are quite incapable of weighing ideas, or even of comprehending any save the most elemental— men whose whole thinking is done in terms of emotion, and whose dominant emotion is dread of what they cannot understand. So confronted, the candidate must either bark with the pack or be lost. . . . All the odds are on the man who is, intrinsically, the most devious and mediocre— the man who can most adeptly disperse the notion that his mind is a virtual vacuum. The Presidency tends, year by year, to go to such men. As democ-racy is perfected, the office represents, more and more closely, the inner soul of the people. We move toward a lofty ideal. On some great and glorious day the plain folks of the land will reach their heart's desire at last, and the White House will be adorned by a downright moron.

Document 4

Source: President Warren G. Harding, c. 1921

I talk to the other side and they seem just as right, and here I am where I started. I know somewhere there is a book that will give me the truth, but, hell, I couldn't read the book. I know somewhere there is an economist who knows the truth, but I don't know where to find him and haven't the sense to know him and trust him when I find him. God! what a job!

Document 5

Source: Klan wedding in Washington, D.C., 1925

FPG/Hulton Archive/Getty Images

Document 6

Source: "The Descent of the Modernists," cartoon by E. J. Pace, in William Jennings Bryan, *Seven Questions in Dispute*, 1924.

Document 7

Source: William Jennings Bryan, undelivered closing statement prepared for the Scopes trial, 1925

Christianity welcomes truth from whatever source it comes and is not afraid that any real truth from any source can interfere with the divine truth that comes by inspiration from God Himself. It is not scientific truth to which Chris-tians object, for true science is classified knowledge, and nothing therefore can be scientific unless it is true.

Evolution is not truth: it is merely an hypothesis— it is millions of guesses strung together. It had not been proven in the days of Darwin; he expressed astonishment that with two or three million species it had been impossible to trace any species to any other species. It had not been proven in the days of [Thomas Henry] Huxley, and it has not been proven up to today.

Part B: Long Essay Questions

Time: 40 minutes

Choose between one of the following three questions.

1. Evaluate the extent to which transatlantic trade developments changed British North American colonial society in the period from 1607–1754.
2. Evaluate the extent to which the Populist movement changed American society in the period from 1865–1912.
3. Evaluate the extent to which the non-violent civil rights movement of the 1950s and 1960s changed American society.

STOP

END OF EXAM

Practice Exam 2

SECTION I

Total time: 1 hour, 35 minutes

Part A: Multiple-Choice Questions

Time: 55 minutes

Questions 1–3 refer to the excerpt below.

"Each public officer who takes an oath to support the Constitution swears that he will support it as he understands it, and not as it is understood by others. It is as much the duty of the House of Representatives, of the Senate, and of the President, to decide upon the constitutionality of any bill or resolution which may be presented to them for passage or approval, as it is of the Supreme Judges when it may be brought before them for judicial decision. The opinion of the Judges has no more authority over Congress than the opinion of Congress has over the Judges; and, on that point, the President is independent of both. The authority of the Supreme Court must not, therefore, be permitted to control the Congress or the Executive when acting in their legislative capacities, but to have only such influence as the force of their reasoning may deserve."

Andrew Jackson, veto message, July 10, 1832

1. Jackson's message seems to be challenging which of the following constitutional principles?
   (a) Division of powers between the states and the federal government
   (b) The principle of judicial review established in Article I of the Constitution
   (c) Separation of powers among the three branches of government
   (d) Congressional authority to legislate

2. The political rhetoric in the excerpt above serves as evidence of what political change in the early nineteenth century?
   (a) The creation of a civil service system based on merit
   (b) Increasing the power of the presidency
   (c) Its firm stance against the extension of slavery into the territories
   (d) Staunch opposition to the expansion of voting rights for unpropertied classes

3. During the era of Jacksonian Democracy, the United States saw
   (a) an accelerated movement toward universal white male suffrage.
   (b) the direct election of senators become a reality with the ratification of the Seventeenth Amendment.
   (c) Andrew Jackson strongly support federally funded internal improvements.
   (d) the elimination of the Second American Party System.

Questions 4–6 refer to the 1976 photo below.

AP Photo/DPG.

An Antibusing Confrontation in Boston, 1975

4. The photo pictured above is most reflective of which of the following changes occurring in the 1970s?
   (a) Blue-collar reaction against antiwar protests at colleges and universities
   (b) Silent majority opposition to federal funding for public education
   (c) Conservative backlash against policies to promote socioeconomic and racial diversity
   (d) The failure of the Great Society Head Start program

5. Which of the following represents a group who consistently fought against the social angst depicted in the image above?
   (a) Civil Rights leaders
   (b) Southern conservatives
   (c) Rebellious counterculture
   (d) Environmentalists

6. The image above best serves as evidence of which of the following historical developments
   (a) Continued challenges to congressional authority over social issues
   (b) Increased clashes over the extent of civil rights in America
   (c) Escalated tension between liberals and conservatives over the size of the federal government
   (d) Increased disputes over the power of states to solve civil rights

Questions 7–10 refer to the excerpt below.

"For the encouraging and increasing of shipping and navigation . . . no goods or commodities whatsoever shall be imported into, or exported out of, any lands, islands, plantations or territories to his Majesty belonging, or in his possession . . . in any other ship or ships, vessel or vessels whatsoever, but such ships and vessels as did truly and without fraud belong only to the people of England."

British Parliament, Navigation Act of 1660

7. What was a major goal of the legislation cited above?
   (a) To subdue increasing unrest in the British North American colonies
   (b) To undermine the increasing power of the Spanish monarchy
   (c) To more tightly control the British textile industry
   (d) To support the imperial economic system of Great Britain

8. The language in the excerpt above was used to support which British economic policy?
   (a) Mercantilism
   (b) Capitalism
   (c) Imperialism
   (d) Market revolution

9. Which of the following describes the historical context of the policy excerpted above?
   (a) The American colonists agreed that this was a reasonable assertion of imperial power
   (b) For several decades, the British government largely allowed the colonists to govern their own affairs
   (c) France declared war on England
   (d) Britain's alliances with North American Indian tribes forced the American colonists to call for closer ties with Britain

10. What event in the eighteenth century was most responsible for forcing the British to consolidate further control over its American colonies through policies such as the one excerpted?
    (a) The spread of Enlightenment ideas
    (b) The invention of new navigational technologies
    (c) Increasing conflicts between the New England and Chesapeake colonies
    (d) The Seven Years' War

Questions 11–13 refer to the excerpts below.

"Here individuals of all nations are melted into a new race of men, whose labors and posterity will one day cause great changes in the world. Americans are the western pilgrims, who are carrying along with them that great mass of arts, sciences, vigour, and industry which began long since in the east; they will finish the great circle."

J. Hector St. John de Crèvecoeur "What Is an American?" in *Letters from an American Farmer*, 1782

"The notorious ignorance in which the great mass of these emigrants have been all their lives sunk, until their minds are dead, makes them but senseless machines; they obey orders mechanically, for it is the habit of their education, in the despotic countries of their birth. And can it be for a moment supposed by any one that by the act of coming to this country, and being naturalized, their darkened intellects can suddenly be illuminated to discern the nice boundary where their ecclesiastical obedience. . . . ends, and their civil independence . . . begins?"

Samuel F. B. Morse, *Imminent Dangers to the United States through Foreign Immigration*, 1835

11. Which of the following best represents the reason for the change described in the two excerpts?
    (a) A general decrease of immigrants from Western Europe
    (b) An increase in animus toward immigrant populations
    (c) New settlement patterns west of the Rocky Mountains
    (d) Wars with European nations, which increased tensions with immigrants

12. What do these two passages have in common?
    (a) The immigrants described in both passages came primarily from Western and Central Europe.
    (b) Both authors voiced concerns that too many immigrants were maintaining their old traditions.
    (c) Crèvecoeur and Morse agreed that immigrants were able to successfully overcome obstacles and would eventually improve American society.
    (d) Both authors urged the U.S. government to adopt policies regulating immigration.

13. What best accounts for increased opposition to immigration in the first half of the nineteenth century?
    (a) Thousands of Chinese arrived in the United States as the railroad industry expanded.
    (b) Immigrants from Southern and Eastern Europe arrived in huge numbers.
    (c) Union members and their leadership feared that immigrants would take jobs from American workers.
    (d) Protestants opposed the influx of large numbers of Roman Catholics into urban areas in the eastern United States.

Questions 14–15 refer to the excerpt below.

"The primary cause of the buffalo's extermination, and the one which embraced all others, was the descent of civilization, with all its elements of destructiveness, upon the whole of the country inhabited by that animal.

"The secondary causes of the extermination of the buffalo may be catalogued as follows: (1) Man's reckless greed, his wanton destructiveness, and improvidence in not husbanding such resources as come to him from the hand of nature readymade. (2) The total and utterly inexcusable absence of protective measures and agencies on the part of the National Government and of the Western States and Territories. (3) The fatal preference on the part of hunters generally, both white and red, for the robe and flesh of the cow over that furnished by the bull, (4) The phenomenal stupidity of the animals themselves, and their indifference to man. (5) The perfection of modern breech-loading rifles and other sporting fire-arms in general."

William T. Hornaday, The Extermination of the American Bison, 1889

14. The above account reflects a growing sentiment in the late nineteenth century that
    (a) natural resources were not inexhaustible.
    (b) the surest way to end Indian resistance was by government-sponsored decimation of the buffalo herds.
    (c) Indians must be confined to small, scattered reservations.
    (d) the advancement of civilization took precedence over the preservation of the environment.

15. What is one way in which American Indians were affected by the actions described in the excerpt above?
    (a) Competition for land and resources intensified
    (b) Assimilation efforts were embraced
    (c) Subsidies were given to American railroad companies
    (d) New farming techniques were introduced in the west

Questions 16–18 refer to the image below.

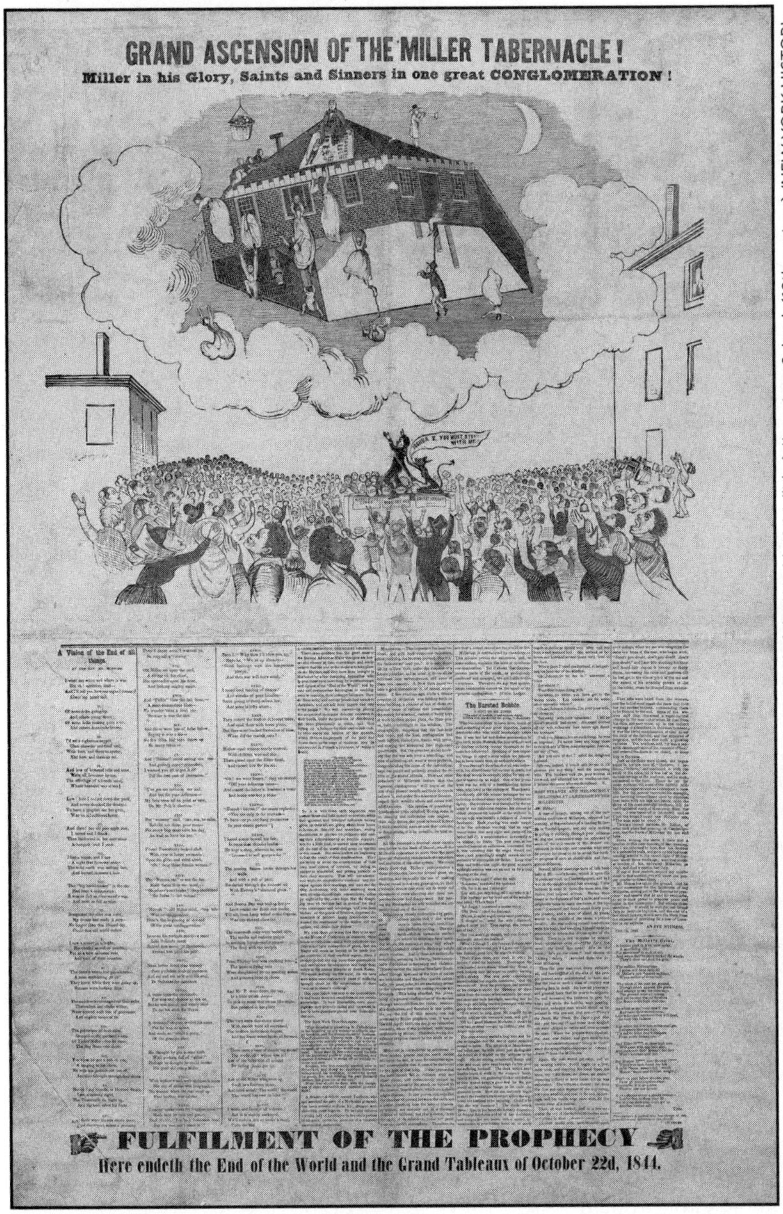

'Grand Ascension of the Miller Tabernacle', Broadside depicting the End of the World, 1844 (litho)/American School, (19th century)/NEW YORK HISTORICAL SOCIETY/Collection of the New-York Historical Society, USA/Bridgeman Images

16. The scene depicted on the broadside above best reflects which of the following historical contexts?
    (a) Protestant evangelism in colonial America
    (b) Enlightenment belief in progress
    (c) the Second Great Awakening
    (d) Romanticism

17. Utopian reformers in America at the time portrayed in the broadside believed most fervently in
    (a) progressivism.
    (b) romanticism.
    (c) perfectionism.
    (d) rationalism.

18. The beliefs of the Millerites would best be reflected later in American history by which of these groups?
    (a) Populists
    (b) Progressives
    (c) Charles Darwin
    (d) Twentieth-century evangelists

Questions 19–21 refer to the excerpt below.

"America is the one country in the world that has taken most care over time to lay out clearly separate paths for the two sexes and also to ensure that the two walk as equals but always on separate paths."

Alexis de Tocqueville, *Democracy in America,* 1848

19. Which of these best accounts for the phenomenon that Tocqueville described in the 1830s?
    (a) The market revolution was changing the nature of work and the relationship between home and the workplace
    (b) Women, both rich and poor, decided that it was better for them to stay home and care for their families
    (c) Slavery in the South and the influx of European immigrants into the North made it possible for women to focus their attention on the home
    (d) In an effort to protect women as the nation became more industrialized, state legislatures began to regulate women's work

20. Which of these was most responsible for bringing women more fully into the public sphere in the mid-nineteenth century?
    (a) As the nation became more divided and the Civil War approached, factories in the North needed more workers
    (b) As a result of the Second Great Awakening, women increasingly were involved in antebellum reform movements
    (c) The expansion of suffrage and the democratization of American society brought women further into the mainstream of American economic life
    (d) As education for women became more accessible, women gained the knowledge and skills that enabled them to enter the workplace

21. Which of the following would not have taken place in the transformative effects described in the excerpt above?
    (a) International migrants
    (b) Urban northern men
    (c) Unmarried northern middle class women
    (d) Wealthy southern women

Questions 22–24 refer to the excerpt below.

"If we call one the natural method, we must call the other the artificial method. If nature's process is rightly named natural selection, man's process is artificial selection. The survival of the fittest is simply the survival of the strong, which implies, and might as well be called, the destruction of the weak. And if nature progresses through the destruction of the weak, man progresses through the *protection* of the weak."

Lester Frank Ward, *Glimpses of the Cosmos*, 1913–1918

22. Based on his views expressed in the passage above, which of these would Ward have been most likely to support?
    (a) Legislation limiting the number of Eastern Europeans who could immigrate to the United States
    (b) The application of Social Darwinism to public policy
    (c) Progressives' efforts to relieve poverty in American cities
    (d) The Chinese Exclusion Act

23. Who would have been most likely to oppose Ward's position?
    (a) Nativists
    (b) Leaders of the Roman Catholic Church
    (c) Settlement house workers
    (d) Political machine bosses

24. In the decades leading to World War I, which of these did NOT fuel the debate between the "natural" and the "artificial" processes that Ward addressed in this passage?
    (a) Conflicts between Native Americans and the U.S. government
    (b) Increased migration of Asians into the United States
    (c) The activism of religious reformers who espoused the Social Gospel
    (d) Passage of legislation that established a quota system to regulate immigration

Questions 25–27 refer to the excerpt below.

"Neither slavery nor involuntary servitude, except as a punishment for a crime whereof the party shall have been duly convicted, shall exist within the United States, or any place subject to their jurisdiction."

Thirteenth Amendment to the U.S. Constitution, 1865

25. This amendment to the Constitution was passed by Congress and ratified in 1865 for which of the following reasons?
    (a) The states of the defeated Confederacy were determined to keep the institution of slavery even after the war ended
    (b) This addition to the Constitution was necessary to banish slavery from states not covered by the Emancipation Proclamation
    (c) Slavery was a common and widespread practice in most of the overseas territories controlled by the United States at this time
    (d) Republicans in Congress were still reluctant to ban slavery in places where it had traditionally existed

26. Which of the following describes actions taken to restrict the freedoms of African Americans after the passing of the 13th Amendment?
    (a) Some states were able to reestablish slavery through elaborate contracts that the federal Justice Department was unable to have declared illegal
    (b) Former slaves were prevented by law from working on any property that was owned by their former masters
    (c) Southern states devised systems of local laws that restricted social, political, and economic freedoms for African Americans for the next century
    (d) Southern legislatures tried to restrict the rights of African Americans, but their efforts were overturned by the Supreme Court in the 1890s

27. Which of the following represents the first real success in overturning laws and customs mandating second-class citizenship for American Americans?
    (a) The Civil Rights Act of 1964
    (b) *Brown v. Board of Education of Topeka, Kansas*
    (c) *Plessy v. Ferguson*
    (d) The economic programs of Johnson's Great Society

Questions 28–30 refer to the excerpt below.

"GROCERY cart and harness for sale—In good order, and one chestnut horse, 8 years old, an excellent saddle horse; can be ridden by a lady. Also, one young man wanted, from 16–18 years of age, able to write. No Irish need apply. Cluff & Tunis, No. 270 Washington-st., corner of Myrtle-av., Brooklyn."

New York Daily Times, March 25, 1854

28. The advertisement above appeared in a New York City newspaper in 1854. What do these employment notices indicate about American society in the middle of the nineteenth century?
    (a) Nativist sentiment continued to be a problem for immigrants coming to the United States
    (b) Equal employment opportunities were available for both men and women during this era
    (c) A strong economy meant employment was available for anyone who was looking for a job
    (d) Few immigrants who arrived in the United States in the first half of the nineteenth century were literate

29. What might explain the attitudes represented by the advertisement above?
    (a) Many immigrants arriving in the United States in the early nineteenth century were discriminated against because they were Catholic and might take jobs from those already here
    (b) There was little land available on the frontier for the huge numbers of immigrants who were coming at this time, so they were flooding urban job markets
    (c) Federal regulations limited immigration, and those who came anyway were in the country illegally
    (d) Most new immigrants refused to live in ethnic communities once they came to the United States, and they threatened the property values of established urban neighborhoods

30. How is the sentiment in this advertisement illustrated by decisions made by Congress in the early twentieth century?
    (a) Attempts were made to reverse what was known as the Great Migration, a movement of southern African Americans from the Deep South to other parts of the country in search of better jobs
    (b) The government passed a series of laws establishing highly restrictive immigration quotas to reduce the numbers of people moving to this country
    (c) Overseas expansion was discouraged by Congress out of fear that it would create new waves of immigrants, particularly to the West Coast
    (d) Congress refused to sign the Treaty of Versailles or participate in the League of Nations primarily out of fear of encouraging new waves of immigration to this country

Questions 31–33 refer to the map below.

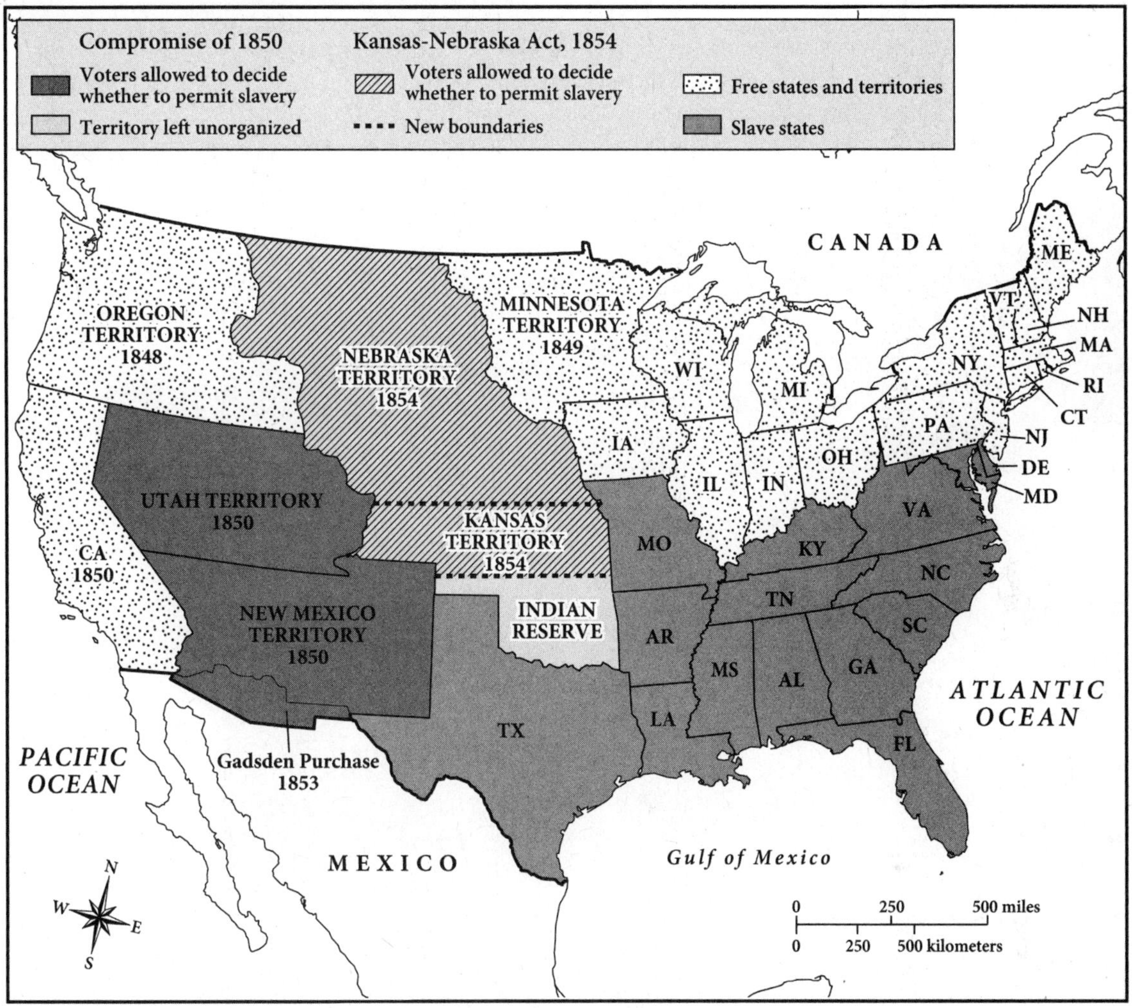

31. The territorial gains referenced in the map above happened in the context of which of the following debates?
    (a) The role of large corporations in America
    (b) Arguments about the superiority of American institutions
    (c) Contestation over European presence in South America
    (d) Debates over the role of the federal government in the economy

32. Northern objections to the Compromise of 1850 came from
    (a) free-soilers, who were opposed to the extension of slavery into any new states or territories.
    (b) Republicans, who insisted that the Compromise of 1850 include the immediate abolition of slavery.
    (c) Know-Nothings, who believed popular sovereignty should decide the issue of slavery in California.
    (d) Whigs, who believed that ending the slave trade in the District of Columbia was a violation of constitutional property guarantees.

33. The controversies surrounding the territorial gains made in the map revealed which of the following historical developments?
    (a) Debates over enslavement in the new territories
    (b) Transportation developments in the new territories
    (c) Foreign relations with European powers
    (d) The impact immigration had on American foreign policy

NPS

Mesa Verse National Park, Colorado

Cahokia Mounds State Historic Site. Painting of imagined reconstruction by William R. Iseminger

Questions 34–35 refer to the images below.

Cahokia Mounds Reconstruction

34. The two civilizations above, which existed in the Southwest and the Mississippi Valley, respectively, before the arrival of Europeans to North America, indicate which of the following about native populations?
   (a) These societies were complex and exhibited diverse economic development and social diversification
   (b) Like most other native societies, these two groups depended on hunting and gathering for subsistence
   (c) These societies were largely mobile due to a scarcity of natural resources
   (d) Large-scale agriculture was favored instead of trade with other villages to support these communities

35. These two civilizations, along with many others of native populations, began to disintegrate after the arrival of Europeans in part because of which of the following conditions?
   (a) Native populations chose to move to areas dominated by Europeans because there were more jobs available in those places
   (b) Europeans brought epidemic diseases that took a heavy toll on native populations and weakened social and political structures in their communities
   (c) Rapid climate change made most of the areas previously settled by native populations unsuitable for traditional agriculture
   (d) The decline of the great buffalo herds made traditional ways of life impossible in the Southwest and the Mississippi Valley

Questions 36–37 refer to the map below.

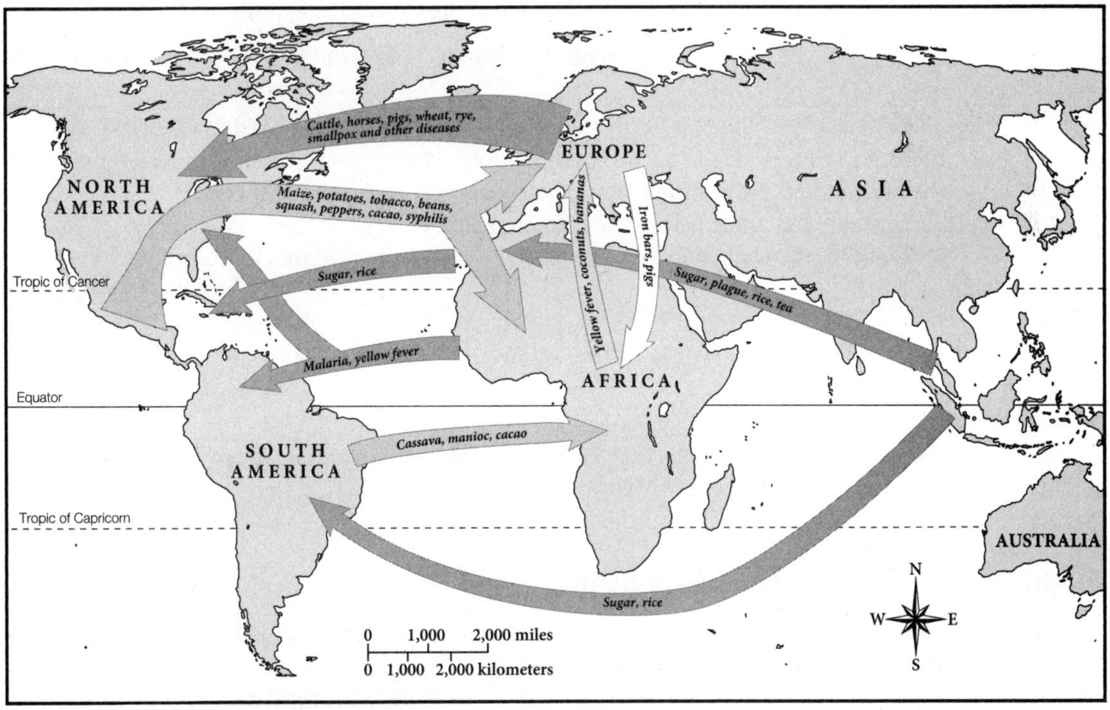

The Columbian Exchange

36. The exchange of goods and the interactions of societies across the Atlantic known as the Columbian Exchange resulted in which of the following?
  (a) Changes occurred on both sides of the Atlantic as the introduction of new agricultural products and animals created new markets and altered lifestyles
  (b) Changes occurred in diets and agriculture, but little in other areas of life for the two regions
  (c) Changes occurred that could ultimately be regarded only as positive, in that both areas benefitted from the introduction of new foods
  (d) There was tremendous population growth on both sides of the Atlantic due to improvements in nutrition

37. Which of the following best represents an economic change as a result of the Columbian Exchange?
  (a) The movement away from mineral sources of wealth
  (b) A decrease in the focus on agriculture
  (c) A change from feudalism to capitalism
  (d) An increase in regional economic development

Questions 38–39 refer to the quotation below.

"This political year features the 'compassionate conservatism' espoused by presidential candidate George W. Bush. ... a coherent principled philosophy. . . . Compassionate conservatives believe that government should have a limited role in people's lives and that competition in the marketplace is the most effective means of producing social and economic progress. Consequently compassionate conservatives believe in low taxes, limited government regulation, and the vast power of the free enterprise system. . . . Government has a responsibility not to redistribute the wealth of citizens but to provide the underprivileged with skills and opportunities to create their own wealth."

Stephen Goldsmith, "+ Is—and Is Not," *Hoover Digest*, 2000

38. The source above was an attempt to explain which of the following beliefs espoused by conservatives?
  (a) A reduced government role in the economy
  (b) The shift in political power from major urban centers to more rural voters
  (c) The elimination of all trade barriers with foreign nations
  (d) A shift from concentrating on U.S. power abroad to a more limited role for the military in general

39. The excerpt above mirrors which conservative critique of the liberal economic programs of the 1960s?
  (a) That government is able to solve economic and cultural crises
  (b) That liberal programs were counterproductive in combating widespread poverty
  (c) That government should get involved in health care
  (d) That a large state government was the source of economic solutions

Questions 40–41 refer to the excerpt below.

"Our nation has been put on notice: We are not immune from attack. We will take defensive measures against terrorism to protect Americans. . . .

"These measures are essential. But the only way to defeat terrorism as a threat to our way of life is to stop it, eliminate it, and destroy it where it grows."

President George W. Bush, September 20, 2011

40. The aftermath of the attack on the World Trade Center and the Pentagon in September 2001 led the U.S. government to do which of the following?
    (a) Concentrate on security at home rather than taking on challenges to U.S. power abroad
    (b) Pass a series of laws aimed at increasing domestic security, which have subsequently come under criticism for threatening individual rights
    (c) Reduce the numbers of women and minorities allowed to serve in the military
    (d) Renew national efforts at finally winning the Cold War with the former Soviet Union

41. What missions undertaken by the United States grew directly out of the World Trade Center and Pentagon attacks in the name of increasing homeland security?
    (a) Lengthy wars in Afghanistan and Iraq
    (b) Efforts to shut down Central American drug cartels
    (c) Tighter immigration controls along the borders of Texas and Mexico
    (d) Tighter quality controls over goods coming in from China and East Asia

Questions 42-43 refer to the photograph below.

Dominique BERRETTY/Gamma-Rapho via Getty Images

Evacuation of Vietnamese civilians in a burning village, c. 1965

42. Images and stories such as the one above led to which of the following historical developments?
   (a) Increased calls for gun control in the United States
   (b) Dramatically increased support for immigration restriction
   (c) Eroding support for the war in Vietnam
   (d) Increasing support for Supreme Court rulings protecting the rights of the accused

43. Which of the following best represents why the United States became involved in the war in Vietnam?
   (a) To contain Soviet expansion in Europe
   (b) A containment of communism in Southeast Asia
   (c) To deter communist North Kora
   (d) To economically rebuild Vietnam

Questions 44–46 refer to the following quotation.

"But the motor age changed advertising to a series of prestigious urges to spend and buy; a bigger car than your neighbor's; a luxury cruise, an all-electric kitchen, a mink coat and diamonds for Mother. . . .

"Advertising also promoted the revolution of rising expectations . . . . Advertisers had taught them it was 'un-American' to be without."

Samuel Eliot Morison, *The Oxford History of the American People,* 1965

44. The growth of consumerism in the 1920s was most fueled by which of the following?
   (a) The widespread introduction of credit cards
   (b) An unparalleled rise in the prices of agricultural commodities
   (c) The introduction of television advertising
   (d) Installment buying

45. The rising expectations that Morison alludes to were most characterized by which of the following in the 1920s?
   (a) The belief that nuclear power would provide cheap energy and make America energy independent
   (b) The consumption of consumer goods
   (c) The optimism brought on by the success of making the world "safe for democracy"
   (d) Immigration restriction

46. Politically the 1920s saw the United States
   (a) return to the progressivism of the prewar era.
   (b) assume leadership of newly created international organizations.
   (c) dominated by conservative leadership.
   (d) play a major role as an international peacekeeper in the Middle East.

Questions 47–49 refer to the following quotation.

"I am convinced that the fifth-column activities of our enemy call for the participation of people who are in fact American citizens.

". . . We believe that any delay in the adoption of necessary protective measures is to invite. . . a Pearl Harbor incident.

". . . We have had no sabotage and no fifth column activities in this state. . . . But I take the view that we are just being lulled into a false sense of security and that the only reason we haven't had a disaster in California is because it has been timed for a different date.

"... I want to say that the consensus among the law enforcement officers of this State is that there is more potential danger among the group of Japanese who are born in this country than from the alien Japanese."

California Attorney General Earl Warren testifying before a U.S. Congressional Committee on Japanese Internment, 1942

47. Ultimately fear of Japanese citizens during World War II led to
    (a) the execution of forty-three Japanese American citizens for sabotage and espionage.
    (b) the deportation of Japanese American citizens from the United States.
    (c) internment of Japanese American citizens in closely guarded camps.
    (d) Japanese American citizens being forced to labor on white-owned farms due to the shortage of agricultural labor.

48. African Americans also suffered discrimination during World War II. Which of the following represents progress made by African Americans prior to the end of the war?
    (a) Racial segregation in the armed forces was ended.
    (b) A federal agency was formed to prevent racial discrimination in hiring for defense plants.
    (c) Schools were integrated.
    (d) African American troops were no longer assigned to the Pacific theater of the war.

49. Which of the following represents a change for some American women during the Second World War?
    (a) Found new employment opportunities in traditionally male industrial jobs
    (b) Served in front-line combat roles with men
    (c) Achieved equal pay for equal work in defense industries
    (d) Were given the right to vote in return for their support of the war effort

Questions 50–52 refer to the image below and excerpt on the next page.

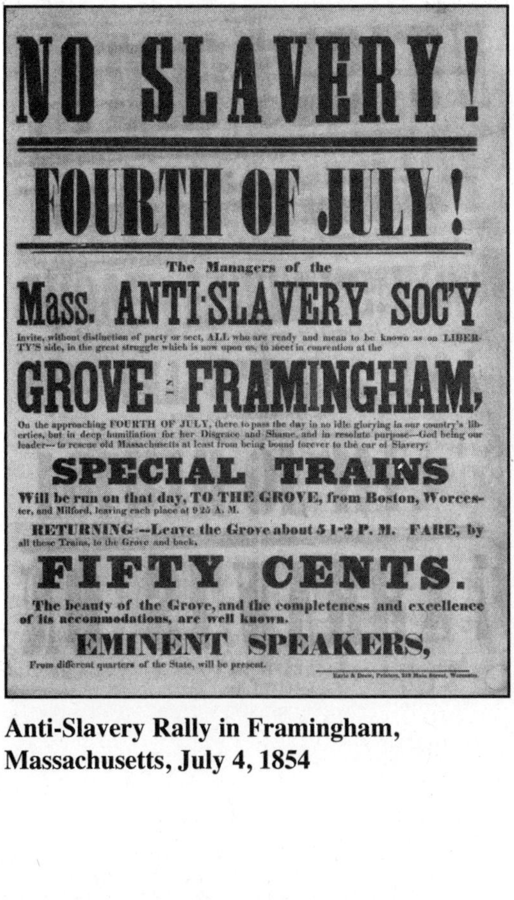

Anti-Slavery Rally in Framingham, Massachusetts, July 4, 1854 (litho)/American School, (19th century)/MASSACHUSETTS HISTORICAL SOCIETY/Massachusetts Historical Society, Boston, MA, USA/Bridgeman Images

Anti-Slavery Rally in Framingham, Massachusetts, July 4, 1854

"Our slaves are black, of another and inferior race. The *status* in which we have placed them is an elevation. They are elevated from the condition in which God first created them, by being made our slaves."

James Henry Hammond, speech before the U.S. Senate, March 4, 1858

50. What do these two sources tell you about the debate over slavery in the 1850s?
    (a) The issue of slavery played little role in sectional tensions after the passage of the Compromise of 1850
    (b) Attitudes toward slavery became more hardened and less open to any compromise during the 1850s
    (c) Southerners were generally able to stop the spread of abolitionist literature by controlling the activities of the antislavery press
    (d) People on both sides of the abolitionist arguments felt the government was working in support on their side

51. Among the arguments used by those opposing the activities of abolitionists was which of the following?
    (a) Slaves were generally better farmworkers than white laborers
    (b) Slaveholders argued enslavement was a positive social good for both the enslaved and slave holders
    (c) The northern economy would not be able to survive without the work of slaves in southern cotton and tobacco fields
    (d) Slaves were critical labor to southern manufacturing and ironworks

52. Which of the following proved to be a major source of disagreement among northern abolitionists in the decade leading up to the Civil War?
    (a) Some abolitionists favored the inclusion of women while others maintained that inclusion would have radicalized the movement
    (b) The groups argued over whether Congress had the power to issue the Fugitive Slave Law that was part of the Compromise of 1850
    (c) Some wanted to shut down efforts to help slaves escape, as they felt it was too dangerous
    (d) They disagreed over whether former slaves would be able to obtain employment in northern manufacturing once they made an escape to freedom

Questions 53–55 refer to the image below.

Dave G. Houser/Getty Images

Marble House, The Vanderbilt Mansion in Newport, Rhode Island, Built 1892

53. Which of the following best represents a common critique of Gilded Age wealth?
   (a) Ostentatious opulence
   (b) Conspicuous consumption
   (c) Scientific management
   (d) Utilitarianism

54. By the late 1800s, the increasing disparity of wealth between the rich and poor led for successful calls to
   (a) place a cap on the maximum income one could attain in a single year.
   (b) nationalize major industries such as steel, oil, and banking.
   (c) impose government regulations on private industry.
   (d) redistribute income by lowering tariffs.

55. In the late nineteenth century, efforts to help the poor came primarily from
   (a) private organizations designed to meet their basic needs.
   (b) the federal government in the form of welfare payments.
   (c) railroad companies who offered free transportation to the west.
   (d) state welfare agencies that provided free housing and food for the needy.

Part B: Short-Answer Questions

Time: 40 minutes

Please answer the following two questions.

1. Using the excerpts below, answer a, b, and c.

"Apprehension seems to exist among the people of the Southern States that by the accession of a Republican Administration their property and their peace and personal security are to be endangered. There has never been any reasonable cause for such apprehension. . . .

"I have no purpose directly or indirectly, to interfere with the institution of slavery in the States where it exists. I believe I have no lawful right to do so, and I have no inclination to do so."

Abraham Lincoln, First Inaugural Address, March 1861

"On the occasion corresponding to this four years ago . . . One eighth of the whole population were colored slaves, not distributed generally over the Union, but localized in the Southern part of it. These slaves constituted a peculiar and powerful interest. . . . To strengthen, perpetuate, and extend this interest was the object for which the insurgents would rend the Union, even by war; while the government claimed no right to do more than to restrict the territorial enlargement of it. . . . The prayers of both could not be answered."

Abraham Lincoln, Second Inaugural Address, March 1865

(a) Briefly explain ONE major difference between Lincoln's First Inaugural Address and his Second Inaugural Address regarding slavery in the 1860s.

(b) Briefly explain ONE specific historical event or development from the period 1844 to 1865 that is not explicitly mentioned in the excerpts could be used to support Lincoln's First Inaugural Address.

(c) Briefly explain ONE specific historical event or development from the period 1844 to 1865 that is not explicitly mentioned in the excerpts could be used to support Lincoln's Second Inaugural Address.

2. Answer a, b, and c.

(a) There were significant political, social, cultural, and economic conflicts in the United States during both the 1920s and 1950s, as Americans debated the institutions and the ideas that would move the nation forward. Briefly explain the reasons for the emergence of ONE example of cultural conflict in the 1920s.

(b) Briefly explain ONE example of cultural conflict in the 1950s.

(c) Briefly explain ONE reason that accounts for a difference in the cultural conflicts of the 1920s and 1950s.

Please choose between question #3 or #4 for your final SAQ question.

3. Using the excerpts below, answer a, b, and c.

"All children born in this country shall be held bond or free only according to the condition of the mother; and that if any Christian shall commit fornication with a Negro man or woman, he or she so offending shall pay double the fines imposed by the former act." (December 1662)

"The conferring of baptism does not alter the condition of the person as to his bondage or freedom." (September 1667)

"Moderate corporal punishment inflicted by master or magistrate upon a runaway servant shall not deprive the master of the satisfaction allowed by the law." (September 1668)

"If any slave resists his master . . . and by the extremity of the correction should chance to die, that his death shall not be accounted a felony, but the master . . . be acquitted." (October 1669)

Virginia Slave Laws, 1660s

(a) Briefly explain ONE reason for the emergence of the ideas expressed in the excerpt above in the period from 1607 to 1754.

(b) Briefly explain ONE event or development that changed the laws excerpted above in the period from 1607 to 1754.

(c) Briefly explain ONE significant outcome of the laws excerpted above in the period from 1607 to 1754.

4. Using the excerpt below, answer a, b, and c.

"The principal attention has been to the stamp bill that has been preparing to lay before Parliament for taxing America.

"I beg leave to give you a Summary of the Arguments which are made in favor of such authority. The House of Commons, say they, is a branch of the supreme legislature of the nation, and which in its nature is supposed to represent, or rather to stand in the place of . . . the great body of the people who are below the dignity of peers. . . . They further urge that the only reason why America has not been heretofore taxed in the fullest manner has been merely on account of their infancy and inability; . . . in short, they say a power to tax is a necessary part of every supreme legislative authority, and that if they have not that power over America. they have none, and then America is at once a kingdom of itself.

"On the other hand, those who oppose the bill say it is true the Parliament have a supreme unlimited authority over every part and branch of the king's dominions, . . . yet we believe a British Parliament will never think it prudent to tax Ireland. . . . 'Tis true they say that the commons of England and of the British Empire are all represented in and by the House of Commons, but this representation is confessedly on all hands by construction and virtually only as to those who have no hand in choosing the representatives, and that the effects of this implied representation here and in America must be infinitely different in the article of taxation. . . . We think, say they, that it will be only to lay a foundation of great jealousy and continual uneasiness, and that to no purpose, as we already by the regulations upon their trade draw from the Americans all that they can spare. At least they say this step should not take place until or unless the Americans are allowed to send members to Parliament."

Jared Ingersoll, *Report on the Debates in Parliament*, 1765

(a) Briefly explain ONE reason for the emergence of the ideas expressed in the excerpt above in the period from 1754 to 1776.

(b) Briefly explain ONE way British North American colonists opposed ideas expressed in the excerpt in the period from 1754 to 1776.

(c) Briefly explain ANOTHER way British North American colonists opposed ideas expressed in the excerpt above from 1754 to 1776.

STOP

END OF SECTION I

Section II

Total time: 1 hour, 40 minutes

Part A: Document-Based Question

Time: 60 minutes

Directions: The following question in based on the accompanying documents. The documents have been edited for this exercise. It is suggested that you spend approximately 15 minutes planning and 45 minutes writing your answer.

Write an essay that does the following:

- States an appropriate thesis that directly addresses all parts of the question.
- Supports the thesis or argument with evidence from all or all but one of the documents AND your knowledge of U.S. history beyond the documents.
- Analyzes all or all but one of the documents.
- Explain the significance of the author's point of view, author's purpose, historical context, and/or audience for at least three documents.
- Uses historical evidence beyond the documents to support your argument.
- Places the argument in the context of broader regional, national, or global processes.
- Incorporates all of the elements above into a convincing essay.

Question: Evaluate the extent to which the ideas of American independence led to change in American politics from 1787–1812.

Document 1

Source: Alexander Hamilton, Constitutional Convention debate, June 18, 1787

All communities divide themselves into the few and the many. The first are the rich and well-born, the other the mass of the people. . . . The people are turbulent and changing; they seldom judge or determine right. Give, therefore, to the first class a distinct, permanent share in the government. They will check the unsteadiness of the second, and, as they cannot receive any advantage by a change, they therefore will ever maintain good government.

Document 2

Source: An Ordinance for the government of the Territory of the United States northwest of the River Ohio, July 13, 1787

Sec. 9. So soon as there shall be five thousand free male inhabitants of full age in the district, upon giving proof thereof to the governor, they shall receive authority, with time and place, to elect a representative from their counties or townships to represent them in the general assembly.

Art. 5. There shall be formed in the said territory, not less than three nor more than five States.

Art. 6. There shall be neither slavery nor involuntary servitude in the said territory, otherwise than in the punishment of crimes whereof the party shall have been duly convicted: *Provided, always*, That any person escaping into the same, from whom labor or service is lawfully claimed in any one of the original States, such fugitive may be lawfully reclaimed and conveyed to the person claiming his or her labor or service as aforesaid.

Document 3

Source: The Anti-federalist Papers, No. 46 "Where Then Is the Restraint?" *Maryland Gazette and Baltimore Advertiser,* November 2, 1788.

My object is to consider that undefined, unbounded and immense power which is comprised in the following clause— "And to make all laws which shall be necessary and proper for carrying into execution the foregoing powers, and all other powers vested by this constitution in the government of the United States; or in any department or offices thereof." Under such a clause as this, can anything be said to be reserved and kept back from Congress? Can it be said that the Congress have no power but what is expressed? "To make all laws which shall be necessary and proper"— or, in other words, to make all such laws which the Congress shall think necessary and proper— or who shalt judge for the legislature what is necessary and proper?

Document 4

Source: Tarring & Feathering an Excise Officer, 1794

Document 5

Source: Treaty of Amity Commerce and Navigation (also known as Jay's Treaty) between the United States and Great Britain, November, 1794

ARTICLE 2. His Majesty will withdraw all His Troops and Garrisons from all Posts and Places within the Boundary Lines assigned by the Treaty of Peace to the United States. This Evacuation shall take place on or before the first Day of June One thousand seven hundred and ninety six, and all the proper Measures shall in the interval be taken by concert between the Government of the United States, and His Majesty's Governor General in America, for settling the previous arrangements which may be necessary respecting the delivery of the said Posts: . . .

ARTICLE 12. His Majesty Consents that it shall and may be lawful, during the time hereinafter Limited, for the Citizens of the United States, to carry to any of His Majesty's Islands and Ports in the West Indies from the United States in their own Vessels, not being above the burthen of Seventy Tons, any Goods or Merchandizes.

Document 6

Source: Map of New Orleans, Louisiana, 1798

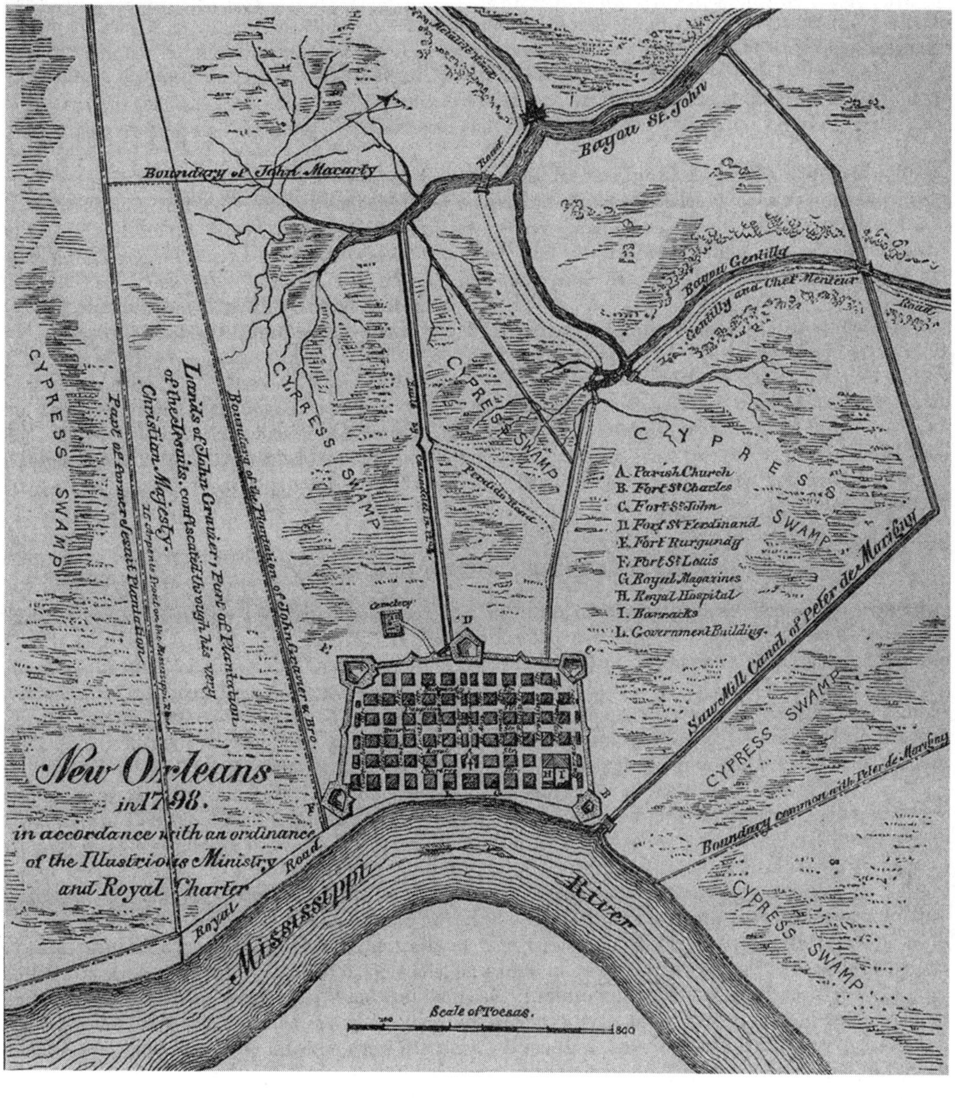

Document 7

Source: Thomas Jefferson, First Inaugural Address, March 4, 1801

Still one thing more, fellow-citizens— a wise and frugal Government, which shall restrain men from injuring one another, shall leave them otherwise free to regulate their own pursuits of industry and improvement, and shall not take from the mouth of labor the bread it has earned. This is the sum of good government, and this is necessary to close the circle of our felicities.

Part B: Long Essay Questions

Time: 40 minutes

Choose between one of the following three questions.

1. Evaluate the relative significance of different factors that changed the federal government's role in the economy from 1787-1820.

2. Evaluate the extent to which the federal government supported the interests of businesses in the period 1865-1900.

3. Evaluate the extent to which the change in innovation and communication changed American society from 1919–1929.

STOP

END OF EXAM

Text Credits

Page 115, Short-Answer Question 2.

United States Department of Homeland Security. *Yearbook of Immigration Statistics: 2010.*Washington, D.C.: U.S. Department of Homeland Security, Office of Immigration Statistics, 2011.

Page 153, Multiple-Choice Questions 5–7.

Cliff Staten, *U.S. Foreign Policy since World War II*, 2005. Courtesy of American Diplomacy Publishers.

Page 177, Multiple-Choice Questions 44–46.

Data from Gray, Lewis Cecil. *History of Agriculture in the Southern United States To 1860.* Vol. II, Carnegie Institute of Washington, 1933.